WELCOME

The Private Collection is an invitation to discover a world away from the ordinary.

In a world that's fast becoming little more than a global village, some places manage to remain just as they were. Unhurried. Uncrowded. Unspoilt. And Unique – by a thousand miles.

Welcome to the third edition of The Private Collection.

Isabelle Van Passel
Editor

Yvan Vermeesch
Publisher

A TRAVELLER

WITHOUT KNOWLEDGE

IS LIKE A BIRD

WITHOUT WINGS.

Mushariff-Ud-Din

WHAT'S IN A NAME?

Whilst XO stands for extraordinary, The Private Collection stands for escapes of distinction – exclusive, sometimes sophisticated, sometimes escapist, sometimes adventurous, but always special. The Private Collection means private and unspoilt surroundings for those people who wish to relax away from the crowds.

This portfolio stands for an indispensable source of inspiration for discerning travellers. It is a unique reference book which guides its readers in the direction of some of the world's finest – and only the finest – escapes, all brought together in a single, beautifully illustrated volume.

The mind, once expanded to the dimensions of larger ideas,
never returns to its original size.

Oliver Wendell Holmes

CONTENTS

A WORLD OF QUALITY

These pages of elegant escapes reflect a world of quality in every sense of the word. Destination, style, theme, duration – these are many in their variety and contrasts. From cruising amid the splendour of Antactica's coastline over walking through extinct volcanoes and rain forests to relaxing on a delightful white powder sand beach.

Throughout, however, The Private Collection publishers continuously strive to single out only those escapes that are the best in their region with location, reputation and aesthetics playing the largest part in the careful selection process.

The preferred travel partners featured in the newly dedicated section of this book have been selected for their exceptional quality to ensure the highest level of personalized service to the sophisticated traveller.

Whatever the selected theme or style of a planned escape, The Private Collection objective is to provide discerning travellers with useful, reliable and current inspiration for their upcoming journeys around the world.

CARIBBEAN

Nowhere evokes such a vision of relaxed sophistication and idyllic palm-fringed beaches as the Caribbean. This being true, the most surprising aspect of the Caribbean to the newcomer is the huge variety from island to island.

The Caribbean is made up of more than thirty countries, each very independent and different from one another. From the white coral beaches of the Bahamas over the lush forested coves of Jamaica to the elegant English charm of Bermuda.

PINK SANDS
Harbour Island

Known for its stunning location set on the pink sand beaches of Harbour Island in the Bahamas, Pink Sands is a true celebrity hideaway. Combining traditions of the past and the most modern amenities and services, the resort is situated on 18 acres with 25 charming one-bedroom and two-bedroom cottages. All of them have a private outdoor patio with teak furniture from which one can enjoy fabulous views of the ocean.

Recreational facilities include a freshwater pool, 3 tennis courts, billiards, fitness studio and a three-mile stretch of private pink-sand beach, sheltered by a barrier reef. Water sports include snorkelling, kayaks, fishing, scuba-diving and waterskiing.

The Garden Terrace Restaurant, the resort's main dining area offers an al fresco setting, where teak furniture and private candlelit corners create an intimate gourmet dining experience. The fashionable Blue Bar overlooking the beach and sea is open daily for lunch. The extensive wine list compliments the gourmet cuisine and offers a wide selection of 'Old' and 'New' world wines.

FACILITIES

Accommodation
25 COTTAGES
(21 ONE-BEDROOM COTTAGES
AND 4 TWO-BEDROOM COTTAGES)

Recreational facilities
FRESHWATER POOL
3 TENNIS COURTS
SNORKELLING
KAYAKS
FISHING
DIVING
WATERSKIING
EXERCISE ROOM

Meeting facilities
NONE

International Airports
NORTH ELEUTHERA AIRPORT (ELH)
20 MINUTES DRIVE AND FERRY-CROSSING AWAY

RESERVATIONS

Prices
COTTAGES FROM 460 EURO PER NIGHT
BREAKFAST AND DINNER INCLUDED

Credit cards
AE, MC, V

GDS Reservation Codes
AMADEUS UI HBIPIN
GALILEO UI 73382
SABRE UI 7739
WORLDSPAN UI 25041

Yearly Closing Dates
NONE

CONTACT DETAILS
PINK SANDS
HARBOUR ISLAND
BAHAMAS
TEL +1 242 333 20 30
FAX +1 242 333 20 60
RESERVATIONS@ISLANDOUTPOST.COM
WWW.PINKSANDS@ISLANDOUTPOST.COM

OWNER: MR CHRIS BLACKWELL
GENERAL MANAGER: MR & MRS CLEMENS &
NANCY VON MERVELDT
SALES EUROPE: MS ANDRÉE EDWARDS-BOWLES

AFFILIATIONS

Bermuda

CAMBRIDGE BEACHES

Somerset

A luxury hideaway overlooking the ocean, this exclusive resort set on a 30-acre peninsula in Bermuda, has been recognised as one of the most romantic locations in the world.

Pastel-pink cottages nestle in colourful gardens; each one individually decorated using only the finest fabrics, furnishings and antiques, and many featuring marble bathrooms complete with whirlpool.

Couples wishing to be pampered can choose from more than 100 health and beauty treatments at the world-class indoor 'Aquarian Baths & Ocean Spa'.

Other features of the prestigious retreat include pink sand beaches, tennis courts, indoor and outdoor swimming pools, a croquet lawn, putting green, gymnasium, water sports centre and, arguably the highlight of a stay at this resort, its superb gourmet cuisine.

Plus, for keen golfers, Cambridge Beaches has membership of all Bermuda's courses and a special package giving exposure to several of them.

Cambridge Beaches: a place for romantics of all ages to rediscover themselves.

FACILITIES

Accommodation
94 LUXURY COTTAGE ROOMS AND SUITES

Recreational facilities
AQUARIAN BATHS & HEALTH SPA
FRESHWATER INDOOR & OUTDOOR
SWIMMING POOLS
CROQUET LAWN
GYMNASIUM
EXERCISE CLASSES
FISHING
GLASS BOTTOM BOAT TRIPS
SCUBA DIVING
SNORKELLING
PARASAILING
WINDSURFING
SAILING
KAYAKS
JET SKIS
5 PINK SAND BEACHES
TENNIS COURTS
MOONLIGHT TRIPS
MOPED & CYCLE RENTAL
GOLF AND HORSEBACK RIDING NEARBY

Meeting facilities
MEETING ROOMS FOR UP TO 160 PEOPLE

International Airports
BERMUDA INTERNATIONAL AIRPORT (BDA)
50 MINUTES DRIVE AWAY

RESERVATIONS

Prices
SUITES FROM 450 EURO PER PERSON PER NIGHT

Credit cards
AE, MC, V

GDS Reservation Codes
NONE

Yearly Closing Dates
NONE

CONTACT DETAILS

CAMBRIDGE BEACHES
30 KINGS POINT ROAD
SOMERSET, MA02
BERMUDA
TEL +441 234 0331
FAX +441 234 3352
CAMBEACH@IBL.BM
WWW.CAMBRIDGEBEACHES.COM

OWNER: THE HON MICHAEL J WINFIELD
GENERAL MANAGER: MR RICHARD QUINN
DIRECTOR OF SALES: MRS NANCY MONIZ

AFFILIATIONS

NONE

GOLDENEYE
Oracabessa

Experience a 'James Bond' holiday. Goldeneye, a Jamaican magical place near Oracabessa, was built by James Bond novelist Ian Fleming in the 1950s. The 18-acre retreat is nestled among tropical forests and lush gardens on a seaside bluff overlooking the Caribbean. Inspiration enough for Fleming to pen 14 of his famous '007' thrillers there.

The 'Ian Fleming House' offers a true private house consisting of 3 bedrooms with private indoor and outdoor sublime bathrooms surrounded by tropical foliage and boasts its own private beach, swimming pool and media entertainment room. Large louver windows and high ceilings encourage the flow of sea breezes throughout the house. The master bedroom features Ian Fleming's original writing desk. The 'Goldeneye Village' consists of 4 further villas ranging from 1 to 3 bedrooms, all featuring great lounges with private bars, ideal for viewing movies and all with access to Goldeneye's other private beach 'Low Cay Beach'.

Wave runners, kayaks and snorkelling gear are at the guests' disposal, as well as the expert instruction. Sunfish sailing, deep sea fishing, jet ski tours and tennis are other ways to spend your free time.

FACILITIES

Accommodation
5 VILLAS WITH ONE TO THREE BEDROOMS

Recreational facilities
SWIMMING POOL WITH THE FLEMING HOUSE
GLASS-BOTTOM BOAT
SNORKELLING
FISHING
BIKING
TENNIS COURT
JET SKI
KAYAKS
CANOE RIDES
GOLDENEYE GARDEN WALKS & TOURS
OUTDOOR MASSAGE & TROPICAL BODY
TREATMENTS AT YOUR VILLA

Meeting facilities
CAN BE RENTED AS AN ENTIRE ESTATE

International Airports
OCHO RIOS AIRPORT (OCJ)
8 MINUTES DRIVE AWAY
MONTEGO BAY INT'L AIRPORT (MBJ)
120 MINUTES DRIVE AWAY

RESERVATIONS

Prices
ROOMS FROM 580 EURO PER NIGHT
(MEALS AND BEVERAGES INCLUDED)

Credit cards
AE, V, MC

GDS Reservation Codes
NONE

Yearly Closing Dates
NONE

CONTACT DETAILS

GOLDENEYE
ORACABESSA
ST. MARY
JAMAICA
TEL +1 876 975 33 54
FAX +1 876 975 36 20
RESERVATIONS@ISLANDOUTPOST.COM
WWW.ISLANDOUTPOST.COM

OWNER: MR CHRIS BLACKWELL
GENERAL MANAGER: MRS JENNY WOOD
SALES EUROPE: MS ANDRÉE EDWARDS-BOWLES

AFFILIATIONS

JAKE'S
Treasure Beach

The concept of Jake's was born in 1993 when the Henzell family incorporated a historical home into a restaurant called Jake's, named after a local parrot. Located on Treasure Beach, on the serene South Coast of Jamaica, Jake's is a "little piece of art coming out of the ground" according to Chris Blackwell, founder of Island Records and Island Outpost.

The resort's 29 rooms and 2 two-bedroom secluded villas, including 4 Honeymoon & Romance Suites, offer an eclectic mix of Jamaican, Mexican, Greek and Catalan styles. The airy cottages were created by theatrical designer Sally Henzell to commune with garden, sea and sky. Each elegant room has been uniquely designed, painted with bright bohemian colors and named after a sea creature.

Hotel facilities include a beach, saltwater pool, private cove, games room with cable TV, CD collection, book and video library and two restaurants and a bar – including Jake's oceanfront restaurant and Jack Sprat, a lively beach-side restaurant.

Jake's is the perfect choice for guests who value openness, imagination, simplicity and romance.

FACILITIES

Accommodation
29 COTTAGES
(18 ONE-BEDROOM UNITS,
4 TWO-BEDROOM AND
1 THREE-BEDROOM COTTAGES)

Recreational facilities
SALTWATER SWIMMING POOL
BEACH
PRIVATE COVE
GAMES ROOM WITH CABLE TV
BOOK AND VIDEO LIBRARY
2 RESTAURANTS AND BAR
SNORKELLING EQUIPMENT
KAYAKS
COVE
EXCURSIONS
CASIA TREE SHOP

Meeting facilities
NONE

International Airports
MONTEGO BAY INT'L AIRPORT (MBJ)
120 MINUTES DRIVE AWAY

RESERVATIONS

Prices
COTTAGES FROM 100 EURO PER NIGHT

Credit cards
AE, MC, V

GDS Reservation Codes
NONE

Yearly Closing Dates
NONE

CONTACT DETAILS

JAKE'S
CALABASH BAY
TREASURE BEACH
ST. ELIZABETH
JAMAICA
TEL +1 876 965 3000
FAX +1 876 965 0552
RESERVATIONS@ISLANDOUTPOST.COM
WWW.ISLANDOUTPOST.COM

OWNER: MR & MS JASON AND SALLY HENZELL
MANAGER: MS YVONNE CLARKE
SALES EUROPE: MS ANDRÉE EDWARDS-BOWLES

AFFILIATIONS

STRAWBERRY HILL
Blue Mountains, Kingston

Strawberry Hill, a unique mountain resort is located in one of the most magnificent natural settings on earth, Jamaica's Blue Mountains. Wrapped in majestic mountains, cooled by the purest air, welcomed by the birds, you'll discover your private Jamaica in an understated atmosphere of island antique furniture, handpainted plates, delicate carved panels and sculpted iron lamps.

12 Georgian-style cottages, located within 26 tropical acres of gardens near Irish Town, range from studios to three bedroom suites all with whitewashed walls, wooden floors, four-poster beds and balconies offering unique vistas of the mountainous terrain.

The first full service Aveda Concept Spa in the Caribbean offers complete personalised treatments, while the breathtaking negative edge swimming pool overlooks the twinkling lights of Kingston 3100 feet below. The invigorating fresh air will inspire you to take a hike through the Blue Mountains to discover hundreds of species of flowering plants and exotic birds.

FACILITIES

Accommodation
12 COTTAGES
(STUDIOS TO THREE-BEDROOM SUITES)

Recreational facilities
AVEDA SPA TREATMENTS
NATURE HIKING TRAILS
SWIMMING POOL
SAUNA
PLUNGE POOL
MOUNTAIN BIKING
COFFEE PLANTATION TOURS
GOURMET RESTAURANT

Meeting facilities
MEETING ROOM FOR UP TO 30 PEOPLE

International Airports
KINGSTON INTERNATIONAL AIRPORT (KIN)
45 MINUTES DRIVE AWAY

RESERVATIONS

Prices
COTTAGES FROM 250 EURO PER NIGHT

Credit cards
AE, V, MC

GDS Reservation Codes
AMADEUS UI KINSTR
GALILEO UI 66482
SABRE UI 21359
WORLDSPAN UI 24102

Yearly Closing Dates
NONE

CONTACT DETAILS

STRAWBERRY HILL
IRISH TOWN
JAMAICA
TEL +1 876 944 8400
FAX +1 876 944 8408
RESERVATIONS@ISLANDOUTPOST.COM
WWW.ISLANDOUTPOST.COM

OWNER: MR CHRIS BLACKWELL
GENERAL MANAGER: MRS CAROLE FULLERTON
SALES EUROPE: MS ANDRÉE EDWARDS-BOWLES

AFFILIATIONS

XO PRIVATE THE PRIVATE COLLECTION

THE CAVES
Negril

The Caves, an exclusive and romantic resort only a few miles away from the bustling Negril strip, is a very private enclave that offers a unique experience. The resort is perched above Negril's natural volcanic formed caves overlooking the Caribbean Sea. The walls of the cliffs feature a series of grottos with ancient fossilized marine life for guests to explore. Below the caves, the water plunges down to depths of 30 feet and a tropical reef system comes right up to the edge of the caves.

10 handcrafted wood and stone thatch-roofed cottages are interwoven with 2 acres of lush vegetation and sea caves, most with sea views. Hotel facilities include Aveda Spa treatments in an open-air gazebo, snorkelling, a private Jacuzzi which can be booked for 2 with views of the stunning sunsets over the sea, and deep-sea fishing, scuba diving and waterskiing can be arranged nearby.

A Caribbean–World cuisine is served in the open-air gazebo or in idyllic spots throughout the resort, such as the furnished cave.

FACILITIES

Accommodation
10 Cottages
(2 One-bedroom Units,
6 One-bedroom Suites,
2 Two-bedroom Suites)

Recreational facilities
Aveda Spa Treatments
Open-air Gazebo
Private Cave Dining Room
Jacuzzi, Sauna, Hot Tub
Saltwater Pool
Floats
Snorkelling Equipment
Bicycles
Kayaks

Meeting facilities
None

International Airports
Montego Bay Int'l Airport (MBJ)
90 minutes drive away

RESERVATIONS

Prices
Rooms from 400 Euro per night
(meals and beverages included)

Credit cards
AE, MC, V

GDS Reservation Codes
None

Yearly Closing Dates
September

CONTACT DETAILS

The Caves
P.O. Box 3113
Lighthouse Road
West End, Negril
Jamaica
Tel +1 876 957 02 70
Fax +1 876 957 49 30
reservations@islandoutpost.com
www.islandoutpost.com

Owner: Mr Chris Blackwell &
Mrs Greer-Ann Saulter
Manager: Mr Pierre Beswick
Sales Europe: Ms Andrée Edwards-Bowles

AFFILIATIONS

COTTON HOUSE
Mustique

Spread over 13 acres of lush vegetation and manicured landscape, Cotton House's 20 delightful rooms and suites provide a haven of relaxation and comfort. Recently refurbished, the hotel offers new decorative touches in every room, as well as the addition of private plunge pools to certain suites. The brand new 2 bedroom Cotton Hill Suite features a private swimming pool and personal butler service.

For active pursuits, seek out the new large infinity swimming pool, tennis courts, horse riding and deep sea diving for a little excitement. For those looking to take it easy, pampering awaits at the 4 treatment rooms of the new "Cotton House Spa" where guests can enjoy the products of E'SPA, Décléor and Leonor Greyl. Original flavours and exotic colours await at the two restaurants of the Cotton House where original cuisine is inspired by Asian tradition and infused with Mediterranean flavours.

The final touches will contribute to making the Cotton House one of the most beautiful hideaways in the Caribbean.

FACILITIES
Accommodation
20 ROOMS, COTTAGES & SUITES
Recreational facilities
SAILING
SCUBA DIVING
SNORKELLING
TENNIS
HORSEBACK RIDING
SPA & FITNESS CENTRE
SWIMMING POOL
PICNIC
Meeting facilities
NONE
International Airports
BARBADOS INTERNATIONAL AIRPORT (BGI)
45 MINUTES FLIGHT AWAY

RESERVATIONS
Prices
ROOMS FROM 606 EURO PER NIGHT
Credit cards
AE, DC, MC, V
GDS Reservation Codes
AMADEUS LW MQS914
GALILEO LW 77887
SABRE LW 24781
WORLDSPAN LW 1914
Yearly Closing Dates
1 SEPTEMBER - 31 OCTOBER 2005

CONTACT DETAILS
COTTON HOUSE
P.O. BOX 349
MUSTIQUE ISLAND
ST. VINCENT & THE GRENADINES
TEL +1 784 456 4777
FAX + 784 456 5887
COTTONHOUSE@CARIBSURF.COM
WWW.COTTONHOUSE.NET

OWNER: MUSTIQUE COMPANY
GENERAL MANAGER: MR NICHOLAS SIMMONDS
DIRECTOR OF SALES: MS FLORENCE DUBOIS

AFFILIATIONS
The Leading Small Hotels
of the World

RAFFLES RESORT CANOUAN ISLAND

Canouan Island

Right in the heart of the Grenadines sits lush and pristine Canouan, which in native Carib-Indian means 'island of turtles'. Raffles Resort Canouan Island is set in its own private 1,200 acres of unspoiled land surrounded by green hills, secluded white sand beaches and sheltered by a large coral reef.

Designed by famous Italian architect Luigi Vietti, this resort's private single and double-storey villas offer 156 luxurious accommodations with ocean vistas of the turquoise-blue Caribbean. The resort's light-infused rooms and elegant suites combine timeless sensibility of colour and harmony. Some suites boast private swimming pools.

Raffles Resort Canouan Island features the 18-hole Trump International Golf Club, Raffles' signature Raffles Amrita Spa, private yacht mooring, water sports centre, a beachfront swimming pool, 2 white sand beaches, tennis courts and 4 inviting gourmet restaurants and charming bars.

FACILITIES

Accommodation
156 ROOMS & SUITES

Recreational facilities
SWIMMING POOL
SCUBA DIVING
AMRITA SPA & FITNESS CENTRE
WINDSURFING
CHILDREN'S POOL
BOAT EXCURSIONS
HYDROBIKES
GOLF COURSE
TENNIS COURTS
KID'S CLUB
4 GOURMET RESTAURANTS & BAR

Meeting facilities
5 MEETING ROOMS FOR UP TO 300 PEOPLE

International Airports
BARBADOS INTERNATIONAL AIRPORT (BGI)
35 MINUTES FLIGHT AWAY

RESERVATIONS

Prices
ROOMS FROM 350 EURO PER NIGHT

Credit cards
AE, MC, V

GDS Reservation Codes
AMADEUS YR CIW908
GALILEO YR 12582
SABRE YR 21272
WORLDSPAN YR 1908

Yearly Closing Dates
NONE

CONTACT DETAILS

RAFFLES RESORT CANOUAN ISLAND
CANOUAN ISLAND
ST. VINCENT AND THE GRENADINES
TEL +1 784 458 8000
FAX +1 784 458 8885
INFO@RAFFLES-CANOUANISLAND.COM
WWW.RAFFLES-CANOUANISLAND.COM

OWNER: CANOUAN RESORTS DEVELOPMENT
GENERAL MANAGER: MR LOUIS SAILER
DIRECTOR OF SALES: MR BRAD BEATY

AFFILIATIONS

The Leading Hotels
of the World®

GRACE BAY CLUB
Providenciales

On Providenciales' beautiful Grace Bay with its white sand beach and multi-hued turquoise water, the luxurious 21-suite Grace Bay Club has pampered guests since 1992. Newly upgraded, the all-suite property has been repeatedly called one of the "best of the best" on one of the "most spectacular beaches in the world".

Oversized accommodations offer private terraces and oceanviews, with featherbeds, Egyptian cotton linens, flat-screen TVs, DVD and CD players.

The Anacaona restaurant offers oceanfront dining with a Caribbean-French menu. The new on-the-beach Lounge at Grace Bay Club is a "hot" spot for tapas and drinks. The circular Anacaona bar is adjacent to dancing to live music.

Most activities focus on the beach and ocean. Guests can also play tennis on the resort's courts, bicycle, or golf at the nearby Provo Golf Club. Water sports can be arranged including catamaran trips, diving, snorkelling, kayaking, sailing and fishing. The Serenity Spa offers distinctive European and Asian-influenced services.

FACILITIES

Accommodation
3 Junior Suites, 2 Deluxe Junior Suites, 12 One-Bedroom Suites and 4 Two-Bedroom Suites

Recreational facilities
White Soft Sandy Beach
Fresh-water Swimming Pool
Jacuzzi
Floodlit Tennis Court
Biking
Windsurfing
Scuba Diving
Deep Sea Fishing
Parasailing
Hobie Cat Sailing
Kayaking
Waterskiing
Snorkelling
Boat Cruises to Cays
Golf Course and Exercise Room nearby
Serenity Spa

Meeting facilities
Meeting Rooms available by Mid 2005

International Airports
Providenciales Int'l Airport (PLS)
15 minutes drive away

RESERVATIONS

Prices
Junior Suites from 360 Euro per night

Credit cards
AE, MC, V

GDS Reservation Codes
Amadeus LX PLSGBC
Galileo LX 58953
Sabre LX 14133
Worldspan LX PLSGB

Yearly Closing Dates
None

CONTACT DETAILS

Grace Bay Club
P.O. Box 128
Providenciales
Turks & Caicos Islands
Tel +1 649 946 5050
Fax +1 649 946 5758
info@gracebayclub.com
www.gracebayclub.com

Owner: Classified
General Manager: Mr Nikheel Advani
Director of sales: Ms Tina Lyra

AFFILIATIONS

THE PALMS
Providenciales

Inspired by the classic estates of Oliver Messel, The Palms lies amidst 12-acres of gardens at the edge of the spectacular 12-mile Grace Bay beach.

Its luxurious guest residences are housed in five separate buildings clad in hand-cut coral stone. The 72 one, two and three-bedroom suites feature no less than 1800 square feet of living space with expansive outdoor terraces, marble floors and vaulted ceilings. Eight extraordinary penthouses are also available with private elevator access and the services of a private butler and chauffeur.

Aromatherapy mists, tropical sorbets and individual iPod minis beside the multi-million dollar serpentine infinity pool ensure a pampered ambiance. Guests can relax in a water banquette and enjoy a full menu without ever having to leave the water. The 15,000 square foot spa is almost a destination in itself with 14 treatment rooms, Yoga/Pilates and Tai Chi studio, fitness centre and traditional barber shop. Pan-Tropical cuisine is featured in the signature restaurant in the Mansion.

FACILITIES

Accommodation
72 SUITES

Recreational facilities
SPA
INFINITY SWIMMING POOL
WHITE SANDY BEACH
CLAY TENNIS COURT
CROQUET LAWN
NON-MOTORIZED WATER SPORTS
FITNESS CENTRE
YOGA, PILATES AND TAI CHI STUDIO
BOUTIQUES
RESTAURANT & POOL BAR

Meeting facilities
MEETING ROOM FOR UP TO 130 PEOPLE

International Airports
PROVIDENCIALES INT'L AIRPORT (PLS)
15 MINUTES DRIVE AWAY

RESERVATIONS

Prices
SUITES FROM 400 EURO PER NIGHT

Credit cards
AE, DC, MC, V

GDS Reservation Codes
NONE

Yearly Closing Dates
NONE

CONTACT DETAILS

THE PALMS
PROVIDENCIALES
TURKS & CAICOS ISLANDS
TEL +1 649 946 8226
FAX +1 649 946 5198
RESERVATIONS@THE PALMSTC.COM
WWW.THEPALMSTC.COM

Owner: THE PALMS LTD.
TURKS & CAICOS ISLANDS
Managing Director: MR WILLIAM K. ANDERSON
Sales Europe: MS ANDRÉE EDWARDS-BOWLES

AFFILIATIONS

NONE

CENTRAL & SOUTH AMERICA

This part of the world conjures up legends of the splendour of the Inca Empire, tales of Spanish conquests, verdant and steaming jungles, pristine white-powder sand beaches and the unmistakable rhythm of its music.

Here is a kaleidoscope of ever contrasting landscapes, from the eternal snows of the Andes, to the dense tropical forests of the Amazon basin, from fertile wine-growing valleys to arid deserts, from immense glaciers to colourful and vibrant cities.

Both Central & South America are enthralling experiences offering elegant explorers plenty of sweet memories to cherish an entire lifetime.

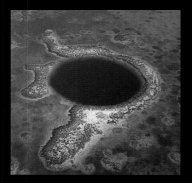

BLANCANEAUX LODGE
Cayo District

Discover a paradise where waterfalls spill into turquoise pools and Mayan ruins spring from the forest. Ensconced in a region of pristine rainforest, Blancaneaux Lodge offers modern comforts in an entirely self-sustained jungle sanctuary.

The Lodge's accommodations mirror the rainforest's vibrant hues. Each bungalow features a thatched roof, artisan-crafted and antique colonial furnishings and a luxurious Japanese bath with views of the jungle sky. Above the river, a kaleidoscope of forest bird life plays against the palmettos. Enjoy the jungle sounds from the private deck.

The hidden Big Rock Falls are a short trip away by car, horse or mountain bike. Hike down to the misty base of the falls, and swim in the warm pools.

In the restaurant, daily specials are offered from the three-acre, self-sustaining organic garden that produces all of the fruits and vegetables used to make traditional Coppola family recipes. Dine on fresh seafood, smoked meats and authentic Napolitan pizzas cooked in a wood-burning Italian oven. Local rum punches await at the Jaguar Bar.

FACILITIES

Accommodation
14 CABAÑAS AND VILLAS

Recreational facilities
BIRD WATCHING IN ANCIENT MAYA CITIES
EXPLORING JUNGLE CAVES
HORSEBACK RIDING
CANOEING

Meeting facilities
NONE

International Airports
BELIZE INTERNATIONAL AIRPORT (BZE)
120 MINUTES DRIVE AWAY
OR 30 MINUTES FLIGHT AWAY

RESERVATIONS

Prices
CABAÑAS FROM 133 EURO PER NIGHT

Credit cards
AE, DC, MC, V

GDS Reservation Codes
NONE

Yearly Closing Dates
NONE

CONTACT DETAILS

BLANCANEAUX LODGE
MOUNTAIN PINE RIDGE RESERVE
P.O. BOX B
CENTRAL FARM
CAYO DISTRICT
BELIZE
TEL +501 824 4912
FAX +501 824 4913
INFO@BLANCANEAUX.COM
WWW.BLANCANEAUX.COM

Owner: MR FRANCIS FORD COPPOLA
General Manager: MRS ANNE WOOD
Director of sales: MRS ANNE WOOD

AFFILIATIONS
NONE

KANANTIK REEF & JUNGLE RESORT

Stann Creek District

The eco-sensitive Kanantik Reef & Jungle Resort, is situated on a quiet palm-fringed gold sandy beach, and is surrounded by 300 private acres of lush, tropical forest. Located on the southern coast of Belize and nearby the Cockscomb Basin Jaguar Preserve, the resort offers the best of both worlds; the fascinating deep forest with its wildlife habitat and the tranquil Caribbean Sea with its 180 miles Barrier reef, ideal for scuba diving and snorkelling.

This enchanting resort consists of 25 luxurious, separate, spacious, air-conditioned cabañas, which are designed for privacy, with a unique blend of Mayan traditional building techniques and contemporary style. The excellent cuisine brings the flair and local flavors together with a splash of the Italian heritage of the owners.

Kanantik is Mayan for "to take care of", and you'll most certainly be taken care of at this lovely resort!

FACILITIES

Accommodation
25 THATCHED ROOF CABAÑAS

Recreational facilities
RIVER CANOEING
SCUBA DIVING
SNORKELLING
COCKSCOMB BASIN JAGUAR PRESERVE
MAYFLOWER WATERFALLS
XUNANTUNICH MAYAN RUINS

Meeting facilities
MEETING ROOM FOR UP TO 50 PEOPLE

International Airports
BELIZE INTERNATIONAL AIRPORT (BZE)
25 MINUTES FLIGHT AWAY TO
KANANTIK PRIVATE AIRSTRIP (KNK)

RESERVATIONS

Prices
CABAÑAS FROM 300 EURO PP PER NIGHT
(ALL INCLUSIVE)

Credit cards
MC, V

GDS Reservation Codes
NONE

Yearly Closing Dates
01 SEPTEMBER - 31 OCTOBER 2005

CONTACT DETAILS

KANANTIK
P.O. BOX 150
DANGRIGA
BELIZE
TEL +501 520 8048
FAX +501 520 8089
INFO@KANANTIK.COM
WWW.KANANTIK.COM

OWNER: G&R DEVELOPMENT CO.
OF BELIZE, LTD.
GENERAL MANAGER: MR ROBERTO FABBRI
DIRECTOR OF SALES: MR ROBERTO FABBRI

AFFILIATIONS
NONE

THE LODGE AT CHAA CREEK

Cayo District

Award-winning Chaa Creek has pioneered natural history travel to Belize since 1981 and is Belize's premier destination for a wide range of Caribbean and Central American adventures.

The 345-acre nature reserve on the Macal River hosts a globally recognized Natural History Centre, Butterfly Farm, miles of trails for walking, birding, mountain biking, horseback riding, a fleet of canoes, an exquisite spa, a conference centre, access to Belize's richest Maya archaeological sites, national parks and reserves. Some 250 species of birds have been sighted within the reserve.

The Jungle Lodge is comprised of 17 charming thatched cottage rooms and 6 elegant suites nestled along the riverside. Beautifully landscaped tropical gardens create a colourful atmosphere while the luxurious Spa promotes a sense of well being.

Travellers indulge in tasty Margaritas under the stars, at the veranda bar, before enjoying candlelight dining at the Chaa Creek restaurant.

FACILITIES

Accommodation
17 COTTAGES, 6 LUXURY SUITES & 10 CASITAS

Recreational facilities
345-ACRE RAINFOREST RESERVE
EXTENSIVE NETWORK OF TRAILS
HIKE IN ANCIENT MAYA TEMPLE SITES
MOUNTAIN BIKE IN THE MAYA MOUNTAINS
HORSEBACK RIDE THROUGH JUNGLE TRAILS
CANOE THE PRISTINE MACAL RIVER
EXPLORE MAYA TEMPLES & CEREMONIAL CAVES
LUXURIATE IN EXQUISITE SPA

Meeting facilities
MEETING ROOM FOR UP TO 50 PEOPLE

International Airports
BELIZE INTERNATIONAL AIRPORT (BZE)
90 MINUTES DRIVE AWAY

RESERVATIONS

Prices
COTTAGES FROM 140 EUR PER NIGHT

Credit cards
AE, MC, V

GDS Reservation Codes
NONE

Yearly Closing Dates
NONE

CONTACT DETAILS

THE LODGE AT CHAA CREEK
RAINFOREST RESERVE,
ADVENTURES CENTRE & SPA
PO BOX 53
SAN IGNACIO, CAYO DISTRICT
BELIZE
TEL +1 501-824-2037
FAX +1 501-824-2501
RESERVATIONS@CHAACREEK.COM
WWW.CHAACREEK.COM

OWNER: MR & MRS MICK AND LUCY FLEMING
GENERAL MANAGER: MR & MRS MICK AND LUCY FLEMING

AFFILIATIONS

NONE

TURTLE INN
Placencia

Just beyond your private deck, the white Caribbean sands dissolve into a clear-water world of unspoiled coral reefs, playful dolphins and bright exotic fish. Hang a hammock from the shady coconut palms and watch colorful iguanas and the gentle tides unfold against the white sand beach. This marine retreat combines natural wonders with luxury amenities, 2 restaurants, attentive staff and fine dining.

Charming cabanas of bleached thatch and native wood mingle with the beach's palm and sea grape. Under the thatched roofs, quiet ceiling fans invite sweet sea air and flora-scents to perfume the tropical interiors. Each Balinese-inspired cabana has artisan-crafted furnishings, a luxury private bath and a panoramic view of the sea.

Bike, hike or take a water taxi down the tip of the peninsula to the sleepy town of Placencia. Enjoy a quick lunch or refreshing drink in the village of Monkey River before continuing your cruise into the jungle. From exotic birds to brightly colored snakes and from wildcats to crocodiles, spectacular wildlife awaits along the river.

FACILITIES

Accommodation
11 ONE-BEDROOM VILLAS, 7 TWO-BEDROOM, 1 FRANCIS COPPOLA PAVILION HOUSE

Recreational facilities
SCUBA DIVING (PADI)
SNORKELLING
MONKEY RIVER TOUR
SWIMMING POOL
SEA KAYAKS
BICYCLES
WIND RUNNERS TO RENT
TOURS TO MAYAN SITES AND JAGUAR PRESERVE

Meeting facilities
NONE

International Airports
BELIZE INTERNATIONAL AIRPORT (BZE)
40 MINUTES FLIGHT AWAY
OR 120 MINUTES DRIVE AWAY

RESERVATIONS

Prices
VILLAS FROM 258 EURO PER NIGHT

Credit cards
AE, MC, V

GDS Reservation Codes
NONE

Yearly Closing Dates
NONE

CONTACT DETAILS

TURTLE INN
PLACENCIA VILLAGE
STANN CREEK DISTRICT
BELIZE
TEL +501 824 4912
FAX +501 824 4913
INFO@BLANCANEAUX.COM
WWW.BLANCANEAUX.COM

OWNER: MR FRANCIS FORD COPPOLA
GENERAL MANAGER: MRS ANNE WOOD
DIRECTOR OF SALES: MRS ANNE WOOD

AFFILIATIONS
NONE

VICTORIA HOUSE
Ambergris Caye

Casual elegance is the very essence of Victoria House. Charming casitas, plantation style rooms and beautiful suites draped in custom mosquito netting are nestled among swaying palm trees and white sand. All of the rooms are air-conditioned and have magnificent beach views and tropical gardens of hibiscus and bougainvillea reminiscent of a Caribbean plantation.

Relax and enjoy Caribbean fusion cuisine served in an intimate poolside setting overlooking azure waters and the world's second largest Barrier Reef. The Fantasea Dive Shop, exclusively located on the pier, offers all water activities and scuba instruction.

Fish, dive, snorkel, bird watch, discover Mayan culture or simply relax and do nothing – the dedicated staff of Victoria House will ensure a perfect stay, and an experience unique to Belize and its people.

Barefoot luxury is Victoria House...

FACILITIES

Accommodation
9 DELUXE PLANTATION ROOMS,
2 LUXURY PLANTATION SUITES
1 HONEYMOON SUITE
10 THATCH ROOF CASITAS
AND 2 LUXURY VILLAS

Recreational facilities
SWIMMING POOL
SAILING
SNORKELLING
FLY FISHING
DEEP SEA FISHING
SCUBA DIVING
SCUBA INSTRUCTION
MAYA RUINS
BIRD WATCHING
BIKING

Meeting facilities
NONE

International Airports
BELIZE INTERNATIONAL AIRPORT (BZE)
20 MINUTES FLIGHT AWAY

RESERVATIONS

Prices
DELUXE ROOMS FROM 215 EURO

Credit cards
AE, DC, MC, V

GDS Reservation Codes
NONE

Yearly Closing Dates
OCTOBER, DATES TBA

CONTACT DETAILS

VICTORIA HOUSE RESERVATIONS
515 LOUISIANA AVENUE, SUITE 300
HOUSTON, TEXAS 77002
UNITED STATES OF AMERICA
TEL +1 713 344 23 40
FAX + 1 713 224 32 87
INFO@VICTORIA-HOUSE.COM
WWW.VICTORIA-HOUSE.COM

OWNER: CLASSIFIED
GENERAL MANAGER: MRS JANET WOOLLAM &
MR BRENT KIRKMAN
DIRECTOR OF SALES: MRS FRANCES BROUSSARD

AFFILIATIONS

NONE

CALA LUNA HOTEL & VILLAS

Tamarindo

Located steps away from the ocean, and surrounded by tropical forests and marine parks in Tamarindo, a small fishing village, Cala Luna Hotel and Villas is a hidden treasure were adventure and tranquillity co-exist.

Visitors are able to walk along the shores of the shell-filles beach in the morning as the fisherman search for lobster, watch as the horizon fills with glorious colours during sunset, or stroll along the stunning beach to the active town centre.

Guests may choose to stay in one of Cala Luna's beautifully decorated deluxe rooms, each featuring a small terrace, a luxurious bathroom, air-conditioning and all the amenities demanded by today's discerning travelers. The spectacular villas have a private pool and garden, private parking, 2 or 3 bedrooms and bathrooms, a kitchen, air-conditioning and offer all the modern amenities.

Cala Luna provides the ability to see natural wonders and can arrange a full complement of sports including surfing, snorkelling, fishing, golf, and adventures.

FACILITIES

Accommodation
20 ROOMS & 16 VILLAS

Recreational facilities
SWIMMING POOL
DEEP SEA FISHING
HORSEBACK RIDING
TURTLE NESTING
KAYAKING
SCUBA DIVING
EXCURSIONS TO VOLCANOES AND MANGROVES
GOLF COURSE NEARBY
RESTAURANT

Meeting facilities
NONE

International Airports
LIBERIA INTERNATIONAL AIRPORT (LIR)
45 MINUTES DRIVE AWAY

RESERVATIONS

Prices
ROOMS FROM 145 EURO PER NIGHT
VILLAS FROM 250 EURO PER NIGHT

Credit cards
AE, MC, V

GDS Reservation Codes
NONE

Yearly Closing Dates
NONE

CONTACT DETAILS

CALA LUNA HOTEL & VILLAS
TAMARINDO
GUANACASTE
COSTA RICA
TEL +506 653 0214
FAX +506 653 0213
SALES@CALALUNA.COM
WWW.CALALUNA.COM

OWNER: MRS GRIET DEPYPERE
GENERAL MANAGER: MRS MERCEDES TRISTAN
DIRECTOR OF SALES: MR DANIEL CHAVARRIA

AFFILIATIONS
NONE

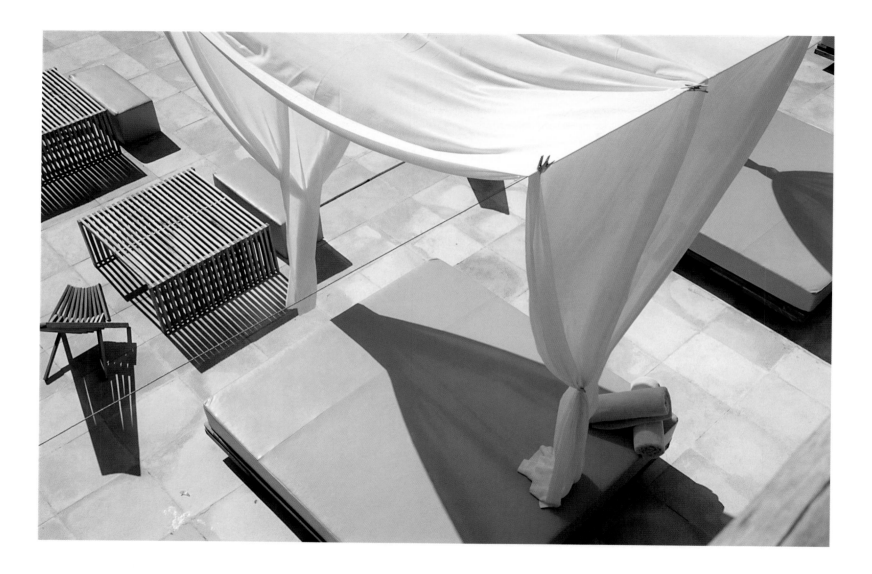

DESEO HOTEL + LOUNGE

Playa del Carmen

Located in the Mexican Caribbean, only 35 minutes south of Cancun on the Maya Riviera, Playa del Carmen is the favourite playground of young urbanites of all latitudes who seek a cool atmosphere, ideal weather, none of the formality of other destinations or the massive tourism of neighbouring beaches.

The 15 rooms and suites – which during the day double as living rooms – are imaginative because of their creative details, which include a basic kit for the beach and partying, king-size beds, hammocks and, air conditioning. Deseo also boasts an Internet service in the reception area, a self-service kitchen, and a library.

On the terrace, guests can relax on the enormous beds, alongside the Jacuzzi and the swimming pool, designed by conceptual artist Silvia Gruner. Entertained by a DJ, who will play ambient music accompanied by the sound of the turf from the turquoise waters of the nearby Caribbean sea, the lounge promises a cosy ambience.

At Deseo, comfort, good music, and amusement are combined with a relaxed atmosphere.

FACILITIES

Accommodation
6 BALCONY ROOMS,
6 LOUNGE VIEW ROOMS
AND 3 SUITES

Recreational facilities
DESEO LOUNGE
WITH KING-SIZE BEDS OUTDOORS
SWIMMING POOL DESIGNED BY SILVIA GRUNER,
AS WELL AS IN SITU VIDEO ART INSTALLATION
JACUZZI
LIVE DJ

Meeting facilities
NONE

International Airports
CANCUN INTERNATIONAL AIRPORT (CUN)
40 MINUTES DRIVE AWAY

RESERVATIONS

Prices
ROOMS FROM 125 EURO PER NIGHT

Credit cards
AE, MC, V

GDS Reservation Codes
AMADEUS DS PCM257
GALILEO DS 39815
SABRE DS 61030
WORLDSPAN DS 08257

Yearly Closing Dates
NONE

CONTACT DETAILS

DESEO HOTEL + LOUNGE
5A AV. Y CALLE 12
PLAYA DEL CARMEN
C.P. 77710
QUINTANA ROO
MEXICO
TEL +52 984 879 36 20
FAX +52 984 879 36 21
INFO@HOTELDESEO.COM
WWW.HOTELDESEO.COM

OWNER: MR MOISÉS MICHA
GENERAL MANAGER: MR ALEJANDRO RUEDA
DIRECTOR OF SALES: MR RAFAEL MICHA

AFFILIATIONS

~ a member of
design hotels

ELIXIR DE CAREYES

Careyes

Three villas, three styles, three atmospheres, all intimate yet grand.

Set in the heights of Costa Careyes, in Mexico's Pacific Coast, the idyllic villas offer superb ocean views and have walking access to Playa Rosa Beach. The three exquisite villas boast cascade lap pools and Jacuzzis. Each living room and dinning room sits under a magnificent Mexican thatched roof. The villas are decorated with original Mexican works of art, elegant hand made textiles, sculptural furniture and giant floor candles. All bedrooms feature balconies and terraces with stunning views of the sea and the forest. Wonderful tropical gardens surround each villa, giving a feeling of privacy and seclusion, amidst an atmosphere of elegant tranquillity.

Each villas has a permanent staff of four who will indulge you with fine food, a combination of delicious Mexican and Mediterranean cuisine. Recreational activities, health programs, yoga sessions, boat trips to nearby beaches and islands, catered parties, all may be arranged.

FACILITIES

Accommodation
3 LUXURY VILLAS EACH WITH 5 BEDROOMS, PRIVATE POOL AND JACUZZI

Recreational facilities
DEEP SEA FISHING
SNORKELLING
KAYAKING
HIKING TRAILS
MOUNTAIN BIKING
HORSEBACK RIDING
SPA & HEALTH CARE CENTRE
GYMNASIUM
YOGA STUDIO
POLO MATCHES (NOV.-APRIL)
OFFICE WITH DSL INTERNET SERVICE

Meeting facilities
MEETING ROOMS FOR UP TO 30 PEOPLE

International Airports
MANZANILLO AIRPORT (ZLO)
60 MINUTES DRIVE AWAY
ORDAZ AIRPORT (PVR)
120 MINUTES DRIVE AWAY

RESERVATIONS

Prices
VILLAS FROM 1,500 EURO PER NIGHT

Credit cards
NONE

GDS Reservation Codes
NONE

Yearly Closing Dates
NONE

CONTACT DETAILS

ELIXIR DE CAREYES
KM.54 CARR.B. DE NAVIDAD-PUERTO VALLARTA
CAREYES JALISCO
MEXICO C.P. 48983
TEL +52 315 35 10344
FAX + 52 315 35 10339
VIVIDEAN@ELIXIRDECAREYES.COM
WWW.ELIXIRDECAREYES.COM

OWNER: CLASIFIED
GENERAL MANAGER: MS VIVIANA DEAN
DIRECTOR OF SALES: MR MARCELO VAZQUEZ

AFFILIATIONS

NONE

HABITA
Mexico City

As a glass box floating high above the crowds, Mexico's first design hotel is breathing some refreshing life into the stagnant hotel scene that greets the modern traveller today. Habita offers a sanctuary for respite and relaxation.

Surrounded by luxury boutiques and the city best restaurants, Habita offers an unparalleled boutique hotel experience. The 32 luxurious rooms and 4 junior suites have been outfitted with every amenity imaginable, including custom pieces by TEN Arquitectos, Eames chairs and a flat screen TV's.

While the Aura restaurant and the Area bar will entice the guest's senses with inventive cuisine, both venues will equally provide the ideal zone of comfort for every occasion. The 6th floor windowless Area Bar, highlighted by a twelve-foot long outdoor fireplace, redefines the modern concept of a roof-top bar.

Should you be inclined to be pampered, retreat to Habita's own Aqua Spa, enjoy a refreshing swim in the roof-top lap pool or relax in the sauna.

Discover. Experience. Indulge. Habita

FACILITIES

Accommodation
32 Rooms & 4 Junior Suites

Recreational facilities
Heated Pool & Solarium
Aqua Spa with Sauna & Outdoor Jacuzzi
Massage Room
Aura Restaurant
Area Bar & Terrace

Meeting facilities
Meeting Room for up to 10 people

International Airports
Mexico City Int'l Airport (MEX)
25 minutes drive away

RESERVATIONS

Prices
Room from 180 Euro per night

Credit cards
AE, MC, V

GDS Reservation Codes
Amadeus LW MEX519
Galileo LW 30272
Sabre LW 55149
Worldspan LW 7519

Yearly Closing Dates
None

CONTACT DETAILS

Hotel Habita
Av. Presidente Masaryk 201
Col. Polanco
C.P. 11560
Mexico D.F.
Mexico
Tel +52 55 52 82 31 00
Fax +52 55 52 82 31 01
INFO@HOTELHABITA.COM
WWW.HOTELHABITA.COM

Owner: Mr Moisés Micha
General Manager: Mr Moisés Micha
Director of Sales: Mr Rafael Micha

AFFILIATIONS

The Leading Small Hotels
of the World

HOTELITO DESCONOCIDO
Jalisco

Located 90 kilometres south of Puerto Vallarta, this magical and truly extraordinary hotel is unique within Mexico. The little unknown hotel is nestled on a beautiful wetland estuary between the towering Sierra Madre Mountains and the Pacific Ocean, and next to one of the best, undeveloped beaches in the country.

Constructed in the style of a Mexican village, Hotelito Desconocido offers guests most unusual accommodations: palafitos, bungalows built on stilts over the edge of the estuary, or snuggled in the sand dunes right on the beach. All, however, are rustically elegant, most romantic and beautifully decorated with local antiques and curios.

This 'pioneering destination concept' combines the essence of a secluded resort with an up-close intimate experience with nature. Enriching the mind, mixed with soft adventure, romantic strolls along the beach and the sound of crushing waves on the Pacific Coast makes this one of the most breathtaking locations in the world.

FACILITIES

Accommodation
24 PALAFITOS

Recreational facilities
HORSEBACK RIDING
BIRDWATCHING TOURS BY BOAT
MOUNTAIN BIKING
KAYAKING & CANOEING
CATAMARAN SAILING
WINDSURFING
SPA SERVICES
BEACH VOLLEYBALL

Meeting facilities
NONE

International Airports
PUERTO VALLARTA INT'L AIRPORT (PVR)
100 MINUTES DRIVE AWAY

RESERVATIONS

Prices
PALAFITOS FROM 305 EURO PER NIGHT

Credit cards
AE, MC, V

GDS Reservation Codes
AMADEUS LX PVRHOD
GALILEO LX 30137
SABRE LX 18922
WORLDSPAN LX PVRHD

Yearly Closing Dates
NONE

CONTACT DETAILS

HOTELITO DESCONOCIDO
NATURAL RESERVE
60 MILES SOUTH OF PUERTO VALLARTA
MEXICO
TEL +52 322 281 40 10
FAX +52 322 281 41 30
HOTELITO@HOTELITO.COM
WWW.HOTELITO.COM

OWNER: MR MARCELLO MURZILLI
GENERAL MANAGER: MR FEDERICO SPADA
DIRECTOR OF SALES: MRS CLAUDIA SILVA

AFFILIATIONS

ALVEAR PALACE
Buenos Aires

The Alvear Palace hotel was inaugurated in 1932 and has remained the meeting point for Buenos Aires' refined society ever since. Located in the heart of the elegant Recoleta neighbourhood, it is surrounded by some of the best restaurants, museums, shops and antique stores in the city.

The Alvear Palace offers traditional hospitality combined with the most up-to-date facilities. The hotel's 105 rooms and 110 suites are sumptuously decorated with attention to every detail: Empire and Louis XVI furniture, Frette Egyptian cotton linen, air-conditioning, intelligent touch screen telephones, cellular phone, cable television, wireless broadband Internet, PC and fax connection whilst Hermès de Paris toiletries are to be found in every bathroom. Moreover, accommodation comes with personal butler service and even a personal shopper is at hand.

Facilities include a state-of-the-art health club featuring an indoor pool, sauna, exercise room, individual gym classes and massage treatments.

Awarded as South America's best hotel by both Travel & Leisure and Condé Nast Traveller.

FACILITIES

Accommodation
105 PALACE ROOMS & 110 SUITES

Recreational facilities
INDOOR SWIMMING POOL
SAUNA
GYMNASIUM
MASSAGE TREATMENTS
INDIVIDUAL GYM CLASSES
BARS & RESTAURANTS

Meeting facilities
16 MEETING ROOMS FOR UP TO 350 PEOPLE

International Airports
BUENOS AIRES INT'L AIRPORT (EZE)
30 MINUTES DRIVE AWAY

RESERVATIONS

Prices
ROOMS FROM 400 EURO PER NIGHT

Credit cards
AE, DC, MC, V

GDS Reservation Codes
AMADEUS LW BUE010
GALILEO LW 45278
SABRE LW 16583
WORLDSPAN LW 7010

Yearly Closing Dates
NONE

CONTACT DETAILS

ALVEAR PALACE
AV. ALVEAR 1891
(C1129AAA) CAPITAL FEDERAL
BUENOS AIRES
ARGENTINA
TEL +54 11 4808 2100
FAX +54 11 4804 9246
INFO@ALVEARPALACE.COM.AR
WWW.ALVEARPALACE.COM

OWNER: CIA. DE SERVICIOS HOTELEROS S.A.
GENERAL MANAGER: MRS OLGA PETRONI
DIRECTOR OF SALES: MR JUAN PEDRIEL

AFFILIATIONS
The Leading Hotels
of the World®

LLAO LLAO RESORT, GOLF – SPA

Bariloche

Llao Llao Hotel & Resort lies between the crystalline waters of Lakes Nahuel Huapi and Moreno with spectacular views of Mounts Lopez, Capilla and the snow-covered Mount Tronador, and is surrounded by ancient cypress woods.

The hotel provides luxurious accommodation in elegant bedrooms, each featuring well-equipped en suite facilities and impressive lake or mountain views. Los Césares à la carte restaurant serves excellent regional and international dishes, while a buffet café provides a more casual atmosphere. The lobby bar, heated by open stone fireplaces, boasts live music in the evenings and is the perfect place to enjoy a leisurely drink or taste delicious pastries.

The leisure facilities of the stunning resort include a challenging 18-hole golf course, a Spa and Health Club, heated indoor and outdoor swimming pools, a sauna and a gymnasium. Mountain bike tours, archery, tango & yoga lessons, windsurfing, canoeing, fly fishing and rafting are just some of the additional options for the more active souls while skiing is equally available in winter.

FACILITIES

Accommodation
147 ROOMS, 11 SUITES AND 1 CABIN

Recreational facilities
18-HOLE GOLF COURSE
LLAO LLAO EXCLUSIVE SPA
HEATED INDOOR SWIMMING POOL
OUTDOOR SWIMMING POOL
SAUNA
GYMNASIUM
HORSE RIDING
BIRD WATCHING
MOUNTAIN BIKING
4X4 DRIVING
GUIDED WALKS & TREKKING
WINDSURFING & CANOEING
FLY FISHING
RAFTING
BOATING
SKIING (WINTER)

Meeting facilitie
6 MEETING ROOMS FOR UP TO 450 PEOPLE

International Airports
SAN CARLOS DE BARILOCHE INT'L AIRPORT (BRC)
50 MINUTES DRIVE AWAY

RESERVATIONS

Prices
ROOMS FROM 200 EURO PER NIGHT

Credit cards
AE, DC, MC, V

GDS Reservation Codes
AMADEUS LW
GALILEO LW
SABRE LW
WORLDSPAN LW

Yearly Closing Dates
NONE

CONTACT DETAILS

LLAO LLAO HOTEL & RESORT
AV. EZEQUIEL BUSTILLO KM. 25
(R8409ALN)
BARILOCHE
RIO NEGRO
ARGENTINA
TEL. +54 2944 448530
FAX +54 2944 445781
VENTAS@LLAOLLAO.COM.AR
WWW.LLAOLLAO.COM

OWNER: CLASSIFIED
GENERAL MANAGER: MR CARLOS BURGOA
DIRECTOR OF SALES: MS FELICITAS MENDIETA

AFFILIATIONS

The Leading Hotels
of the World®

EXPLORA EN ATACAMA

San Pedro de Atacama

In the midst of the driest desert on earth, the explora Atacama is situated within a stone's throw of snow-capped volcanoes, shimmering salt pans and the Andes.

The explora en Atacama lodge features 50 stylish, design rooms with Jacuzzi's and boasting spectacular views of the desert, mountains and volcanoes. The high standard restaurant serves international cuisine whilst the bar and lounge area form a perfect place to exchange the adventure experiences of the day. Four spectacular outdoor swimming pools are thé place to cool off.

A stay at explora en Atacama comes on an all-inclusive basis and includes a number of excursions per day, tailored to one's personal interests by multi-lingual guides. On offer are horse riding in the sand dunes, sunset hiking to the Moon Valley, volcano climbing, cultural excursions, relaxing in explora's private hot springs, and much, much more.

Atacama is the ultimate destination for those looking for both adventure and natural beauty.

FACILITIES

Accommodation
50 DELUXE ROOMS,
WITH JACUZZI AND SITTING AREA

Recreational facilities
4 OUTDOOR SWIMMING POOLS
35 DIFFERENT EXPLORATIONS
SAUNA
LIBRARY
GAMES ROOM
MASSAGE SERVICES

Meeting facilities
MEETING ROOM FOR UP TO 100 PEOPLE

International Airports
SANTIAGO INTERNATIONAL AIRPORT (SCL)
FOLLOWED BY A 2,5 HOUR FLIGHT
FROM SCL TO CJC.
EXPLORA WILL TRANSPORT GUESTS VIA A ONE
HOUR VAN RIDE TO EXPLORA EN ATACAMA

RESERVATIONS

Prices
FROM 1,300 EURO PP DOUBLE OCCUPANCY
FOR A 4 NIGHTS PROGRAMME
(PROGRAMME INCLUDES: RETURN AIRPORT
TRANSFERS, ACCOMMODATION, FULL BOARD,
ALL DRINKS, DAILY EXPLORATIONS WITH
BILINGUAL GUIDES, EQUIPMENT,
HORSES, VEHICLES)

Credit cards
AE, DC, MC, V

GDS Reservation Codes
NONE

Yearly Closing Dates
NONE

CONTACT DETAILS

EXPLORA RESERVATIONS OFFICE
AV. AMERICO VESPUCIO 80, PISO 5
LAS CONDES
SANTIAGO
CHILE
TEL +56 22 06 60 60
FAX +55 22 28 46 55
RESERVEXPLORA@EXPLORA.COM
WWW.EXPLORA.COM

GENERAL MANAGER: MR FELIPE CRUZ
SALES MANAGER EUROPE: MRS XIMENA ZAMORA

AFFILIATIONS

NONE

THE PRIVATE COLLECTION

EXPLORA EN PATAGONIA

Torres del Paine National Park

The explora en Patagonia lodge is an architecturally remarkable hotel in a showpiece location: a biosphere reserve of waterfalls, glaciers, thick forests, and granite pillars that soar more than 2,000 metres above the Patagonian steppes.

The hotel features 50 modernist rooms and suites with large windows boasting spectacular views. Some rooms have a Jacuzzi bath. The main ground level of the hotel houses the reception, lounge, bar and restaurant in a single-plan area. Outside, a wooden plank walkway leads down to an indoor swimming pool, massage room, sauna, and adjacent outdoor Jacuzzis.

The main draw of a stay at explora en Patagonia is to take full advantage of Torres del Paine National Park's outstanding natural attractions. Excursions include hikes to the magnificent Lago Grey Glacier, a trekking out to the primitive rock paintings at Lago Sarmiento, horse riding, boating excursions on Lake Pehoe or discovering the wildlife in the region.

Staying at explora en Patagonia is truly … an 'out of this world' experience!

FACILITIES

Accommodation
50 DELUXE ROOMS & SUITES

Recreational facilities
HEATED INDOOR LAP POOL
21 DIFFERENT EXPLORATIONS
SAUNA
MASSAGE SERVICES
2 OUTDOOR JACUZZIS
LIBRARY
GAMES ROOM

Meeting facilities
MEETING ROOM FOR UP TO 60 PEOPLE

International Airports
SANTIAGO INTERNATIONAL AIRPORT (SCL)
FOLLOWED BY A 4 HOUR FLIGHT FROM SCL
TO PUQ, EXPLORA WILL TRANSPORT GUESTS
VIA A 6 HOURS VAN RIDE TO
EXPLORA EN PATAGONIA

RESERVATIONS

Prices
FROM 1,200 EURO PP DOUBLE OCCUPANCY
FOR A 4 NIGHTS PROGRAMME
(PROGRAMME INCLUDES : RETURN AIRPORT
TRANSFERS, ACCOMMODATION, FULL BOARD,
ALL DRINKS, DAILY EXPLORATIONS WITH
BILINGUAL GUIDES, EQUIPMENT, BOATS,
HORSES, VEHICLES)

Credit cards
AE, DC, MC, V

GDS Reservation Codes
NONE

Yearly Closing Dates
NONE

CONTACT DETAILS

EXPLORA RESERVATIONS OFFICE
AV. AMERICO VESPUCIO 80, PISO 5
LAS CONDES SANTIAGO
CHILE
TEL +56 22 06 60 60
FAX +55 22 28 46 55
RESERVEXPLORA@EXPLORA.COM
WWW.EXPLORA.COM

GENERAL MANAGER: MR FELIPE CRUZ
SALES MANAGER EUROPE: MRS XIMENA ZAMORA

AFFILIATIONS

NONE

The modern thoroughbred horse takes its ancestry from Europe, and its unparalleled speed, grace and endurance from careful breeding.

CLP offers a stable of championship winners that is second to none. The right helicopter with the right support for every specific purpose, customized to each client's individual specifications.

CONSULTANCY • SALES • FINANCE • LEASING • INSURANCE • MAINTENANCE • FRACTIONAL OWNERSHIP

Boomsesteenweg 93 • B-2610 Wilrijk • Belgium
Tel. +32 (0)3 827 77 77 • Fax +32 (0)3 820 91 66
Mobile +32 (0)486 70 80 90
kris@heli.bz • www.heli.bz

AGENT FOR EUROCOPTER, WORLD LEADER

EUROPE

Whether you wish to immerse yourself in culture, escape deep into the countryside or soak up the sun on a picturesque island, Europe will oblige.

Its converted castles, restored monastries and refurbished palaces are all testimony to the fascinating history whilst the gourmet cuisine and vintage wines reflect the irrepressible joie de vivre.

THE PRIVATE COLLECTION

ALMDORF SEINERZEIT

Patergassen

Almdorf Seinerzeit is a rare gem, offering the romantic charm of a rustic mountain hideaway combined with all the comforts of a deluxe hotel.

This mountain fantasy is the brain child of your enchanting, enthusiastic hosts, Mr & Mrs Steiner, who decided to create a very special place to stay. The hideaway is located on an idyllic piece of land in the Nockerberge national park, overlooking a sublime glacial valley and comprises a cluster of small, individual chalets snuggled on a gentle mountain slope, looking out to a picture-perfect panorama.

Every lovely chalet, decorated in a cozy Alpine style is like a charming little home featuring an open fireplace plus wood-burning stove, well-equipped kitchinette, dining room, parlour, two bedrooms, and two bathrooms. Naturally perfect for families, the adorable chalets are just as popular amongst couples.

Guests can dine in the romantic restaurant or have their chosen meals brought to their chalet at no extra charge. Breakfast will be delivered and served outside on your terrace, where you can relax.

FACILITIES

Accommodation
16 LUXURY CHALETS AND 4 DELUXE CHALETS

Recreational facilities
ALPINE SKIING
CROSS-COUNTRY SKIING
SAUNA
AUNTHENTIC HAY & HERB SPA
MASSAGE TREATMENTS
MOUNTAIN BIKING
FISHING
GUIDED WALKS
GOLF, SWIMMING POOL AND
TENNIS COURTS NEARBY

Meeting facilities
NONE

International Airports
KLAGENFURT AIRPORT (KLU)
45 MINUTES DRIVE AWAY

RESERVATIONS

Prices
CHALET FROM 200 EURO PER NIGHT
DELUXE CHALETS FROM 425 EURO PER NIGHT

Credit cards
AE, DC, MC, V

GDS Reservation Codes
NONE

Yearly Closing Dates
3 APRIL – 13 MAY 2005
2 NOVEMBER – 18 DECEMBER 2005

CONTACT DETAILS

ALMDORF SEINERZEIT
FELLACHER ALM
A-9564 PATERGASSEN
AUSTRIA
TEL +43 4275 7201
FAX +43 4275 72016
OFFICE@ALMDORF.COM
WWW.ALMDORF.COM

OWNER: MR & MRS KARL AND ISABELLE STEINER
GENERAL MANAGER: MR KARL STEINER
DIRECTOR OF SALES: MRS ISABELLE STEINER

AFFILIATIONS

NONE

DIE SWAENE
Bruges

'The Swan' is a true sanctuary overlooking one of the most picturesque canals in Bruges. Secluded and quiet, this little gem is conveniently located in the heart of the city.

Considered one of the most romantic and peaceful hotels in Europe, the lovely property features 30 elegantly furnished rooms, all individually decorated.

Public rooms reflect an atmosphere of times past. The impressive lounge, with its fine painted ceiling, is the restored meeting room of the original Guild of Tailors, dating from 1779. It's the perfect place to enjoy an appetizer, a drink before dinner or to savour one of the many exclusive cognacs later in the evening. The restaurant, located in a 17th Century vaulted room, offers a wonderful dining experience and serves some of the finest food in Bruges.

A magnificent new wing, The Pergola, has recently opened with 8 rooms and 2 suites at water level. Its sunny terrace follows the canal to provide an entrancing view of the ceaseless water-borne activity.

The Swan has everything to make your visit a lasting, most enjoyable experience.

FACILITIES

Accommodation
30 Rooms & Suites

Recreational facilities
Indoor Swimming Pool
Sauna
Gymnasium
Lounge & Bar
Restaurant
Horse & Carriage Rides
Boat Trips
Biking
3 Golf Courses nearby

Meeting facilities
Meeting Room for up to 20 people

International Airports
Ostend-Bruges Airport (OST)
20 minutes drive away
Brussels National Airport (BRU)
60 minutes drive away

RESERVATIONS

Prices
Rooms from 185 Euro per night
Suites from 350 Euro per night

Credit cards
AE, DC, MC, V

GDS Reservation Codes
Amadeus LX BRUDSW
Galileo LX 45514
Sabre LX 155
Worldspan LX BRUDS

Yearly Closing Dates
None

CONTACT DETAILS

Die Swaene
Steenhouwersdijk 1
B-8000 Brugge
Belgium
Tel +32 50 342 798
Fax +32 50 336 674
INFO@DIESWAENE-HOTEL.COM
WWW.DIESWAENE.COM

Owner: Family Hessels
General Manager: Mr Koen Hessels
Director of sales: Mrs Marijke Termote

AFFILIATIONS

HOTEL DE TUILERIEËN

Bruges

This elegant 15th Century mansion, converted into a stylish luxury hotel, enjoys a privileged location alongside one of the most picturesque canals in what many consider to be the most beautiful city in all of Western Europe: Bruges!

Hotel De Tuilerieën retained its dignity and historical significance, but meanwhile offers a truly luxurious experience with all modern comforts. The well known interior designer, Pieter Porters, has transformed each room into a masterpiece. All feature a direct-dial telephone, mini bar, safe, television, air-conditioning, marble bathrooms, turndown service and every amenity to make one's stay a most comfortable one.

For those in a more leisurely-oriented frame of mind, the property boasts an indoor swimming pool, a sauna, a steam bath and a Jacuzzi.

Elegantly appointed rooms, exceptional and friendly service, an enjoyable Champagne breakfast buffet and a lovely decor in a most romantic setting. A stay at Hotel De Tuilerieën is truly a unique experience!

FACILITIES

Accommodation
45 ROOMS & SUITES

Recreational facilities
INDOOR SWIMMING POOL
SAUNA
TURKISH STEAM BATH
JACUZZI
LOUNGE, BAR & RESTAURANT
HORSE & CARRIAGE RIDES
BOAT TRIPS
BIKING
3 GOLF COURSES NEARBY

Meeting facilities
MEETING ROOM FOR UP TO 50 GUESTS

International Airports
OSTEND-BRUGES AIRPORT (OST)
20 MINUTES DRIVE AWAY
BRUSSELS NATIONAL AIRPORT (BRU)
60 MINUTES DRIVE AWAY

RESERVATIONS

Prices
ROOMS FROM 259 EURO PER NIGHT
SUITES FROM 390 EURO PER NIGHT

Credit cards
AE, DC, MC, V

GDS Reservation Codes
AMADEUS LX BRUDET
GALILEO LX 25115
SABRE LX 15867
WORLDSPAN LX OSTDT

Yearly Closing Dates
NONE

CONTACT DETAILS

HOTEL DE TUILERIEËN
DIJVER 7
B-8000 BRUGGE
BELGIUM
TEL +32 50 343 691
FAX +32 50 340 400
INFO@HOTELTUILERIEEN.COM
WWW.HOTELTUILERIEEN.COM

OWNER: MR & MRS LUC RAMMANT
GENERAL MANAGER: MRS PATRICIA HOMBLÉ
DIRECTOR OF SALES: MRS PATRICIA HOMBLÉ

AFFILIATIONS

HOTEL MANOS PREMIER

Brussels

The sophistication of this beautiful mansion, combined with the owner's creativity and imagination in its decoration, has made the Manos Premier an exclusive world-class hotel and a favourite meeting place.

The generously proportioned bedrooms are reminiscent of the atmosphere found in a bourgeois mansion. Furnished with antiques and other pieces of furniture chosen personally by the owner, each exquisite room is like a unique painting.

The same individuality is found in the elegant cigar Bar or in the Kolya bar, with its lounge-like atmosphere where ethnic and baroque influences mix to achieve a high cosmopolitan character and where jazz music can be heard at different times. The quest for perfection is also evident in the Lella spa centre which invites guests to relax in an area that is worthy in comparison to the Alhambra. The Kolya restaurant has established a reputation for itself and in the original setting of the dining room guests can experience the best culinary creations.

FACILITIES

Accommodation
50 ROOMS & SUITES

Recreational facilities
LELLA SPA CENTRE FEATURING
JACUZZI, SAUNA, HAMMAM,
MASSAGE AND FITNESS ROOM
GARDEN WITH CHILDREN'S PLAYGROUND
RESTAURANT LOUNGE KOLYA
CIGAR BAR
NEAR CITY & FAMOUS SHOPPING AREA

Meeting facilities
6 MEETING ROOMS FOR UP TO 100 PEOPLE

International Airports
BRUSSELS NATIONAL AIRPORT (BRU)
20 MINUTES DRIVE AWAY

RESERVATIONS

Prices
ROOMS FROM 295 EURO PER NIGHT

Credit cards
AE, DC, MC, V

GDS Reservation Codes
NONE

Yearly Closing Dates
NONE

CONTACT DETAILS
HOTEL MANOS PREMIER
CHAUSSÉE DE CHARLEROI 100 -106
B-1060 BRUSSELS
BELGIUM
TEL +32 2 537 96 82
FAX +32 2 539 36 55
MANOS@MANOSHOTEL.COM
WWW.MANOSHOTEL.COM

OWNER: MR CONSTANTIN POULGOURAS
GENERAL MANAGER: MR CONSTANTIN POULGOURAS
DIRECTOR OF SALES: MRS NANCY NAVEAU

AFFILIATIONS
NONE

THE PAND
Bruges

The Pand is tucked away amidst a romantic leafy square, in one of Bruges' most beautiful and tranquil corners.

The 18th Century carriage house has been converted into a wonderful 'boutique' hotel, furnished with exclusive fabrics, antiques and objects of art. In the library and the elegant lounges, guests can relax by the open fire place, in most comfortable sofas.

All 24 rooms are delightfully furnished with many antiques and objects of art. The 9 suites are decorated with the stunning fabrics of Ralph Lauren.

Breakfast is true feast every morning and is served in the country-style breakfast room. Eggs are prepared to order on granny's AGA stove whilst bread is freshly baked in-house.

The Pand is staffed by individuals who value your stay as much as you do and are always on hand to accommodate your every need. There's a strong commitment to excellence in the art of friendly hospitality at the Pand.

FACILITIES

Accommodation
15 ROOMS & 11 JUNIOR SUITES

Recreational facilities
LOUNGES & BAR
BIKING
HORSE & CARRIAGE RIDES
BOAT TRIPS
FITNESS & JOGGING TRACK
3 GOLF COURSES NEARBY

Meeting facilities
MEETING ROOM FOR UP TO 20 PEOPLE

International Airports
OSTEND-BRUGES AIRPORT (OST)
20 MINUTES DRIVE AWAY
BRUSSELS NATIONAL AIRPORT (BRU)
60 MINUTES DRIVE AWAY

RESERVATIONS

Prices
ROOMS FROM 150 EURO PER NIGHT
JUNIOR SUITES FROM 225 EURO PER NIGHT

Credit cards
AE, DC, MC, V

GDS Reservation Codes
AMADEUS LX ZGJBRU
GALILEO LX 43385
SABRE LX 37313
WORLDSPAN LX BRUGG

Yearly Closing Dates
NONE

CONTACT DETAILS

THE PAND
PANDREITJE 16
B-8000 BRUGGE
BELGIUM
TEL +32 50 340 666
FAX +32 50 340 556
INFO@PANDHOTEL.COM
WWW.PANDHOTEL.COM

OWNER: FAMILY VANHAECKE
GENERAL MANAGER: MRS CHRIS VANHAECKE &
MS LYNE VANHAECKE
DIRECTOR OF SALES: MS LYNE VANHAECKE

AFFILIATIONS

ALMYRA
Pafos

Almyra is set in 8 acres of landscaped gardens on a sun-drenched headland on Cyprus' southwest coast, with views across the bay.

Almyra, meaning 'the taste of the sea', brings a complete reinvention of the resort experience. Contemporary style and comfort combine with state-of-the-art amenities, attending to every need of the modern traveller. While simple, practical and understated, Almyra's rooms are also about comfort, style and convenience. The Kyma' suites have each a private terrace lined with modern, pale-cushioned seating and full-size day beds facing the sea.

There is a freshwater swimming pool and a children's pool at the property whilst other leisure activities on offer include water sports, tennis, table tennis, gym, sauna, Jacuzzi. Three golf courses can also be found within easy reach from the hotel.

Three restaurants are on site at Almyra and offer a variety of local and international cuisine, but the place to be for a sundowner is the Helios lobby bar with its lovely sea view terrace.

FACILITIES

Accommodation
190 ROOMS & SUITES

Recreational facilities
OUTDOOR SWIMMING POOL
CHILDREN'S SWIMMING POOL
SCUBA DIVING
SAILING, WATERSKIING, WINDSURFING,
TENNIS COURT
TABLE TENNIS
INDOOR GYM, SAUNA & JACUZZI
CHILDREN'S CLUB
SIGHTSEEING EXCURSIONS
GOLF COURSES NEARBY

Meeting facilities
MEETING ROOMS FOR UP TO 250 PEOPLE

International Airports
LARNACA INTERNATIONAL AIRPORT (LCA)
90 MINUTES DRIVE AWAY
PAPHOS INTERNATIONAL AIRPORT (PFO)
15 MINUTES DRIVE AWAY

RESERVATIONS

Prices
ROOMS FROM 180 EURO PER NIGHT
SUITES FROM 450 EURO PER NIGHT

Credit cards
AE, DC, MC, V

GDS Reservation Codes
AMADEUS DS PFOPAP
GALILEO DS 41964
SABRE DS 87794
WORLDSPAN DS PFOPP

Yearly Closing Dates
NONE

CONTACT DETAILS

ALMYRA
POSEIDONOS AVENUE
CY-8042 PAFOS
CYPRUS
TEL +357 26 93 30 91
FAX +357 26 94 28 18
ALMYRA@THANOSHOTELS.COM
WWW.THANOSHOTELS.COM

OWNER: THANOS HOTELS
GENERAL MANAGER: MR BURKHARD WOLTER
DIRECTOR OF SALES: MR THANOS MICHAELIDES

AFFILIATIONS

 a member of
design hotels

ANASSA
Polis

Anassa stands close to where Aphrodite is said to have bathed in the waters of eternal beauty, an area of majestic hills, idyllic coves and sleepy villages.

Reflecting the style of a classical Greek village, whitewashed walls, domes and courtyards provide a striking contrast to the deep blue see beyond. All the suites have sea views, whilst some feature their own private plunge pools on the terrace. The interiors mirror the colourful history of Cyprus, complete with Greek motifs, Roman mosaics and spacious marble bathrooms.

The Spa offers thalasso therapy, aromatherapy, reflexology, massage and an indoor pool. Alternative leisure facilities include 2 outdoor swimming pools, a full range of water sports, cruises aboard a private yacht, tennis and squash, a gymnasium and a children's club.

Freshly-caught fish as well as fresh produce form the basis of Anassa's delicious dining options. The 4 restaurants serve a wide choice of cuisine from contemporary French specialties and traditional favourites to fusion Mediterranean and Asian dishes.

FACILITIES

Accommodation
177 STUDIO SUITES & SUITES

Recreational facilities
2 OUTDOOR SWIMMING POOLS
1 INDOOR SWIMMING POOL
SCUBA DIVING
SAILING
TENNIS AND SQUASH COURTS
TABLE TENNIS
INDOOR GYM
SPA SPECIALISED IN THALASSO THERAPY
CHILDREN'S CLUB IN HIGH SEASON
SIGHTSEEING EXCURSIONS
JEEP SAFARIS
3 GOLF COURSES NEARBY

Meeting facilities
3 MEETING ROOMS FOR UP TO 500 PEOPLE

International Airports
LARNACA INTERNATIONAL AIRPORT (LCA)
120 MINUTES DRIVE AWAY
PAPHOS INTERNATIONAL AIRPORT (PFO)
45 MINUTES DRIVE AWAY

RESERVATIONS

Prices
STUDIO SUITES FROM 250 EURO PER NIGHT
SUITES FROM 840 EURO PER NIGHT

Credit cards
AE, DC, MC, V

GDS Reservation Codes
AMADEUS LW PE0852
GALILEO LW 63788
SABRE LW 42255
WORLDSPAN LW 0852

Yearly Closing Dates
NONE

CONTACT DETAILS

ANASSA
P.O. BOX 66006
CY-8830 POLIS
CYPRUS
TEL + 357 26 888 000
FAX + 357 26 322 900
ANASSA@THANOSHOTELS.COM
WWW.THANOSHOTELS.COM

OWNER: THANOS HOTELS
GENERAL MANAGER: MR JAN VERDUYN
DIRECTOR OF SALES: MR THANOS MICHAELIDES

AFFILIATIONS

The Leading Hotels of the World

THE ANNABELLE
Pafos

This elegant resort sits on the edge of the beach with views out towards the picturesque fishing harbour of Pafos.

The stylish interiors are equally inviting, the 218 luxurious rooms and suites tastefully appointed in cool pastel shades, each with its own private terrace or balcony and equipped with all the amenities demanded by today's discerning travellers. The Annabelle boasts studio suites with private plunge pools, garden suites with outdoor whirlpools as well as opulently decorated superior suites and a presidential suite.

The daytime focus tends to be on the water, although the swimming pools and water sports are supplemented by a gym, tennis and squash courts, a kiddies club, as well as the Andromeda Health and Beauty centre, with body treatments such as aromatherapy, thalasso therapy and reflexology.

For the evenings, the wealth of acclaimed dining possibilities includes restaurants specialising in Mediterranean and Cypriot cuisine, as well as international theme buffets. Live music encourages guests to dance the night away.

FACILITIES

Accommodation
218 ROOMS & SUITES

Recreational facilities
2 OUTDOOR SWIMMING POOLS
SWIM-IN GROTTO
SCUBA DIVING
TENNIS COURT, SQUASH COURT
INDOOR GYM
TABLE TENNIS
POOL TABLE
CHILDREN'S CLUB
HEALTH & BEAUTY CENTRE
SIGHTSEEING EXCURSIONS
JEEP SAFARIS
GOLF COURSES NEARBY

Meeting facilities
4 MEETING ROOMS FOR UP TO 400 PERSONS

International Airports
LARNACA INTERNATIONAL AIRPORT (LCA)
90 MINUTES DRIVE AWAY
PAPHOS INTERNATIONAL AIRPORT (PFO)
15 MINUTES DRIVE AWAY

RESERVATIONS

Prices
STUDIO SUITES FROM 280 EURO PER NIGHT
SUITES FROM 900 EURO PER NIGHT

Credit cards
AE, DC, MC, V

GDS Reservation Codes
AMADEUS PH PFOANN
GALILEO PH 57802
SABRE PH 36130
WORLDSPAN PH PFOAH

Yearly Closing Dates
NONE

CONTACT DETAILS

THE ANNABELLE
POSEIDON AVENUE
CY-8042 PAFOS
CYPRUS
TEL + 357 269 383 33
FAX + 357 269 455 02
THE-ANNABELLE@THANOSHOTELS.COM
WWW.THANOSHOTELS.COM

OWNER: THANOS HOTELS
GENERAL MANAGER: MR KEN FLOCKHART
DIRECTOR OF SALES: MR THANOS MICHAELIDES

AFFILIATIONS

ARIA HOTEL
Prague

The Aria Hotel is a world-class property in Mala Strana, Prague's stunning left-bank neighborhood of Baroque palaces, churches, and gardens wedged in between the Vltava River and Prague Castle.

The four guestroom floors of the Aria Hotel are each dedicated to a different musical genre; Jazz, Opera, Classical or Contemporary Music. Each of the 52 rooms and suites celebrates an individual artist or composer who was particularly influential in their genre from Dvorak to Elvis, Mozart to Billie Holiday. Each room offers original artwork, a selection of books and a flat screen computer with the biography of the honored artist as well as a collection of his music.

From the music library to the private screening room, guests can explore the Aria's array of imaginative opportunities to experience the joy of music. Guests are welcome to gather with friends for an evening of movies and music in the intimate music box entertainment chamber, with sofa seating, plasma screen, surround sound and option of DVD or video projection.

FACILITIES

Accommodation
52 ROOMS, INCLUDING 9 SUITES

Recreational facilities
ROOF TERRACE
RESTAURANT & LOBBY BAR
LIBRARY WITH FIREPLACE
MUSIC LIBRARY
SCREENING ROOM
GYMNASIUM
STEAM BATH
CULTURAL VISITS
CENTRAL LOCATION

Meeting facilities
MEETING ROOM FOR UP TO 12 PEOPLE
SCREENING ROOM FOR UP TO 40 PEOPLE

International Airports
PRAGUE INTERNATIONAL AIRPORT (PRG)
35 MINUTES DRIVE AWAY

RESERVATIONS

Prices
ROOMS FROM 350 EURO PER NIGHT
SUITES FROM 425 EURO PER NIGHT

Credit cards
AE, DC, MC, V

GDS Reservation Codes
AMADEUS UZ PRG308
GALILEO UZ 59835
SABRE UZ 52996
WORLDSPAN UZ PRG08

Yearly Closing Dates
NONE

CONTACT DETAILS

ARIA HOTEL
TRZISTE 9
CZ-118 00 PRAGUE 1
CZECH REPUBLIC
TEL +420 225 334 111
FAX +420 225 334 666
STAY@ARIA.CZ
WWW.ARIA.CZ

OWNER: HK HOTELS
GENERAL MANAGER: MR JOZEF JUCK
DIRECTOR OF SALES: MR PETR MAREK

AFFILIATIONS
NONE

HOTEL LE PALAIS
Prague

The Hotel Le Palais is a real treasure for sophisticated travellers wanting to discover a delightful gem of the 19th Century 'Belle Epoque' architecture that boasts a peaceful location to discover Prague.

The historically accurate restoration of the original structure and the gentle weave of modern elements generate an unequalled ambience. Large parts of this beautiful building were created by the Bohemian painter Ludek Marold and are therefore classified as historical monuments.

The 60 spacious rooms and 12 suites with their elegant and homely ambience and their luxurious, generous marble bathrooms offer first-class accommodation. The suites have been lovingly restored and individually furnished, and offer splendid views over Prague. All accommodation feature state-of-the-art equipment and every amenity demanded by discerning travellers.

An elegant à la carte restaurant with silent open terrace boasts wonderful views of Prague whilst a spacious and well-equipped health club and relax centre complete the offer.

FACILITIES

Accommodation
60 Rooms & 12 Suites

Recreational facilities
Fitness Centre
Massage
Sauna
Jacuzzi & Steam Bath
Hydrojet & Aroma Showers
Solarium
Beauty Salon
Library
Restaurant & Lobby Bar

Meeting facilities
Meeting Rooms for up to 80 People

International Airports
Prague International Airport (PRG)
35 minutes drive away

RESERVATIONS

Prices
Rooms from 325 Euro per night
Suites from 380 Euro per night

Credit cards
AE, DC, MC, V

GDS Reservation Codes
Amadeus LW PRGO51
Galileo LW 53244
Sabre LW 46586
Worldspan LW 3051

Yearly Closing Dates
None

CONTACT DETAILS
Hotel Le Palais
U Zvonarky 1
CZ-120 00 Prague 2 - Vinohrady
Czech Republic
Tel +420 234 634 111
Fax +420 234 634 635
INFO@PALAISHOTEL.CZ
WWW.PALAISHOTEL.CZ

Owner: Classified
General Manager: Mr Jiri Gajdosik
Director of sales: Mrs Lenka Darázs

AFFILIATIONS

The Leading Small Hotels
of the World

THE PRIVATE COLLECTION

RIVERSIDE HOTEL
Prague

The Riverside Hotel opened in 2002 and is located on the left bank of the Vltava River, a short walk to the National Theatre and a pleasant twenty minutes stroll to the Old Town Square.

Built at the beginning of the 20th Century in late eclectic style with rich decoration of the façade, the interior of the Riverside Hotel is contemporary in design with 45 lavishly decorated rooms and suites. All deluxe rooms and suites overlook the river with views on the Charles Bridge, the Castle and the historical city of Prague.

Start you day with breakfast in the privacy of your room or in the breakfast room. Enjoy a drink or a light snack in the Hemingway Bar, the place to see and to be seen. For other meals the many restaurants, bistros and cafes in the area are just steps away.

FACILITIES

Accommodation
13 SUITES & 32 ROOMS

Recreational facilities
BREAKFAST RESTAURANT
BAR
CENTRAL LOCATION
HORSE & CARRIAGE RIDES
BOAT TRIPS
CULTURAL VISITS
EXCURSIONS

Meeting facilities
NONE

International Airports
PRAGUE INTERNATIONAL AIRPORT (PRG)
25 MINUTES DRIVE AWAY

RESERVATIONS

Prices
STANDARD ROOM FROM 230 EURO PER NIGHT

Credit cards
AE, DC, MC, V

GDS Reservation Codes
NONE

Yearly Closing Dates
NONE

CONTACT DETAILS
JANACKOVO NABREZI 15
CZ-150 00, PRAGUE 5
CZECH REPUBLIC
TEL +420 225 994 611
FAX + 420 225 994 615
INFO@RIVERSIDEPRAGUE.COM
WWW.RIVERSIDEPRAGUE.COM

OWNER: ORCO HOTEL COLLECTION
GENERAL MANAGER: MR JEAN-FRANCOIS PELOUARD

AFFILIATIONS

THE PRIVATE COLLECTION

HOTEL SCHLÖSSLE
Tallinn

The Hotel Schlössle is at the centre of Tallinn's beautiful medieval old town. Only steps away from the historic Town Hall Square, and shopping streets, walk up to the palace of feudal lords and barons dating back to the Danish King Waldemar II and the Czars.

The medieval architecture featuring vaulted cellars, limestone stairways, massive wooden beams, antique furnishings, and green and plum colour décor gives this unique hotel a luxurious baronial atmosphere. Blossoming trees in the sun-dappled courtyard and the glow of the fireside combine to impart an inimitable sense of luxury and charm.

Guests at this lovely property are treated to imaginative meals, a fine selection of champagne and wines, and even to a traditional Estonian sauna.

All 24 rooms and suites have been individually designed and boast luxury furnishings, an en-suite bathroom, ISDN-lines, trouser press, hairdryer, safe and mini bar. Many guests re-book the same room time after time.

FACILITIES

Accommodation
24 ROOMS AND SUITES

Recreational facilities
SAUNA
IN-ROOM MOVIES
RESTAURANT 'STENHUS'

Meeting facilities
MEETING ROOM FOR UP TO 60 PEOPLE

International Airports
TALLINN INTERNATIONAL AIRPORT (TLL)
15 MINUTES DRIVE AWAY

RESERVATIONS

Prices
ROOMS FROM 307 EURO PER NIGHT
SUITES FROM 505 EURO PER NIGHT

Credit cards
AE, DC, MC, V

GDS Reservation Codes
AMADEUS XL TLLGTP
GALILEO XL 92390
SABRE XL 42029
WORLDSPAN XL 40051

Yearly Closing Date
NONE

CONTACT DETAILS

SCHLÖSSLE HOTEL
PÜHAVAIMU 13-15
10123 TALLINN
ESTONIA
TEL + 372 699 7700
FAX + 372 699 7777
GRANDPALACE@
SCHLOSSLE-HOTELS.COM
WWW.SCHLOSSLE-HOTELS.COM

Owner: SCHLÖSSLE HOTEL GROUP
General Manager: MR PETER KNOLL
Director of sales: MRS EVELIN BÖTKER

AFFILIATIONS

SUMMIT HOTELS AND RESORTS

LE CHALET DU MONT D'ARBOIS
Megève

On the heights of Megève, nestled amongst the pine trees, the lovely rooms of the Chalet du Mont d'Arbois, felted and enhanced by the warmth of wood, offers comfort and calm in an exceptionally natural setting.

The cuisine is both classic and innovative, featuring a spit over a crackling wood fire. Winter as well as summer. guests can experience a world of pleasure and relaxation for all the family to enjoy. The privileged domain offers a wide range of activities such as skiing at 200 m, a private 18 holes golf course, tennis as well as a fitness and beauty centre, beauty workshop, sauna, Jacuzzi, Turkish bath, indoor and outdoor heated swimming pool; everything travellers need to ensure total relaxation after an invigorating day out in the Alpine air.

Megève, the star of resorts and a village boasting a unique cachet, awaits guests for an unforgettable holiday on the Mont d'Arbois plateau.

FACILITIES

Accommodation
24 ROOMS IN THE MAIN CHALET AND 12 ROOMS & SUITES IN ADJACENT CHALETS

Recreational facilities
PRIVATE 18-HOLE GOLF AT 300 M
SPA, BEAUTY AND HEALTH CENTRE
INDOOR AND OUTDOOR HEATED SWIMMING POOL
JACUZZI
SAUNA & HAMMAM
TENNIS COURT AT 100 M
SKI STATION AT 300 M

Meeting facilities
MEETING ROOMS FOR UP TO 50 PEOPLE

International Airports
GENEVA INTERNATIONAL AIRPORT (GVA)
60 MINUTES DRIVE AWAY
ANNECY-MEYTHE AIRPORT (NCY)
60 MINUTES DRIVE AWAY

RESERVATIONS

Prices
ROOMS FROM 345 EURO PER NIGHT

Credit cards
AE, DC, MC, V

GDS Reservation Codes
AMADEUS WB GVACHA
GALILEO WB 13798
SABRE WB 47528
WORLDSPAN WB H507

Yearly Closing Date
15 APRIL - 15 JUNE 2005
15 SEPTEMBER - 15 DECEMBER 2005

CONTACT DETAILS

LE CHALET DU MONT D'ARBOIS
447 CHEMIN DE LA RACAILLE
F-74120 MEGÈVE
FRANCE
TEL +33 450 21 25 03
FAX +33 450 21 24 79
MONTARBOIS@RELAISCHATEAUX.FR
WWW.CHALET-MONTARBOIS.COM

OWNER: MR & MRS BENJAMIN AND NADINE DE ROTHSCHILD
GENERAL MANAGER: MR ALEXANDRE FAIX
DIRECTOR OF SALES: MRS CLAIRE RAMOS

AFFILIATIONS

RELAIS & CHATEAUX

CHÂTEAU DE BAGNOLS
Lyon

Dating from the 13th Century, the Château de Bagnols is set among vineyards, forests and green hills in the heart of the Beaujolais countryside in south eastern France.

With its towers, moat, honey-coloured stone known as pierre dorée and entrance across a drawbridge, Château de Bagnols is one of France's major historic monuments. The 21 unique rooms and suites, together with the salons and gardens, have been painstakingly restored, revealing wall paintings created during the Château's finest period, when nearby Lyon was one of Europe's great Renaissance cities.

Nothing has been left to chance, nothing is too much trouble – especially in the kitchen. Lyon is world famous for its cuisine and food markets, and the Château's Chef is justly proud of his seductive candle light dinner menus which are served in front of one of Europe's largest gothic chimneys.

A roman swimming pool, a magnificent landscaped garden, vineyards, golf courses, wine tasting, horseback riding, biking, hiking and cultural excursions are just some of the possible leisure activities on offer to complement your stay.

FACILITIES

Accommodation
21 ROOMS & SUITES

Recreational facilities
ROMAN SWIMMING POOL
WINE TASTINGS
HIKING & BIKING
GOLF
HOT AIR BALLOONING
HELICOPTER TOURS
TENNIS
HORSEBACK RIDING
HORSE CARRIAGE EXCURSIONS
GUIDED CULTURAL VISITS

Meeting facilities
4 MEETING ROOMS FOR UP TO 20 PEOPLE

International Airports
LYON INTERNATIONAL AIRPORT (LYS)
40 MINUTES DRIVE AWAY

RESERVATIONS

Prices
ROOMS FROM 425 EURO PER NIGHT

Credit cards
AE, DC, MC, V

GDS Reservation Codes
AMADEUS LW LYS620
GALILEO LW 52631
SABRE LW 36102
WORLDSPAN LW 0620

Yearly Closing Dates
02 JANUARY – 02 APRIL 2005

CONTACT DETAILS

CHÂTEAU DE BAGNOLS
F-69620 BAGNOLS
FRANCE
TEL +33 474 714 000
FAX +33 474 714 049
INFO@BAGNOLS.COM
WWW.ROCCOFORTEHOTELS.COM

OWNER: LADY HELEN HAMLYN
GENERAL MANAGER: MR FRANCO MORA
DIRECTOR OF SALES: MRS ELENA BRUNO

AFFILIATIONS

The Leading Small Hotels
of the World

CHÂTEAU DE MIRAMBEAU

Mirambeau

Located in one of the best known areas of south west France, the Charente-Maritime area, the grand Château de Mirambeau stands proudly in between the famous cities of Cognac and Bordeaux.

The castle itself lies in the heart of 8 hectares of parkland and its towers dominate the whole surrounding countryside. Its galleries, spires, chapel and stone porticoes are an invitation to think back to the history of bygone centuries. The style and architecture allow for guests to experience the atmosphere of ancient château life.

The rooms and suites are spacious and decorated with refined antique furnishings and four-poster beds, and feature marble bathrooms and every modern amenity to provide discerning guests with a most comfortable and enjoyable stay.

On the leisure side, the hotel boasts a Wellness Centre with swimming pool, sauna, Jacuzzi, solarium and gymnasium. Within the lovely landscaped gardens and parkland, two tennis courts and an outdoor swimming pool can also be found.

CHÂTEAU DU DOMAINE ST MARTIN
Vence

Overlooking the French Riviera and located between Nice and Cannes, le Château du Domaine St Martin offers exquisite accommodation in a relaxed environment. All the 47 junior suites and villas are distinctively decorated and boast a sweeping panoramic view over the Mediterranean Sea. The fine furnishings and artwork coupled with the immaculate attention to detail throughout the hotel reflect the elegant and intimate French charm.

The one Michelin Star gourmet restaurant 'La Commanderie' with its shaded terrace offers some of the finest French cuisine and wines. During the summer, guests can enjoy light grilled Mediterranean dishes at the 'L'Oliveraie', situated in the park among the century olive trees. The hotel also features an overflow and heated swimming pool, 2 clay tennis courts, jeu de boules and a helicopter pad.

The Château du Domaine St Martin is synonymous with pleasure, fine dining, well being and perfection.

FACILITIES

Accommodation
47 JUNIOR SUITES AND VILLAS

Recreational facilities
HEATED OVERFLOW SWIMMING POOL
2 CLAY TENNIS COURTS
BODY AND BEAUTY TREATMENTS
JEU DE BOULES
HELICOPTER PAD FOR PANORAMIC FLIGHTS
GOURMET RESTAURANT
(ONE STAR MICHELIN)
BAR
CULTURAL VISITS & EXCURSIONS

Meeting facilities
2 MEETING ROOMS FOR UP TO 70 PEOPLE

International Airports
NICE INTERNATIONAL AIRPORT (NCE)
20 MINUTES DRIVE AWAY

RESERVATIONS

Prices
JUNIOR SUITES FROM 245 EURO PER NIGHT

Credit cards
AE, MC, V

GDS Reservation Codes
AMADEUS WB XCGCSM
GALILEO WB 13187
SABRE WB 47307
WORLDSPAN WB CD28

Yearly Closing Dates
15 OCTOBER 2004 – 13 FEBRUARY 2005

CONTACT DETAILS

CHÂTEAU DU DOMAINE ST MARTIN
AV. DES TEMPLIERS, BP 102
F-06140 VENCE
FRANCE
TEL +33 4 93 58 02 02
FAX +33 4 93 24 08 91
RESERVATIONS@CHATEAU-ST-MARTIN.COM
WWW.CHATEAU-ST-MARTIN.COM

OWNER: S.A. HOTEL DU CAP – EDEN ROC
GENERAL MANAGER: MR PHILIPPE PERD
DIRECTOR OF SALES: MRS VALÉRIE MULLER

AFFILIATIONS

RELAIS &
CHATEAUX

THE PRIVATE COLLECTION

COUR DES LOGES

Lyon

Four of the finest Renaissance houses in Old Lyon, contemporary art works, 9 interior courtyards, hanging gardens and intimate passageways constitute Cour des Loges.

But it is not so much the nobility of the place, where each stone, each step seems impregnated with history that gives rise to the unique nature of Cour des Loges, but it is rather due to the combination of centuries and the marriage of styles; a subtle harmony between the Renaissance spirit and contemporary creativity.

Very special cares has been taken with the interior decoration and in improving the comfort of the guests, while preserving the magic and charm of this exceptional spot. At the hearth of the capital of gastronomy, the sumptuously decorated rooms of Cour des Loges offer exceptional style and comfort.

FACILITIES

Accommodation
62 ROOMS, INCLUDING 10 SUITES & APARTMENTS

Recreational facilities
INDOOR HEATED SWIMMING POOL
SAUNA
HANGING GARDENS
CENTRAL LOCATION
CULTURAL VISITS
SHOPPING

Meeting facilities
6 MEETING ROOMS FOR UP TO 85 PEOPLE

International Airports
LYON INTERNATIONAL AIRPORT (LYS)
40 MINUTES DRIVE AWAY

RESERVATIONS

Prices
ROOMS FROM 230 EURO PER NIGHT
SUITES FROM 440 EURO PER NIGHT

Credit cards
AE, DC, MC, V

GDS Reservation Codes
NONE

Yearly Closing Dates
NONE

CONTACT DETAILS

COUR DES LOGES
6 RUE DU BOEUF
F-69005 LYON
FRANCE
TEL 00 33 4 72 77 44 44
FAX 00 33 4 75 40 93 61
CONTACT@COURDESLOGES.COM
WWW.COURDESLOGES.COM

OWNER: MR GEORGES-ERIC TISCHKER
GENERAL MANAGER: MR GEORGES-ERIC TISCHKER
DIRECTOR OF SALES: MRS VÉRONIQUE PELLICIER

AFFILIATIONS

NONE

GRAND-HOTEL DU CAP-FERRAT

St-Jean Cap-Ferrat

The Grand-Hotel du Cap-Ferrat is nestled peacefully on the tip of the Cap-Ferrat peninsula, from where its guests can enjoy magnificent views of the sea. Set in the shade of pine trees dominating the peninsula, in a private park at the very end of the coast and brimming with a myriad of glorious flowers, the hotel was built in 1908 at the height of the Belle Epoque.

The hotel's terraced gardens slope downwards towards the sea and the beach club, where the wonderful heated seawater pool with its al fresco restaurant is to be found. The restaurant 'Le Cap' tempts one with inventive Mediterranean gourmet delights.

The hotel is the epitome of privacy and discretion and its elegant furnishings and luxurious bedrooms with bathrooms made of rare marble, combine beautifully with the graceful architecture of the palace itself.

The Villa Rose-Pierre is a superb private residence comprising 6 bedrooms, a dining room, a private swimming pool, sauna and fitness room, and a team of staff is at the exclusive disposal of the villa's occupants.

FACILITIES

Accommodation
44 ROOMS, 9 SUITES &
ONE 6-ROOM PRIVATE VILLA

Recreational facilities
OUTDOOR SEAWATER OLYMPIC-SIZED
SWIMMING POOL
CHILDREN'S POOL
TENNIS COURT
JOGGING TRACK
ALL-TERRAIN BICYCLES
BOUTIQUE
15 ACRE PRIVATE PARK OF PINE TREES
AND CYPRESS

Meeting facilities
2 MEETING ROOMS FOR UP TO 40 PEOPLE

International Airports
NICE INTERNATIONAL AIRPORT (NCE)
20 MINUTES DRIVE AWAY

RESERVATIONS

Prices
ROOMS FROM 205 EURO PER NIGHT
SUITES FROM 740 EURO PER NIGHT

Credit cards
AE, DC, MC, V

GDS Reservation Codes
AMADEUS LX NCEBEL
GALILEO LX 21547
SABRE LX 33570
WORLDSPAN LX NCEBE

Yearly Closing Dates
3 JANUARY - 1 MARCH 2005

CONTACT DETAILS

GRAND-HOTEL DU CAP-FERRAT
71 BD GÉNÉRAL DE GAULLE
F-06230 ST-JEAN CAP-FERRAT
FRANCE
TEL +33 (0)4 93 76 50 50
FAX +33 (0)4 93 76 04 52
RESERV@GRAND-HOTEL-CAP-FERRAT.COM
WWW.GRAND-HOTEL-CAP-FERRAT.COM

OWNER: CLASSIFIED
GENERAL MANAGER: MR MICHEL A. GALOPIN
DIRECTOR OF SALES: MR GILLES FOUILLEROUX

AFFILIATIONS

HOTEL DU CASTELLET

Le Castellet

A stone's throw from the village of Le Castellet with its terraced vineyards and azure skies, the Hotel du Castellet is a blend of hacienda, medina and Italian palazzo, surveying the Mediterranean Sea and overlooking a park of several hectares.

A stay at Hotel du Castellet is an invitation to savour total comfort and serenity in a Provencal atmosphere, enhanced by elegant fabrics, colourful patinas and stylish furnishings, warm moments of enjoyment around the piano or the fireplace. The pleasure of staying in guest-rooms or suites, all with terraces or gardens and the sea as the background, is a real lullaby for your dreams and a chance for replenishment in a setting of serenity.

Hotel du Castellet also provides unique facilities such as a private International Airport and 4 spectacular holes of golf, facing the splendid bay of Bandol.

Guests can enjoy diner in the popular restaurant and discover the cuisine of Chef Hervé Sauton, a reflection of the elegant and refined place.

FACILITIES

Accommodation
34 ROOMS & 13 JUNIOR SUITES

Recreational facilities
OUTDOOR SWIMMING POOL
INDOOR SWIMMING POOL
FITNESS CENTRE
MASSAGE AND BEAUTY TREATMENTS
STEAM BATH
GOLF COURSES
PUTTING GREEN
2 CLAY TENNIS COURTS
JOGGING PATH
MOUNTAIN BIKE CIRCUIT
LUXURY BOUTIQUE
HELICOPTER FLIGHTS

Meeting facilities
4 MEETING ROOMS FOR UP TO 110 PEOPLE

International Airports
MARSEILLE INT'L AIRPORT (MRS)
45 MINUTES DRIVE AWAY
LE CASTELLET AIRPORT (CTT)
5 MINUTES DRIVE AWAY

RESERVATIONS

Prices
ROOMS FROM 260 EURO PER NIGHT
JUNIOR SUITES FROM 400 EURO PER NIGHT

Credit cards
AE, DC, MC, V

GDS Reservation Codes
AMADEUS LW TNT631
GALILEO LW 50996
SABRE LW 64024
WORLDSPAN LW 0631

Yearly Closing Dates
NONE

CONTACT DETAILS

HOTEL DU CASTELLET
3001 ROUTE DES HAUTS DU CAMP
F-83330 LE CASTELLET
FRANCE
TEL +33 4 94 98 37 77
FAX + 33 4 94 98 37 78
INFOS@HOTELDUCASTELLET.COM
WWW.HOTELDUCASTELLET.COM

OWNER: CLASSIFIED
PRESIDENT: MR PHILIPPE GURDJIAN
GENERAL MANAGER: MR DIDIER BRU

AFFILIATIONS

The Leading Small Hotels
of the World

99

HOTEL LANCASTER
Paris

The Hotel Lancaster, in rue de Berri, just off the Champs-Elysées in the heart of Paris, is one of Europe's most charming hotels, with an undisputed reputation for impeccable standards and service.

Until today, the Lancaster has been run as it always was, like a luxurious private home, filled with a fascinating collection of furniture , antique clocks, paintings, chandeliers, lamps, tapestries, velvets, silk and damask, crystal and porcelain... With its 60 individually-styled and decorated bedrooms, the Lancaster remains a favourite of connoisseurs, and its courtyard, once the stables of the private house, is one of the prettiest in Paris.

A must is the newly renovated intimate restaurant, overseen by 3 Michelin star Chef, Michel Troisgros, where inventive flavours and meticulous details revive timeless classics.

The spacious, elegant and newly refurbished bedrooms, cosy bar, garden courtyard and small private dining salons blend to create the feel of an elegant private home.

FACILITIES

Accommodation
60 ROOMS, INCLUDING 11 SUITES

Recreational facilities
FITNESS CENTRE
SAUNA
COURTYARD GARDEN
JUST OFF THE CHAMPS ELYSÉES AVENUE

Meeting facilities
MEETING ROOM FOR UP TO 14 PEOPLE

International Airports
PARIS CHARLES DE GAULLE AIRPORT (CDG)
60 MINUTES DRIVE AWAY

RESERVATIONS

Prices
DOUBLE ROOMS FROM 410 EURO PER NIGHT
SUITES FROM 790 EURO PER NIGHT

Credit cards
AE, DC, MC, V

GDS Reservation Codes
AMADEUS LW PAR615
GALILEO LW31688
SABRE LW22463
WORLDSPAN LW 615

Yearly Closing Dates
NONE

CONTACT DETAILS

HOTEL LANCASTER
7, RUE DE BERRI
F-75008 PARIS
FRANCE
TEL +33 140 76 40 76
FAX +33 140 76 40 00
RESERVATIONS@HOTEL-LANCASTER.FR
WWW.HOTEL-LANCASTER.FR

OWNER: MR & MRS ANDRIEU
GENERAL MANAGER: MR DENYS COURTIER
DIRECTOR OF SALES: MR JOHN W. PETCH

AFFILIATIONS
The Leading Small Hotels
of the World

HOTEL LE BEAUVALLON

Ste. Maxime

Hotel Le Beauvallon is a Belle-Époque palace, first constructed in 1914, and commands stunning views over the Bay of St Tropez, eight minutes away by boat from the hotel's private pontoon.

Refreshing and lacking for nothing, the 58 rooms and 12 suites reflect the elegance and refined luxury that is the spirit of the hotel. Most offer panoramic views of the gardens and the Bay of St Tropez beyond, whilst others overlook the greens of the Beauvallon Golf Course and the surrounding hills.

Dining at Le Beauvallon is a gourmets' dream. With its terrace and magical views across the bay, the gastronomic restaurant "Les Colonnades" offers menus that are Mediterranean in flavour and yet influenced by the finest of international cuisine. Six hectares of landscaped gardens unfurl like a green carpet as far as the Mediterranean coastline to Beach Club, a private playground for guests of Le Beauvallon featuring: swimming pool, heated Jacuzzi, gymnasium, boutiques, restaurant and bar. The Beach Restaurant sits literally on the water's edge and offers a delectable selection of Mediterranean summertime dishes.

FACILITIES

Accommodation
58 ROOMS & 12 SUITES

Recreational facilities
OUTDOOR SWIMMING POOL
HEATED OUTDOOR JACUZZI
PRIVATE BEACH & WATER SPORTS
SPA & GYMNASIUM
BOUTIQUES & JEU DE BOULES
PRIVATE FERRY TO ST. TROPEZ
SNOOKER AND GAMES ROOM
PRIVATE SCREENING ROOM
18-HOLE GOLF COURSE NEXT DOOR
CLAY COURT TENNIS CLUB NEXT DOOR

Meeting facilities
MEETING ROOMS FOR UP TO 235 PEOPLE

International Airports
TOULON/HYÈRES AIRPORT (TLN)
45 MINUTES DRIVE AWAY
NICE INTERNATIONAL AIRPORT (NCE)
75 MINUTES DRIVE AWAY
GRIMAUD HELIPORT
15 MINUTES DRIVE AWAY

RESERVATIONS

Prices
ROOMS FROM 205 EURO PER NIGHT
SUITES FROM 495 EURO PER NIGHT

Credit cards
AE, DC, MC, V

GDS Reservation Codes
AMADEUS YX LTTBEA
GALILEO YX 67779
SABRE YX 29683
WORLDSPAN YX TLNLB

Yearly Closing Dates
NOVEMBER 2004 – MARCH 2005

CONTACT DETAILS

HOTEL LE BEAUVALLON
BAIE DE ST. TROPEZ
BEAUVALLON-GRIMAUD
F-83120 STE. MAXIME
FRANCE
TEL +33 4 94 55 78 88
FAX +33 4 94 55 78 78
COMMERCIAL@LEBEAUVALLON.COM
WWW.HOTEL-LEBEAUVALLON.COM

OWNER: CLASSIFIED
GENERAL MANAGER: MR OLIVIER VALENTIN
DIRECTOR OF SALES: MS VÉRONIQUE LENOIR-GOMES

AFFILIATIONS

NONE

HOTEL MEURICE

Paris

Always ranking amongst the most elegant hotels in the world, the Hotel Meurice embodies a rebirth of a French palace with exceptional style and quality combined with contemporary chic. It boasts an extraordinary location facing the Tuileries Gardens and the very hearth and soul of Paris's stylish 1st district.

This luxury hotel offers travellers and Parisians a wonderful choice of memorable moments. In the sumptuous two stars Michelin Le Meurice Restaurant, Chef Yannick Alleno showcases the best of French cuisine. With deep leather armchairs and dark woodwork, the intimate Bar Fontainebleau is an ideal setting for sipping cocktails and socializing.

Located above the interior garden, the exclusive Espace Bien-Etre Caudalie Spa features the latest exercise equipment, dry saunas, steam and whirlpool baths, and the only Caudalie 'vinotherapy' Spa in Paris where guests can pamper themselves with the unique, rejuvenating effects of grape seed based treatments.

In every aspect, Hotel Meurice exemplifies modern excellence. Tekst

FACILITIES

Accommodation
160 ROOMS, INCLUDING 40 SUITES
AND JUNIOR SUITES

Recreational facilities
FITNESS CENTRE
JACUZZI
2 SAUNAS
2 STEAM BATHS
BEAUTY CENTRE CAUDALIE
GASTRONOMIC RESTAURANT
(TWO STARS MICHELIN)
WINTER GARDEN
BAR
PRIVATE DINING ROOMS

Meeting facilities
4 MEETING ROOMS FOR UP TO 200 PEOPLE

International Airports
PARIS CHARLES DE GAULLE AIRPORT (CDG)
60 MINUTES DRIVE AWAY

RESERVATIONS

Prices
ROOMS FROM 650 EURO PER NIGHT

Credit cards
AE, DC, MC, V

GDS Reservation Codes
AMADEUS LW PAR625
GALILEO LW 40399
SABRE LW 01193
WORLDSPAN LW 0625

Yearly Closing Dates
NONE

CONTACT DETAILS

HOTEL MEURICE
228, RUE RIVOLI
F-75001 PARIS
FRANCE
TEL +33 1 44 58 10 10
FAX +33 1 44 58 10 15
RESERVATIONS@MEURICEHOTEL.COM
WWW.MEURICEHOTEL.COM

OWNER: DORCHESTER HOTELS
GENERAL MANAGER: MR DOMINIQUE BORRI
DIRECTOR OF SALES: MRS CHRISTINE ODILE

AFFILIATIONS

The Leading Hotels
of the World®

HOTEL MONTALEMBERT
Paris

The chic Hotel Montalembert, precursor of the design-led movement, is a historic landmark and the most stylish hotel on Paris' Left Bank.

The hotel dates from 1926 when it was built in the Beaux-Arts style. It was restored and hailed as a smashing success, borrowing sophisticated elements of Bauhaus and post-modern design in honey beiges, creams, and golds. Simple lines, hand-crafted pieces, and top-quality fabrics and amenities make this a very special place to stay in Paris.

The 48 rooms and 8 suites are each decorated in their unique way with contemporary lighting, photographs and engravings. The full bathrooms are luxurious with deep tubs, chrome fixtures, Cascais marble, and tall pivoting mirrors.

The hotel's lounge, with a fireplace corner and splendid library, provides a serene ambiance, while the restaurant, is inviting and intimate, serving fine, inventive cuisine. Hotel guests gather at the cafe-bar, in the library and on the outdoor dining terrace from which one can observe Parisian life.

FACILITIES

Accommodation
56 ROOMS, INCLUDING 8 SUITES

Recreational facilities
RESTAURANT & BAR
SAINT-GERMAIN-DES-PRÈS AREA
A FEW STEPS AWAY FROM THE MUSÉE D'ORSAY
AND THE MUSÉE DU LOUVRE

Meeting facilities
MEETING ROOM FOR UP TO 20 PEOPLE

International Airports
PARIS CHARLES DE GAULLE AIRPORT (CDG)
60 MINUTES DRIVE AWAY

RESERVATIONS

Prices
ROOMS FROM 320 EURO PER NIGHT
SUITES FROM 660 EURO PER NIGHT

Credit cards
AE, DC, MC, V

GDS Reservation Codes
AMADEUS PH PARHMH
GALILEO PH 31662
SABRE PH 24443
WORLDSPAN PH PARHM

Yearly Closing Dates
NONE

CONTACT DETAILS

HOTEL MONTALEMBERT
3, RUE DE MONTALEMBERT
F-75007 PARIS
FRANCE
TEL +33 145 49 68 68
FAX +33 145 49 69 49
WELCOME@MONTALEMBERT.COM
WWW.MONTALEMBERT.COM

OWNER: WESTMONT HOSPITALITY GROUP
GENERAL MANAGER: MR ALEXANDRE FOUGEROLE
DIRECTOR OF SALES: MR VINCENT TISSIER

AFFILIATIONS

HOTEL ROYAL – ROYAL PARC EVIAN

Evian

The prestigious Belle Epoque palace Hotel Royal is nestled in a 19-hectares magnificent park overlooking Lake Geneva.

The spectacular hotel, created at the beginning of the last century, has retained its majesty and is today a temple of refinement, good taste and 'art de vivre'. The elegant lounges, arched ceilings, frescos and domes give this hotel its uniqueness.

The Hotel Royal is a classic health spa resort offering numerous personalised, relaxing body and beauty treatments, and vacation activities including indoor and outdoor swimming pools, sauna, Turkish bad, Jacuzzi, tennis courts, archery, shooting club, climbing wall and the 18-hole championship Evian Masters golf course.

With 8 restaurants, the Royal Parc Evian invites food lovers on a journey of fine dining experiences. Guests can even enjoy light, energy-giving health spa cuisine that adheres the resort's philosophies of Synergetic Cuisines.

FACILITIES

Accommodation
154 ROOMS & SUITES

Recreational facilities
BETTER LIVING INSTITUTE
FORM AND RELAXATION CENTRE
CHILDREN'S AND JUNIOR'S CLUB
EVIAN MASTER GOLF CLUB
MUSICAL INTERLUDES
CASINO
8 RESTAURANTS

Meeting facilities
MEETING ROOM FOR UP TO 300 PEOPLE

International Airports
GENEVE INTERNATIONAL AIRPORT (GVA)
45 MINUTES DRIVE AWAY

RESERVATIONS

Prices
ROOMS FROM 160 EURO PP PER NIGHT

Credit cards
AE, DC, MC, V

GDS Reservation Codes
AMADEUS LW GVA009
GALILEO LW 8436
SABRE LW 4796
WORLDSPAN LW 0609

Yearly Closing Dates
1 DECEMBER 2004 - 31 JANUARY 2005

CONTACT DETAILS

THE ROYAL – ROYAL PARC EVIAN
RIVE SUD DU LAC DE GENÈVE
F-74501 EVIAN
FRANCE
TEL +33 450 26 85 00
FAX +33 450 75 61 00
RESERVATION@ROYALPARCEVIAN.COM
WWW.ROYALPARCEVIAN.COM

OWNER: DANONE GROUP
GENERAL MANAGER: MR ROGER MERCIER
DIRECTOR OF SALES: MR FRANCK RATEL

AFFILIATIONS

HOTEL SAN REGIS

Paris

The Hotel San Regis is a peaceful haven of luxury and comfort in the elegant 8th arrondissement. Located in the Golden Triangle, a few steps away from the Champs-Elysées and the avenue Montaigne Haute-Couture boutiques, the San Regis breaths history, but comfort is not outdated and today's modern amenities have been harmoniously integrated in the hotel.

The rooms and suites interiors are ravishing in colour, textures and imagination, the rich patinas of the cabinet-maker's craft contrasting with the luxuriance of antique furnishings. The works of art and original paintings display the owner's passion for this house of character.

The 'Boiseries Lounge', 'Winter Garden' and 'English Bar' inspire undeniable warmth. Contiguous, the intimate restaurant decorated in the style of a library, serves a fine classic cuisine inspired by the Provence region. The discreet, efficient service will fulfil the guest's highest expectations, giving a feeling of well-being in a setting that is as luxurious as it is calm.

FACILITIES

Accommodation
44 ROOMS & SUITES

Recreational facilities
JUST OFF THE CHAMPS-ELYSÉES AVENUE
SIGHTSEEING & EXCURSIONS

Meeting facilities
NONE

International Airports
PARIS CHARLES DE GAULLE AIRPORT (CDG)
60 MINUTES DRIVE AWAY

RESERVATIONS

Prices
ROOMS FROM 315 EURO PER NIGHT
SUITES FROM 620 EURO PER NIGHT

Credit cards
AE, DC, MC, V

GDS Reservation Codes
AMADEUS LX PARSAN
GALILEO LX 24563
SABRE LX 28321
WORLDSPAN LX 16558

Yearly Closing Dates
NONE

CONTACT DETAILS

HOTEL SAN REGIS
12, RUE JEAN GOUJON
F-75008 PARIS
FRANCE
TEL +33 (0)1 44 95 16 16
FAX +33 (0)1 45 61 05 48
MESSAGE@HOTEL-SANREGIS.FR
WWW.HOTEL-SANREGIS.FR

OWNER: MR ELIE GEORGES
GENERAL MANAGER: MR MAURICE GEORGES
DIRECTOR OF SALES: MR JOSEPH GEORGES

AFFILIATIONS

HOTEL ROYAL RIVIERA

St. Jean-Cap-Ferrat

Perched on the Saint-Jean-Cap-Ferrat peninsula, in the exclusive resort of Saint-Jean-Cap-Ferrat, between Monaco and Nice, the Hôtel Riviera was originally built as a palace in 1904. Today it is a classic in the modern idiom, providing all the intimacy of a private Mediterranean villa with the supreme glamour of a grand palace.

A simple, yet elegant French contemporary style imbues the hotel's spacious, air-conditioned rooms and suites. Many have a private balcony and have all ample windows framing tableaux which epitomise the beauty of the surrounding area.

Surrounded by a sumptuous Mediterranean scented garden, you can enjoy a private sandy beach, outdoor heated swimming pool, fitness centre and a personalised treatment at the amazing Décleor Wellness Centre in a charming intimate atmosphere.

A hotel of unashamed style and luxury, the Hôtel Royal Riviera marks a return to the elegance, fine service and supremely tasteful comfort that was once the hallmark of the French Riviera.

FACILITIES

Accommodation
95 Rooms & Suites,
including 16 at L'Orangerie

Recreational facilities
Outdoor Pool
Private Beach
Decléor Wellness Centre
Fitness Centre
Water Sports
Tennis
Casino at 5 minutes' walk
Golf Courses nearby

Meeting facilities
Meeting Rooms for up to 120 people

International Airports
Nice International Airport (NCE)
20 minutes drive away

RESERVATIONS

Prices
Rooms from 250 Euro per night
Junior Suites from 500 Euro per night

Credit cards
AE, DC, MC, V

GDS Reservation Codes
Amadeus LW NCE024
Galileo LW 23917
Sabre LW 28279
Worldspan LW 0624

Yearly Closing Dates
01 December 2004 – 16 January 2005

CONTACT DETAILS

Hotel Royal Riviera
3, avenue Jean Monnet
F-06230 St-Jean Cap-Ferrat
France
Tel +33 493 76 31 00
Fax +33 493 01 23 07
resa@royal-riviera.com
www.royal-riviera.com

Owner: Westmont Hospitality Group
General Manager: Mr Bruno Mercadal
Director of Sales: Mrs Sandrine Camia

AFFILIATIONS
The Leading Small Hotels
of the World

LA BASTIDE DE MARIE
Menerbes

Bastide de Marie is ideally located in the heart of the regional natural park of the Luberon, where famous writer Peter Mayle wrote his book 'A Year in Provence'. This 18th century structure, surrounded by 15 hectares of vineyards, is a standing invitation to discover the subtle fragrances of the Provence.

It is neither a small hotel nor a host house, think of it moreover as a beautiful property where you come to stay with a friend to spend a few hours or a few days lazing around, sipping the wine of the property. All the rooms and suites are elegantly decorated with Provencal furniture discovered in the region's many antiques shop.

In the cool evening air, you may feel like having a game of jeu de boules or getting a taste for the subtle flavours of local products hinted with the scent of olive oil. Bastide de Marie is the faithful reflection of this tradition. It opens its doors to a relaxing world where you long to stay for as long as possible.

FACILITIES

Accommodation
14 ROOMS & SUITES

Recreational facilities
SWIMMING POOL
WINE CELLAR
COOKING LESSONS
LOCATED IN THE HEARTH OF
LUBERON NATURAL PARK
GUIDED CULTURAL VISITS TO TYPICAL VILLAGES
ANTIQUARIES SHOPPING
GOLF COURSE NEARBY

Meeting facilities
NONE

International Airports
MARSEILLE INTERNATIONAL AIRPORT (MRS)
60 MINUTES DRIVE AWAY

RESERVATIONS

Prices
ROOMS FROM 390 EURO PER NIGHT
SUITES FROM 600 EURO PER NIGHT

Credit cards
AE, DC, MC, V

GDS Reservation Codes
NONE

Yearly Closing Dates
15 NOVEMBER 2004 – 15 MARCH 2005

CONTACT DETAILS

LA BASTIDE DE MARIE
ROUTE DE BONNIEUX
QUARTIER VERRERIE
F-84560 MENERBES
FRANCE
TEL +33 4 90 72 30 20
FAX +33 4 90 72 54 20
CONTACT@BASTIDEMARIE.COM
WWW.C-H-M.COM

OWNER: JOCELYNE & JEAN LOUIS SIBUET
GENERAL MANAGER: MRS MIREILLE BAUD
DIRECTOR OF SALES: MRS VÉRONIQUE PELLICIER

AFFILIATIONS

NONE

HOTEL LA VILLA
Calvi

La Villa, a beautiful Mediterranean Villa-style property of sun-blenched terracotta, sits on a hill with a stunning mountainous backdrop and is surrounded by typical gardens of dense, shrubby maquis vegetation. From this vantage point, the magnificent swimming pool and restaurant terrace command superb views out to sea and across to the Citadel of Calvi.

Perched on the hills of Calvi, it offers a peaceful setting, only 5 minutes drive from the town centre, which offers a wide choice of shops, restaurants and a smart marina.

The Mediterranean style interior decoration of the rooms is simple, light and wrought iron furnishings add an elegant yet discreet touch. All rooms are spacious and contemporary styled and benefit from a lovely balcony or terrace.

The Michelin starred restaurant serves a variety of cuisine, and during fine weather, guests can dine on the stunning pool terrace.

FACILITIES

Accommodation
52 Rooms & Suites

Recreational facilities
Swimming Pools
Tennis Courts
Spa & Massage
Beauty Centre
Sailing
Waterskiing
Biking & Mountain Biking
Hiking
Hunting
Canoeing, Kayaking & Rafting
Restaurant (one star Michelin)

Meeting facilities
Meeting Room for up to 100 people

International Airports
Calvi Ste Catherine Airport (CLY)
15 minutes drive away

RESERVATIONS

Prices
Rooms from 326 Euro per night
Suites from 520 Euro per night

Credit cards
AE, DC, V

GDS Reservation Code
Amadeus WB CLYLVH
Galileo WB 14399
Sabre WB 32482
Worldspan WB CD33

Yearly Closing Dates
1 November 2004 – 31 March 2005

CONTACT DETAILS

Hotel La Villa
Chemin de Notre Dame de la Serra
F-20260 Calvi
France
Tel +33 (0)4 95 65 10 10
Fax +33 (0)4 95 65 10 50
reservation@hotel-lavilla.com
www.hotel-lavilla.com

Owner: Mr Jean-Pierre Pinelli
General Manager: Mr Jean-Pierre Pinelli

AFFILIATIONS

RELAIS &
CHATEAUX.

LE BRISTOL PARIS

Paris

Strolling along the famous rue du Faubourg Saint-Honoré, in the heart of Paris, Le Bristol appears, offering peace and tranquillity among the world renowned fashion houses, art galleries and antique shops. The Champs Elysées is just around the corner.

Richly decorated, fine furnishings and artwork of an old world charm combined with ultra modern comfort, Le Bristol offers 164 rooms and suites, all of which feature impressive marble bathrooms.

For the ultimate in relaxation, Le Bristol's swimming pool overlooks Parisian rooftops. The decor will lull you into a dream of the Art Deco era recalling transatlantic voyages of days gone by. Sauna and a fully equipped fitness centre are just next to the pool. The Anne Semonin Spa offers personalized natural skin care therapy.

Exquisite views onto the French gardens make Le Bristol an ideal meeting place and offers 600 square metres of modular capacity.

Refined and creative French cuisine is served in Le Bristol's Winter Restaurant and in the Summer Restaurant (two stars Michelin) which opens onto the splendid French gardens.

FACILITIES

Accommodation
164 ROOMS, INCLUDING 73 SUITES

Recreational facilities
SWIMMING POOL
SAUNA
FITNESS CENTRE
BEAUTY SALON ANNE SÉMONIN
GASTRONOMIC RESTAURANT
(TWO STARS MICHELIN)
BAR
BUSINESS CENTRE
PARKING
HAIRDRESSER

Meeting facilities
6 MEETING ROOMS FOR UP TO 180 PEOPLE

International Airports
PARIS CHARLES DE GAULLE AIRPORT (CDG)
60 MINUTES DRIVE AWAY
PARIS ORLY AIRPORT (ORY)
30 MINUTES DRIVE AWAY

RESERVATIONS

Prices
DOUBLE ROOMS FROM
610 EURO PER NIGHT

Credit cards
AE, DC, MC, V

GDS Reservation Codes
AMADEUS LW PAR012
GALILEO LW 8428
SABRE LW225593
WORLDSPAN LW 0612

Yearly Closing Dates
NONE

CONTACT DETAILS

LE BRISTOL PARIS
112, RUE DU FAUBOURG SAINT-HONORÉ
F-75008 PARIS
FRANCE
TEL +33 153 43 43 00
FAX +33 153 43 43 01
RESA@LEBRISTOLPARIS.COM
WWW.LEBRISTOLPARIS.COM

OWNER: CLASSIFIED
GENERAL MANAGER: MR PIERRE FERCHAUD
DIRECTOR OF SALES: MRS CATHERINE HODOUL-BAUDRY

AFFILIATIONS

The Leading Hotels
of the World®

LE MOULIN DE L'ABBAYE

Brantôme

One of the most romantic towns in France, Brantôme, truly merits its nickname of 'the Venice of Périgord', featuring a Benedictine abbey tucked into the cliffs, narrow streets lined with gray-stone houses and an ancient footbridge spanning the River Dronne.

Le Moulin de l'Abbaye stands for the romanticism of a mill and the nobleness of a site, the poetry of a village house dating back to the 12th century, the elegance of refined decor and the magic of undisputed beauty. Fine dining in the Moulin's restaurant is a real treat, whether served on the beautiful terrace or in the elegant dining room, both enjoy the idyllic riverside setting and culinary delights. Sixteen elegantly appointed rooms, three apartments; each named after a Bordeaux grand cru are found in three buildings; the mill, an adjacent home, and a delightful riverside house across the bridge.

Walking around Brantôme, its unique atmosphere, its old abbey and beautiful dwellings is sure to be an unforgettable experience.

FACILITIES

Accommodation
16 ROOMS & 3 SUITES

Recreational facilities
CULTURAL VISITS
CYCLING
EXCURSIONS
VISITS TO VINEYARDS AND MARKETS
IN THE REGION
KAYAKING
HORSEBACK RIDING
FISHING
GUIDED CULTURAL VISITS
EXCURSIONS TO PERIGORD

Meeting facilities
MEETING ROOM FOR UP TO 25 PEOPLE

International Airports
BORDEAUX INT'L AIRPORT (BOD)
50 MINUTES DRIVE AWAY

RESERVATIONS

Prices
ROOMS FROM 200 EURO PER NIGHT
SUITES FROM 270 EURO PER NIGHT

Credit cards
AE, DC, MC, V

GDS Reservation Codes
AMADEUS WB PGXMOU
GALILEO WB 12445
SABRE WB 43404
WORLDSPAN WB SW08

Yearly Closing Dates
24 OCTOBER 2004 – 3 MAY 2005

CONTACT DETAILS

LE MOULIN DE L'ABBAYE
1 ROUTE DE BOURDEILLES
F-24310 BRANTÔME
FRANCE
TEL +33 (0) 5 53 05 80 22
FAX +33 (0) 5 53 05 75 27
MOULIN@RELAISCHATEAUX.COM
WWW.MOULIN-ABBAYE.COM

OWNER: MR REGIS BULOT
GENERAL MANAGER: MR BERNARD DESSUM
DIRECTOR OF SALES: MRS DAVINA BULOT

AFFILIATIONS

RELAIS &
CHATEAUX

THE PRIVATE COLLECTION

LES FERMES DE MARIE
Megève

Set in the heart of a two-hectare park, Les Fermes de Marie is a cosy Savoyard chalet style village, nestled in the French Alps in the heart of Megève. Hotelier couple Jocelyne and Jean Louis Sibuet reconstructed and refurbished a traditional farmhouse to create this unusual hotel and spa, which offers a charming intimate atmosphere.

This enchanting village makes guests feel instantly at home, with its inviting corners, the elegant bar, the library, the cosy fireplace lounges and the gastronomy restaurants The luxuriously appointed and spacious rooms are all uniquely decorated with charming furniture and good taste.

The world-famous spa provides tailor-made programmes combining personal treatments and the eponymous house beauty line, based on rare mountain plants such as edelweiss and arnica.

Definitely, this mountain vacation is a destination in itself, as it offers a magnificent setting for relaxation, indulgence and total attention to the art of fine living.

FACILITIES

Accommodation
71 ROOMS IN 10 CHALETS,
INCLUDING SUITES AND APARTMENTS

Recreational facilities
BEAUTY FARM WITH SPA
ALPINE SKI, SNOWSHOE,
CROSS-COUNTRY SKIING, ICE SPORT,
HUSKY SAFARI IN WINTER
TREKKING, GOLF, HORSEBACK RIDING,
WATER SPORTS IN SUMMER

Meeting facilities
5 MEETING ROOMS FOR UP TO 150 PEOPLE

International Airports
GENEVA INTERNATIONAL AIRPORT (GVA)
50 MINUTES DRIVE AWAY

RESERVATIONS

Prices
ROOMS FROM 134 EURO PER NIGHT
SUITES FROM 258 EURO PER NIGHT

Credit cards
AE, DC, MC, V

GDS Reservation Codes
NONE

Yearly Closing Dates
15 APRIL – 1 JUNE 2005
25 OCTOBER – 1 DECEMBER 2005

CONTACT DETAILS

LES FERMES DE MARIE
CHEMIN DE RIANTE COLLINE
F-74120 MEGÈVE
FRANCE
TEL 00 33 4 50 93 03 10
FAX 00 33 4 50 93 09 84
CONTACT@FERMESDEMARIE.COM
WWW.C-H-M.COM

OWNER: JOCELYNE & JEAN LOUIS SIBUET
GENERAL MANAGER: MRS BRIGITTE FLAMENT
DIRECTOR OF SALES: MRS VÉRONIQUE PELLICIER

AFFILIATIONS

NONE

LES SOURCES DE CAUDALIE
Martillac - Bordeaux

There is no word in English for 'Caudalie'. Nor does Les Sources de Caudalie have any equivalent! It is a unique concept that brings together the sophistication of the grape, the art of haute cuisine, the Grand Cru Château Smith Haute Lafitte and thermal springs.

9 suites and 40 rooms whose individual decoration and furnishing was overseen with a great sense of detail and comfort. All are air-conditioned and have a private bathroom, telephone, television, mini-bar and safe. There is a fitness centre, heated outdoor swimming pool and two restaurants. Relax in the Caudalie Vinotherapie Spa which offers anti-aging face, slimming and body tonic treatments based on the grape seed extracts.

'La Grand' Vigne' for refined classics and 'La Table du Lavoir' with a country inn-flavour. Don't forget to stop at the 'French Paradox' bar where guests are able to taste top wines by the glass, and at 'La Tour des Cigares', offering a selection of fine cigars, Cognac and vintage ports.

The Caudalie can offer the perfect programme to fit your every need.

FACILITIES

Accommodation
40 ROOMS AND 9 SUITES

Recreational facilities
CAUDALIE VINOTHERAPY SPA
THERMAL POOL & HAMMAM
HEALTH & BEAUTY TREATMENTS
INDOOR AND HEATED OUTDOOR
SWIMMING POOL
FITNESS CENTRE & TENNIS
GOLF PITCH AND PUT
PRIVATE CYCLING & JOGGING TRACK
CIGAR TASTING CLUB
COUNTRY INN & GASTRONOMIC RESTAURANT
WINEBAR & WINE TASTING
COOKING & TASTING CLASSES
GUIDED TOUR OF THE
CHÂTEAU SMITH HAUT LAFITTE

Meeting facilities
2 MEETING ROOMS FOR UP TO 40 PEOPLE

International Airports
BORDEAUX INTERNATIONAL AIRPORT (BOD)
20 MINUTES DRIVE AWAY

RESERVATIONS

Prices
ROOMS FROM 185 EURO PER NIGHT
SUITES FROM 305 EURO PER NIGHT

Credit cards
AE, DC, MC, V

GDS Reservation Codes
AMADEUS LX BODSCL
GALILEO LX 18506
SABRE LX 48502
WORLDSPAN LX BODSC

Yearly Closing Dates
NONE

CONTACT DETAILS

LES SOURCES DE CAUDALIE
CHEMIN DE SMITH HAUT LAFITTE
F-33650 BORDEAUX-MARTILLAC
FRANCE
TEL +33 5 57 83 83 83
FAX +33 5 57 83 83 84
SOURCES@SOURCES-CAUDALIE.COM
WWW.SOURCES-CAUDALIE.COM

OWNER: CATHIARD FAMILY
GENERAL MANAGER: MR JÉRÔME TOURBIER
DIRECTOR OF SALES: MRS ALICE CATHIARD

AFFILIATIONS

VILLA GALLICI

Aix-en-Provence

Villa Gallici is located in the ancient and famous city of Aix-en-Provence, surrounded by the enchanting scenery of the Provence. This 18th Century manor house has been transformed into a luxurious hotel only in 1991 by three friends of whom two were professional decorators. The goal was to create an establishment where the guests were truly privileged.

The 18 rooms and 4 suites, elegantly decorated with period pieces, are spacious and well-lit and feature every modern day comfort. All rooms look onto the Sainte-Victoire Mountains whilst the suites boast a private garden or terrace. Not one room is furnished alike so that every stay is always a new experience for the guests.

The restaurant serves traditional Provencal, French and Mediterranean cuisine. In Summer, the dishes are served on the terrace near the swimming pool, and in Winter in the elegant dining room, beside the windows or the open fire place.

FACILITIES

Accommodation
18 ROOMS & 4 SUITES

Recreational facilities
SWIMMING POOL
GARDEN
BAR & RESTAURANT
MANY SIGHTSEEING OPTIONS NEARBY

Meeting facilities
NONE

International Airports
MARSEILLE INTERNATIONAL AIRPORT (MRS)
30 MINUTES DRIVE AWAY

RESERVATIONS

Prices
ROOMS FROM 280 EURO PER NIGHT

Credit cards
AE, DC, MC, V

GDS Reservation Codes
AMADEUS WB QXBHVG
GALILEO WB 13180
SABRE WB 47303
WORLDSPAN WB CD19

Yearly Closing Dates
NONE

CONTACT DETAILS

VILLA GALLICI
AVENUE DE LA VIOLETTE
F-13100 AIX-EN-PROVENCE
FRANCE
TEL +33 442 232 923
FAX +33 442 963 045
GALLICI@RELAISCHATEAUX.COM
WWW.VILLAGALLICI.COM

OWNER: BAGLIONI HOTELS SPA
GENERAL MANAGER: MR GIUSEPPE ARTOLLI
DIRECTOR OF SALES: MS ALESSANDRA RUGGERI

AFFILIATIONS

RELAIS &
CHATEAUX.

VILLA MARIE
Ramatuelle

Overlooking the beautiful turquoise bay of Pamplona, hiding in the St Tropez hills, the Villa Marie is a beautiful secluded villa, surrounded by three hectares of pinewood.

The stylish rooms boast private terraces with superb views and are uniquely decorated with touches of Mediterranean refinement. White stone, antique Florentine furniture, ochre's and warm colours decorate the Villa Marie and create a charming intimate atmosphere. With its large spaces, cosy patios and magnificent landscaped gardens, Villa Marie offers a peaceful haven away from a busy world.

Guests can stroll along to the swimming pool in a natural preserved environment made up with big rocks and the sea as the only horizon. For an even more relaxing stay, the 6 private cabins of the spa centre with pine, jasmine and rose essence offer a true sense of well-being.

FACILITIES

Accommodation
41 ROOMS & SUITES

Recreational facilities
SWIMMING POOL
BEAUTY TREATMENTS
PAMPLONE BEACHES NEARBY
LOCATED NEARBY ST TROPEZ

Meeting facilities
NONE

International Airports
TOULON AIRPORT (TLN)
60 MINUTES DRIVE AWAY

RESERVATIONS

Prices
ROOMS FROM 200 EURO PER NIGHT

Credit cards
AE, DC, MC, V

GDS Reservation Codes
NONE

Yearly Closing Dates
15 NOVEMBER 2004 – 15 MARCH 2005

CONTACT DETAILS

VILLA MARIE
CHEMIN DU VAL RIANT
F-83350 RAMATUELLE
FRANCE
TEL +33 4 94 97 40 22
FAX +33 4 94 97 37 55
CONTACT@VILLAMARIE.FR
WWW.C-H-M.COM

OWNER: JOCELYNE & JEAN LOUIS SIBUET
GENERAL MANAGER: MRS LAURENCE VITTE
DIRECTOR OF SALES: MRS VÉRONIQUE PELLICIER

AFFILIATIONS

NONE

HOTEL LOUIS C. JACOB
Hamburg

For more than 200 years, the Hotel Louis C. Jacob has stood for exclusive pleasure, the charm of private atmosphere and excellent service. In a unique location on the banks of the river Elbe and within easy reach of Hamburg's city centre, it is comfortably removed from the hustle and bustle of the city; tradition and modern hotel comfort have been successfully combined.

Timeless elegance and hanseatically reticent design are characteristics of the style of the hotel, which allows the guests to immerse themselves in an unforgettable world. The hotel has 85 exclusively furnished rooms and suites, some of which have spectacular views over the river Elbe.

A unique view of the Elbe is afforded from below the fresh green canopy of the famous lime-tree terrace. From there, guests can enjoy the summer at its most unforgettable. The modern kitchen of the chef, Thomas Martin, is creative and refined but not over-fashionable. Critics tend to classify the Jacob's Restaurant as the best address in Northern Germany.

FACILITIES

Accommodation
66 ROOMS & 19 SUITES

Recreational facilities
GOURMET RESTAURANT (1 MICHELIN STAR)
WORLD-FAMOUS LIME TREE TERRACE
HISTORIC ICE CELLAR
JACOBS BAR
WINE BAR WITH GARDEN
LOBBY WITH FIREPLACE
CITY & HARBOUR TOURS
WELLNESS AREA FEATURING SAUNA,
JACUZZI
JOGGING PATH ALONG THE RIVER ELBE
LIMOUSINE SERVICE
CITY SHUTTLE
GOLF & POLO CLUBS NEARBY
PRIVATE ART COLLECTION

Meeting facilities
6 MEETING ROOMS FOR UP TO 200 PEOPLE

International Airports
HAMBURG INTERNATIONAL AIRPORT,
20 MINUTES DRIVE AWAY

RESERVATIONS

Prices
ROOMS FROM 225 EURO PER NIGHT
JUNIOR SUITES FROM 405 EURO PER NIGHT
SUITES FROM 685 EURO PER NIGHT

Credit cards
AE, DC, MC, V

GDS Reservation Codes
AMADEUS LW HAM 732
GALILEO LW 68439
SABRE LW 2557
WORLDSPAN LW 0732

Yearly Closing Dates
NONE

CONTACT DETAILS

HOTEL LOUIS C. JACOB
ELBCHAUSSEE 401 – 403
D – 22609 HAMBURG
GERMANY
TEL +49 40 822 55 0
FAX + 49 40 822 55 444
JACOB@HOTEL-JACOB.DE
WWW.HOTEL-JACOB.DE

OWNER: ARKONA AG
GENERAL MANAGER: MR JOST DEITMAR
DIRECTOR OF SALES & MARKETING: MR MARC BRAUER

AFFILIATIONS

The Leading Small Hotels
of the World

DANAI BEACH RESORT & VILLAS

Halkidiki

With extraordinary views out over the azure Aegean, this exclusive clifftop hideaway is perfect for those seeking refuge from the hurly-burly of city life. Set like a jewel in the most serene gardens and woodlands, the Danai Beach Resort is the ultimate haven in a most beautiful and striking part of northern Greece, often called the Greek Riviera.

Its traditionally tiled roofs blaze red amidst a veritable forest of towering pines that scent the air with their unique and bracing perfume. At the foot of the cliffs on which the resort perches, is its own beach glistening golden under brilliant skies, with its charming bar. And for those who wish to walk a few steps for a refreshing swim, the magnificent outdoor pool is situated at the heart of the complex.

60 spacious suites and villas, some with private plunge pools, are all decorated to the highest standards. With cool marble floors and chic and luxurious furnishings, each suite and villa has its own personalised décor and all the very latest amenities to satisfy the hedonist in us all.

FACILITIES

Accommodation
60 SUITES & VILLAS

Recreational facilities
ST. BARTH WELLNESS & SPA
TENNIS
GYMNASIUM
SWIMMING POOL
SAUNA
SAILING & WINDSURFING
FISHING
SNORKELLING
SCUBA DIVING NEARBY
WINE & OLIVE OIL TASTINGS
RESTAURANTS & BARS
SIGHTSEEING EXCURSIONS

Meeting facilities
MEETING ROOM FOR UP TO 50 PEOPLE

International Airports
MACEDONIA INTERNATIONAL AIRPORT (SKG)
50 MINUTES DRIVE AWAY

RESERVATIONS

Prices
SUITES FROM 320 EURO PER NIGHT
VILLAS FROM 1,250 EURO PER NIGHT

Credit cards
AE, DC, MC, V

GDS Reservation Codes
AMADEUS LW SKG807
GALILEO LW 18490
SABRE LW 50565
WORLDSPAN LW 0807

Yearly Closing Dates
NONE

CONTACT DETAILS

DANAI BEACH RESORT & VILLAS
NIKITI
GR-63088 HALKIDIKI
GREECE
TEL +30 2 3750 22 310
FAX +30 2 3750 22 591
TEL +30 2 3103 41 810 (WINTER)
FAX +30 2 3103 47 450 (WINTER)
INFO@DBR.GR
WWW.DBR.GR

OWNER: MR KIMON RIEFENSTAHL
GENERAL MANAGER: MR KIMON RIEFENSTAHL

AFFILIATIONS

The Leading Small Hotels
of the World

ELOUNDA GULF VILLAS & SUITES

Elounda

Located on the hillside overlooking the magnificent Gulf of Mirabello is the exclusive "Elounda Gulf Villas & Suites" a luxury resort that comprises of just 14 villas, all with private pools with Jacuzzi, and 10 elegant suites.

All Villas and Suites have stunning sea views and are individually designed and decorated. The villas have two to four master bedrooms while some have their own private sauna, Turkish bath & gym room. Each villa has its own private swimming pool with Jacuzzi and sun terrace. The Suites range from 1 to 2 master bedrooms with en-suite bathrooms and are close to the main swimming pool with Jacuzzi and the children's pool.

The elegant "Argonauts" Bar and the à la carte "Argo" Restaurant offer delicious cocktails and tasteful international and Cretan meals. All guests have complimentary access to the Elixir Fitness Gallery, which has gym room, sauna, and steam bath, massage room and outdoor Jacuzzi.

FACILITIES

Accommodation
14 LUXURY VILLAS WITH PRIVATE POOLS & 10 ELEGANT SUITES

Recreational facilities
SWIMMING POOL
OUTDOOR HEATED JACUZZI
14 PRIVATE SWIMMING POOLS WITH JACUZZI
CHILDREN'S POOL
RESTAURANT & BAR
ELIXIR FITNESS GALLERY
MASSAGE ROOM
SAUNA & STEAM BATH
WATER SPORTS NEARBY

Meeting facilities
MEETING ROOM FOR UP TO 90 PEOPLE

International Airports
HERAKLION AIRPORT (HER)
60 MINUTES DRIVE AWAY

RESERVATIONS

Prices
SUITES FROM 200 EURO PER NIGHT
VILLAS FROM 500 EURO PER NIGHT

Credit cards
AE, MC, V

GDS Reservation Codes
AMADEUS LX HEREGU
GALILEO LX 64106
SABRE LX 65450
WORLDSPAN LX HEREG

Yearly Closing Dates
1 NOVEMBER 2004 – 31 MARCH 2005

CONTACT DETAILS

ELOUNDA GULF VILLAS
RESERVATIONS OFFICE
CANDIA TOWER
AG. DIMITRIOU SQUARE
GR-71 202 HERAKLION
CRETE
GREECE
TEL +30 2810 227721
FAX +30 2810 227811
INFO@ELOUNDAVILLAS.COM
WWW.ELOUNDAVILLAS.COM

OWNER: KAPA ANAPTIXIAKI S.A.
GENERAL MANAGER: MRS ANNA KADIANAKIS
DIRECTOR OF SALES: MRS CHARITINI KADIANAKIS

AFFILIATIONS

ANDRÁSSY HOTEL
Budapest

The Andrássy Hotel is an elegant Bauhaus building located in a prestigious neighbourhood on Andrassy Avenue. This broad boulevard is close to the main business districts and is walking distance away from the main sights of Budapest, the Museum of Fine Arts and the world famous Széchenyi Thermal & Spa Bath.

Located on Budapest's foremost address, the boutique Andrássy Hotel and Zebrano Restaurant have played host to world leaders, poets & musicians, and those who simply like to enjoy life. The hotels' 70 spacious guestrooms and suites are beautifully decorated in Art Deco style and offer every modern comfort, and beds designed to dream. Guests enjoy 24-hours personalized service, luxury in-room amenities, oversized bathrooms, private balconies and individual air-conditioning.

The popular restaurant Zebrano serves colourful, light and international cuisine in a warm and relaxed setting. The fashionable summer terrace offers fantastic dining in a beautiful garden.

FACILITIES

Accommodation
70 ROOMS & SUITES

Recreational facilities
A FEW STEPS AWAY FROM THE CITY PARK WITH JOGGING TRAILS AND THE SZÉCHENYI THERMAL & SPA BATH
SIGHTSEEING & EXCURSIONS
ZEBRANO RESTAURANT & BAR

Meeting facilities
2 MEETING ROOMS FOR UP TO 16 PEOPLE

International Airports
BUDAPEST INTERNATIONAL AIRPORT (BUD)
30 MINUTES DRIVE AWAY

RESERVATIONS

Prices
ROOMS FROM 134 EURO PER NIGHT

Credit cards
AE, DC, MC, V

GDS Reservation Codes
AMADEUS LX BUDAND
GALILEO LX 52945
SABRE LX 61017
WORLDSPAN LX BUDAN

Yearly Closing Dates
NONE

CONTACT DETAILS

ANDRÁSSY HOTEL
ANDRÁSSY ÚT 111
H-1063 BUDAPEST
HUNGARY
TEL +36-1-4622 100
FAX +36-1-3229 445
WELCOME@ANDRASSYHOTEL.COM
WWW.ANDRASSYHOTEL.COM

Owner: ORCO HOTEL COLLECTION
General Manager: MR RAOUL GRANSIER
Director of sales: MS ILDIKÓ BUDEA

AFFILIATIONS

CASTELLO DI VELONA
Montalcino

Set high on a gentle hill in the heart of the peaceful Tuscan countryside, the Castello di Velona is the breathtaking site of a newly reconstructed luxury boutique hotel, an 11th century aristocratic charming country mansion surrounded by vineyards and olive groves.

22 suites and 2 double rooms provide every comfort for the sophisticated traveller. All the rooms are unique, decorated in a different colour, but all with romantic fireplaces, elegant antique furniture and sweeping views of the beautiful Tuscan countryside. Lovers of fine food will enjoy tasting typical regional delicious Italian cuisine, served in summertime under the olive and cypress trees and in winter in the intimate castle's restaurant, in front of the massive log fire.

The Castello is the confluence of history, art, viniculture and gastronomy: only 15 minutes from Montalcino and 30 minutes from Siena. Ideally located, it is the perfect venue for your Tuscany experience.

FACILITIES

Accommodation
2 Double Rooms & 18 Suites

Recreational facilities
Outdoor Swimming Pool
with Hydromassage
Wine Tasting
Biking
Horseback Riding nearby
Sightseeing and Excursions
Library
Restaurant
Panoramic Terrace
Helipad

Meeting facilities
Meeting Rooms for up to 25 people

International Airports
Florence International Airport (FLR)
90 minutes drive away

RESERVATIONS

Prices
Rooms from 210 Euro per night
Suites from 320 Euro per night

Credit cards
AE, DC, MC, V

GDS Reservation Codes
Amadeus LX SAYCAS
Galileo LX 64339
Sabre LX 61559
Worldspan LX SAYCA

Yearly Closing Dates
30 November 2004 – 10 February 2005

CONTACT DETAILS

Castello di Velona
Loc. La Velona
I-53024 Montalcino (SI)
Italy
Tel +39 0577 800101
Fax +39 0577 835661
Info@castellodivelona.it
www.castellodivelona.it

Owner: Podere Castello srl
General Manager: Mr Alessandro Ercolani
Director of sales: Ms Barbara Fenu

AFFILIATIONS

CONTINENTALE
Florence

The Continentale, with its exclusive visual and designer characteristics, recalls and emphasizes the positive cosmopolitan character of the utmost Italian spirit, creates a glamorous environment and a fascinating experience. The hotel proposes itself as an intimate and cosy 'drawing room', a meeting place for the new international nomads where the spaces rich with a contemporary and detailed interpretation, evoke a feeling of the 1950's.

A property marvellously located overlooking the Ponte Vecchio and the Corridoio Vasariano, equipped with 43 rooms, a spectacular Penthouse and a large number of rooms with a terrace that overlook the river or the Florentine roofs; The Sky Lounge 'Terrazza dei Consorti' for total relaxation or for a cocktail, with a breathtaking view of the sunset over the River Arno, makes for an unforgettable 'must'. The design of the rooms, in a balanced mix between hi-tech and soft design creates a mood with modern lightness and brightness outlined through the use of soft long veils hung around the beds.

FACILITIES

Accommodation
43 ROOMS, INCLUDING 1 PENTHOUSE SUITE

Recreational facilities
HOME THEATRE LOUNGE
SKY LOUNGE ROOF TOP TERRACE
FITNESS CENTRE WITH SAUNA
RELAX ROOM
BAR

Meeting facilities
NONE

International Airports
FLORENCE INTERNATIONAL AIRPORT (FLR)
15 MINUTES DRIVE AWAY

RESERVATIONS

Prices
ROOMS FROM 290 EURO PER NIGHT

Credit cards
AE, DC, MC, V

GDS Reservation Codes
AMADEUS DS FLRCON
GALILEO DS 20424
SABRE DS 35486
WORLDSPAN DS 19422

Yearly Closing Dates
NONE

CONTACT DETAILS

CONTINENTALE
VICOLO DELL'ORO 6R
I-50123 FLORENCE
ITALY
TEL +39 055 27262
FAX +39 055 283139
CONTINENTALE@LUNGARNOHOTELS.COM
WWW.LUNGARNOHOTELS.COM

OWNER: LUNGARNO HOTELS / FERRAGAMO FAMILY
MANAGER: MR ALESSIO IANNA

AFFILIATIONS

a member of
design hotels

GRAND HOTEL MAJESTIC
Pallanza

Built in 1870 on the elegant west shores of Lake Maggiore, this graceful, privately-owned hotel dreamily evokes 'La Belle Epoque'. It perfectly combines the graciousness and romance of the past with state-of-the art facilities and amenities thanks to a recent, radical renovation.

Moments away from the picturesque town of Pallanza, its privileged position directly on the waterfront affords it breathtaking, unparalleled views of the Borromee Islands, the surrounding mountains and the lake itself.

90 elegant rooms and junior suites offer all the amenities and comforts one expects from a hotel of this category. Facilities include an in-door swimming pool with sliding doors to the gardens, a tiny private beach, private jetty, a tennis court, a fitness and beauty centre and panoramic terrace.

La Beola restaurant offers innovative, gourmet dining and in summer, the outdoor restaurant on the hotel portico seduces with its romantic atmosphere.

FACILITIES

Accommodation
90 ROOMS & JUNIOR SUITES

Recreational facilities
INDOOR SWIMMING POOL
TENNIS COURT
PRIVATE BEACH
BEAUTY & WELNESS CENTRE
FITNESS CENTRE
GOURMET RESTAURANT
PANORAMIC BAR
PRIVATE JETTY

Meeting facilities
MEETING ROOM FOR UP TO 240 PEOPLE

International Airports
MILAN MALPENSA INT'L AIRPORT (MXP)
45 MINUTES DRIVE AWAY

RESERVATIONS

Prices
ROOMS FROM 180 EURO PER NIGHT

Credit cards
AE, DC, MC, V

GDS Reservation Codes
AMADEUS LX MXPGMG
GALILEO LX 52965
SABRE LX 39223
WORLDSPAN LX MXPGM

Yearly Closing Dates
OCTOBER 2004 – APRIL 2005

CONTACT DETAILS

GRAND HOTEL MAJESTIC
VIA VITTORIO VENETO, 32
I-28922 VERBANIA-PALLANZA (VB)
LAKE MAGGIORE
ITALY
TEL +39 0323 50 43 05
FAX +39 0323 55 63 79
INFO@GRANDHOTELMAJESTIC.IT
WWW.GRANDHOTELMAJESTIC.IT

OWNER: S.A.V. SOCIETÀ ALBERGHI VERBANIA SPA
GENERAL MANAGER: MRS CRISTINA ZUCCARI
DIRECTOR OF SALES: MRS MARIE-FRANCE BALLY

AFFILIATIONS

HOTEL ALLELUJA
Punta Ala

A delightful Mediterranean-style hotel decorated in soft pastel colours, the Alleluja's 38 rooms and extensive grounds offer an understated luxury, and within easy reach of the fashionable port of Punta Ala and its magnificent golf course, only 3 kilometres away and reputed as one of Italy's finest.

The typically low Tuscan farmhouse style building housing the hotel, creates a warm, stylish atmosphere. The main drawing room is embellished by a large fireplace and wide windows offering a magnificent view over the entire park.

Guests can enjoy a leisurely stroll down to the stunning beach to soak up the sun, followed by a delicious lunch at the superb beachside restaurant. Or, if they prefer, they can stretch out by the hotel swimming pool or play a few sets of tennis on the hotel's court. The hotel's elegant gastronomic restaurant enjoys an excellent reputation for its cuisine, while the piano bar provides nightly entertainment to accompany after dinner liqueurs.

FACILITIES

Accommodation
38 Rooms including 1 Suite

Recreational facilities
Swimming Pool
Tennis Court
Private White Sand Beach
Beach Bar Service
18-hole Golf Course nearby
Horse Back Riding in high season
Beach Sports
Visits to Archeologic Sites
in the surroundings

Meeting facilities
Meeting Room for up to 20 people

International Airports
Pisa International Airport (PSA)
90 minutes drive away
Fiumicino International Airport (FCO)
180 minutes drive away

RESERVATIONS

Prices
Rooms from 340 Euro per night

Credit cards
AE, DC, MC, V

GDS Reservation Codes
None

Yearly Closing Dates
15 October 2004 - 24 April 2005

CONTACT DETAILS
Hotel Alleluja
Via del Porto
I-58040 Punta Ala
Italy
Tel +39 0564 922050
Fax +39 0564 920734
ALLELUJA.PUNTAALA@BAGLIONIHOTELS.COM
WWW.BAGLIONIHOTELS.COM

Owner: Baglioni Hotels SPA
General Manager: Ms Pia Hellqvist
Director of sales: Ms Alessandra Ruggeri

AFFILIATIONS
None

HOTEL DE RUSSIE
Rome

Located on the fashionable Via del Babuino, next to the Piazza del Popolo and close to the Spanish Steps, the Rocco Forte Hotel de Russie is a tranquil oasis from which to visit the key attractions of this historic and eternal city.

The simple but sophisticated design gives all spacious 125 bedrooms a unique charm: soft colours, thick drapes, luxurious beds with linen sheets, en-suite bathrooms tiled with stylish mosaics, and the latest amenities to help you enjoy your stay. Most rooms overlook the gardens and the piazza or the famous Roman rooftops.

'Le Jardin du Russie' restaurant offers a wide range of mouth watering traditional Italian cuisine which can be enjoyed outside on the terrace during the warmer months. In addition, the Stravinskij Bar spills on to the Piazzetta Valadier and has an extensive selection of refreshments and Roman delicacies.

The elegant décor, picturesque terraced gardens and relaxing spa offer a peaceful sanctuary in which to retreat from the hustle and bustle of the city.

FACILITIES

Accommodation
125 ROOMS, INCLUDING 31 SUITES

Recreational facilities
TERRACED GARDENS
SPA WITH HYDROPOOL, JACUZZI, SAUNA, TURKISH STEAM BATH, BEAUTY TREATMENTS AND GYM
RESTAURANT LE JARDIN DU RUSSIE
AMAZINGLY CENTRAL LOCATION
GUIDED CULTURAL VISITS

Meeting facilities
6 MEETING ROOMS FOR UP TO 90 PEOPLE

International Airports
FIUMICINO INTERNATIONAL AIRPORT (FCO)
45 MINUTES DRIVE AWAY
CIAMPINO INTERNATIONAL AIRPORT (CIA)
40 MINUTES DRIVE AWAY

RESERVATIONS

Prices
ROOMS FROM 420 EURO PER NIGHT

Credit cards
AE, DC, MC, V

GDS Reservation Codes
AMADEUS LW ROM160
GALILEO LW 25135
SABRE LW 50313
WORLDSPAN LW 2160

Yearly Closing Dates
NONE

CONTACT DETAILS

HOTEL DE RUSSIE
VIA DEL BABUINO, 9
I-00187 ROMA
ITALY
TEL +39 06 328881
FAX +39 06 32888888
RESERVATIONS@HOTELDERUSSIE.IT
WWW.ROCCOFORTEHOTELS.COM

OWNER: SIR ROCCO FORTE
GENERAL MANAGER: MR MARTIN ESLNER
DIRECTOR OF SALES: MRS ELENA BRUNO

AFFILIATIONS

The Leading Hotels of the World®

HOTEL MAJESTIC ROMA
Rome

Inaugurated in 1889, the Hotel Majestic Roma situated in the heart of the eternal city on the famed Via Veneto, still continues to be the home away from home for many celebrities and political figures with its recognized reputation for impeccable standards and service.

All the spacious guestrooms and suites are well appointed and designed with sumptuous Italian furnishings and fabrics, Carrara marble baths with Jacuzzi and luxurious amenities in all suites, and modern comforts for today's discerning travellers, including internet access and air conditioning.

Facilities include the brand new 24-hour access fitness centre equipped with state of the art cardiovascular equipment and free weights, personal trainer and massage treatments.

La Veranda Restaurant welcomes guests in a warm and stylish atmosphere and features Italian cuisine prepared with flair and imagination. Don't miss the nightly live musical entertainment at La Ninfa where one can enjoy refreshing cocktails and tasty culinary specialities.

FACILITIES

Accommodation
98 ROOMS, INCLUDING 13 SUITES

Recreational facilities
FITNESS CENTRE
RESTAURANT LA VERANDA
LA NINFA BRASSERIE
GUIDED CULTURAL VISITS
PRIVATE MUSEUM VISITS
PERSONAL SHOPPER
CENTRAL LOCATION
POLO GAME NEARBY
HORSEBACK RIDING NEARBY
TENNIS NEARBY
GOLF COURSE NEARBY

Meeting facilities
4 MEETING ROOMS FOR UP TO 140 PEOPLE

International Airports
FIUMICINO INTERNATIONAL AIRPORT (FCO)
25 MINUTES DRIVE AWAY
CIAMPINO INTERNATIONAL AIRPORT (CIA)
30 MINUTES DRIVE AWAY

RESERVATIONS

Prices
ROOMS FROM 390 EURO PER NIGHT

Credit cards
AE, DC, MC, V

GDS Reservation Codes
AMADEUS LW ROM111
GALILEO LW 9832
SABRE LW 34562
WORLDSPAN LW 2111

Yearly Closing Dates
NONE

CONTACT DETAILS

HOTEL MAJESTIC ROMA
VIA VENETO 50
I-00187 ROME
ITALY
TEL +39 06 421 441
FAX +39 06 488 0984
INFO@HOTELMAJESTIC.COM
WWW.HOTELMAJESTIC.COM

OWNER: MR GIANLUCA VIOLANTE AND
MS ALESSANDRA VIOLANTE
GENERAL MANAGER: MR GREGOIRE SALAMIN
DIRECTOR OF SALES: MS LAURA FIORE

AFFILIATIONS

The Leading Hotels of the World

 THE PRIVATE COLLECTION

HOTEL SAVOY
Florence

A warm welcome awaits you at the Rocco Forte Hotel Savoy in the heart of Florence. Located on the historic Piazza della Repubblica, close to the landmark Duomo and just a few steps away from the main fashion houses, museums and galleries, this is the ideal base from which to visit the key attractions of this beautiful and historic city.

The hotel's elegant décor offers a chance to experience the best that Florence has to offer. All spacious bedrooms are stylishly designed to offer maximum comfort and many have large walk-in wardrobes and superb panoramic views of the Piazza or the Duomo. The bathroom mosaics, crisp Italian linen and parquet floors combine to create a cool and soothing ambience.

L'Incontro Restaurant and Bar which spills out on to the Piazza allows you to relax and savour the surrounding atmosphere as you dine. The menu offers delicious traditional Florentine dishes and the wine list proposes the best of Italian and Tuscan wines.

As a tribute to the designer fashion houses in the magic city you find quirky prints of shoes throughout the charming hotel!

FACILITIES

Accommodation
107 ROOMS, INCLUDING 9 SUITES

Recreational facilities
PANORAMIC GYM OVERLOOKING DUOMO
L'INCONTRO BAR & RESTAURANT
AMAZINGLY CENTRAL LOCATION
GUIDED CULTURAL VISITS
EXCURSIONS TO TUSCANY

Meeting facilities
2 MEETING ROOMS FOR UP TO 70 PEOPLE

International Airports
FLORENCE INTERNATIONAL AIRPORT (FLR)
15 MINUTES DRIVE AWAY

RESERVATIONS

Prices
ROOMS FROM 310 EURO PER NIGHT

Credit cards
AE, DC, MC, V

GDS Reservation Codes
AMADEUS LW FLR 109
GALILEO LW 25483
SABRE LW 50493
WORLDSPAN LW 2109

Yearly Closing Dates
NONE

CONTACT DETAILS

HOTEL SAVOY
PIAZZA DELLA REPUBBLICA 7
I-50123 FLORENCE
ITALY
TEL +39 055 27351
FAX +39 055 2735888
RESERVATIONS@HOTELSAVOY.IT
WWW.ROCCOFORTEHOTELS.COM

OWNER: SIR ROCCO FORTE
GENERAL MANAGER: MR DAVIDE BERTILACCIO
DIRECTOR OF SALES: MRS ELENA BRUNO

AFFILIATIONS
The Leading Hotels
of the World®

BAUER IL PALAZZO
Venice

Housed primarily in an 18th Century palace on the Grand Canal, 'Bauer Il Palazzo' has been converted into a private mansion featuring 76 luxurious rooms and suites, with tapestry-covered walls, gilt mirrors and carved stucco ceilings.

Some palatial rooms and junior suites have either a view of the Grand Canal or the Lagoon. The deluxe suites may have either an internal courtyard view or a characteristic Venetian 'Calle' outlook. The executive and presidential suites have panoramic views whilst the royal and gran canal suites command spectacular views of the Grand Canal.

For those with a more active frame of mind, there's a fitness centre featuring sauna, steam room and outdoor Jacuzzi with a spectacular view and sun deck. De Pisis is a delightful, terraced gourmet restaurant directly on the Grand Canal which offers both indoor and al fresco dining. Bar Foyer is an intimate bar where you can stop for a cocktail or meet for tea whilst Settimo Cielo is a panoramic terrace and lounge, with a breathtaking view of the lagoon, where breakfast is served.

FACILITIES

Accommodation
15 PALATIAL ROOMS
23 PALATIAL ROOMS WITH VIEW
38 SUITES

Recreational facilities
FITNESS CENTRE
SAUNA, STEAM ROOM AND SOLARIUM
MASSAGE & SPA SERVICES
OUTDOOR JACUZZI
BREAKFAST RESTAURANT WITH HIGHEST TERRACE IN VENICE
BARS & GOURMET RESTAURANT
LOCATED DIRECTLY ON THE GRAND CANAL, ONLY 2 MINUTES WALKING TO SAN MARCO SQUARE

Meeting facilities
MEETING ROOMS AVAILABLE AT THE BAUER HOTEL

International Airports
VENICE INTERNATIONAL AIRPORT (VCE)
30 MINUTES DRIVE BY WATER TAXI

RESERVATIONS

Prices
ROOMS FROM 430 EURO PER NIGHT
ROOMS WITH VIEW FROM 610 EURO PER NIGHT
SUITES FROM 560 EURO PER NIGHT

Credit cards
AE, DC, MC, V

GDS Reservation Codes
AMADEUS LW VCE127
GALILEO LW 53000
SABRE LW 006437
WORLDSPAN LW 2127

Yearly Closing Dates
NONE

CONTACT DETAILS

BAUER IL PALAZZO
S. MARCO 1413/D
I-30124 VENEZIA
ITALY
TEL +39 041 5207022
FAX +39 041 5207557
INFO@ILPALAZZOVENEZIA.COM
WWW.ILPALAZZOVENEZIA.COM

OWNER: MRS FRANCESCA BORTOLOTTO POSSATI
GENERAL MANAGER: MR DANILO ZUCCHETTI
DIRECTOR OF SALES: MRS SANDRA JAEGER

AFFILIATIONS
The Leading Small Hotels
of the World

LUNA HOTEL BAGLIONI
Venice

Full of charm and character and reputed to be one of the oldest hotels in the city built in the 14th Century, the Luna Hotel was previously referred to as the 'Locanda della Luna'. Located just 10 metres from the vibrant buzz and beauty of the Piazza San Marco.

The light galleried reception with marble floor and tasteful Murano Glass chandeliers offers a cosy location in which to relax and plan the day ahead. Alternatively, the lounge bar overlooking the side canal provides the ideal venue for guests to share their experiences of the day.

The rooms and suites at the Luna Hotel are well-appointed and provide all of the amenities expected from a five star hotel. Room types vary from good sized double room up to the one bedroom suites with roof top terrace complete with sun lounger and enviable panoramic views across Venice.

The private landing stage of the hotel allows the gondolas and motorboats direct access to the entrance of the hotel making the temptation to hire a gondola hard to resist.

FACILITIES

Accommodation
109 ROOMS, INCLUDING 12 SUITES AND 9 JUNIOR SUITES

Recreational facilities
BARS & RESTAURANTS
AMAZINGLY CENTRAL LOCATION, PERFECT FOR SIGHTSEEING

Meeting facilities
2 MEETING ROOMS FOR UP TO 170 PEOPLE

International Airports
VENICE INTERNATIONAL AIRPORT (VCE)
20 MINUTES DRIVE BY WATER TAXI

RESERVATIONS

Prices
ROOMS FROM 336 EURO PER NIGHT

Credit cards
AE, DC, MC, V

GDS Reservation Codes
AMADEUS LW VCE148
GALILEO LW 92633
SABRE LW 15295
WORLDSPAN LW 2148

Yearly Closing Dates
NONE

CONTACT DETAILS

LUNA HOTEL BAGLIONI
SAN MARCO 1243
I-30124 VENICE
ITALY
TEL +39 041 5289840
FAX +39 041 5287160
LUNA.VENEZIA@BAGLIONIHOTELS.COM
WWW.BAGLIONIHOTELS.COM

OWNER: BAGLIONI HOTELS SPA
GENERAL MANAGER: MR ABEL DAMERGI
DIRECTOR OF SALES: MS ALESSANDRA RUGGERI

AFFILIATIONS
The Leading Hotels of the World®

MASSERIA SAN DOMENICO

San Domenico

Against a backdrop of a cobalt blue sky and sea, the whitewashed Masseria San Domenico stands proud, evoking its historic past. Situated in the 'heel' of Italy, recently hailed the 'new Tuscany', the building was once a watchtower, used in the 15th Century as a defence against the Turks. Having been carefully restored, the Masseria stands amidst 100 hectares of olive groves, orchards and countryside that is still wild and unspoilt.

The Masseria San Domenico is simply the best hotel in the area, a great example of fine restoration, full of antique artefacts and renowned for its traditional cooking using organic, locally and home grown produce and regional delicacies.

The hotel's centrepiece is the magnificent pool, which is filled with naturally filtered seawater, reflecting the philosophy of the hotel's unique Thalassotherapy Spa. For golf enthusiasts who want to experience a challenging round of golf whilst enjoying views over the Adriatic Sea, the course lies just 20 steps away.

FACILITIES

Accommodation
25 Rooms, 14 Junior Suites & 11 Suites

Recreational facilities
Spa Thalassotherapy Centre
Gym, Sauna, Steam Bath
Salted Water Swimming Pool
Massage Treatments
Private Beach
Motor Boat Rental
Bikes
18-Hole Golf Course
2 Tennis Courts
Bar & Restaurant
Sightseeing Excursions
Spirits and Cigars Bar

Meeting facilities
Meeting Room for up to 150 people

International Airports
Brindisi International Airport (BDS)
30 minutes drive away
Bari International Airport (BRI)
45 minutes drive away

RESERVATIONS

Prices
Rooms from 330 Euro per night

Credit cards
AE, DC, MC, V

GDS Reservation Codes
Amadeus LW BDS165
Galileo LW 64904
Sabre LW 30488
Worldspan LW 2165

Yearly Closing Dates
January and February

CONTACT DETAILS

Masseria San Domenico
Litoranea 379
I-72010 Savelletri di Fasano
(Brindisi)
Italy
Tel +39 080 4827769
Fax +39 080 4827978
INFO@MASSERIASANDOMENICO.COM
WWW.MASSERIASANDOMENICO.COM

Owner: Mr and Mrs Melpignano
General Manager: Mrs Marisa Melpignano
Director of sales: Mrs Viola Melpignano

AFFILIATIONS

The Leading Small Hotels
of the World

PALAZZO SASSO
Ravello

The Palazzo Sasso is set on the Amalfi Coast, south of Naples, with spectacular views over the Mediterranean sea. Ravello itself being a charming little town, boldly laid out on a steep hillside. The glorious surroundings of clear blue sea, a profusion of flowers, and pastel-painted houses offer visitors a peaceful haven from a busy world.

Originally, a 12th Century villa built for the noble Sasso family, has been tastefully refurbished to the highest standards, yet retains of its medieval and baroque features. The hotel has been recognised internationally with prestigious awards for its commitment to the very best in service and hospitality.

Accommodation at the hotel comprises 34 rooms and 10 suites, all of deluxe standard. Most of them have Jacuzzis and wonderful sea views. There is a stunning outdoor swimming pool and the rooftop features a magnificent sun terrace, with hydromassage plunge pools. One can relax at the hotel's new Spa offering a steam bath, hydrotherapy pool, sauna and treatment rooms.

FACILITIES

Accommodation
44 ROOMS, INCLUDING 10 SUITES

Recreational facilities
OUTDOOR HEATED SWIMMING POOL
ROOFTOP SUN TERRACE WITH 2 JACUZZI POOLS
OUTDOOR FITNESS FACILITIES
SPA WITH HYDROTHERAPY, STEAM BATH
SAUNA & TREATMENT ROOMS
ROSSELLINIS, ONE MICHELIN STAR RESTAURANT
CAFFÈ DELL'ARTE AND TERRAZZA BELVEDERE
LIMOUSINE AND HELICOPTER SERVICE
BOAT TRIPS & GUIDED EXCURSIONS

Meeting facilities
MEETING ROOM FOR UP TO 60 PEOPLE

International Airports
NAPLES INTERNATIONAL AIRPORT (NAP)
60 MINUTES DRIVE AWAY

RESERVATIONS

Prices
ROOMS FROM 390 EURO PER NIGHT
SUITES FROM 825 EURO PER NIGHT

Credit cards
AE, DC, MC, V

GDS Reservation Codes
AMADEUS PH NAPPALS
GALILEO PH 87149
SABRE PH 40823
WORLDSPAN PH NAPPS

Yearly Closing Dates
01 NOVEMBER 2004 – 17 MARCH 2005

CONTACT DETAILS

PALAZZO SASSO
VIA SAN GIOVANNI DEL TORO 28
I-84010 RAVELLO, AMALFI COAST
ITALY
TEL +39 089 81 81 81
FAX +39 089 85 89 00
INFO@PALAZZOSASSO.COM
WWW.PALAZZOSASSO.COM

OWNER: NEPTUNIA SRL.
GENERAL MANAGER: MR STEFANO GEGNACORSI
DIRECTOR OF SALES: MR STEFANO GEGNACORSI

AFFILIATIONS

REGINA HOTEL BAGLIONI
Rome

Housed in a magnificent, liberty-style building, the Regina Hotel has always attracted a clientele in search of elegance and finesse. Guests are guaranteed prompt, impeccable service during their stay, and are able to wander through the magnificently furnished rooms which once hosted famous figures such as Queen Margherita.

The 143 rooms and suites offer guests every imaginable comfort and charming views of the capital, with the stunning 200 square metres suite on the 8th floor boasting an amazing panorama of the roofs of Rome, a totally soundproofed glass outer wall and relaxing Jacuzzi on the spacious sunroof.

Not to be forgotten are the 'Le Grazie del Canova' restaurant which covers four rooms of which each single one has been infused with warmth and furnished with a particular attention to detail in keeping with the Liberty-style of the building. Also, Caffè Regina is the cocktail bar by excellence, serving the famous Regina cocktail.

FACILITIES

Accommodation
143 ROOMS, INCLUDING 8 SUITES AND 4 JUNIOR SUITES

Recreational facilities
RESTAURANT & BAR
NUMEROUS EXCURSION AND SIGHTSEEING POSSIBILITIES

Meeting facilities
3 MEETING ROOMS FOR UP TO 80 PEOPLE

International Airports
FIUMICINO INTERNATIONAL AIRPORT (FCO) 25 MINUTES DRIVE AWAY

RESERVATIONS

Prices
ROOMS FROM 300 EURO PER NIGHT

Credit cards
AE, DC, MC, V

GDS Reservation Codes
AMADEUS XL ROMREC
GALILEO XL 92658
SABRE XL 16026
WORLDSPAN XL 5298

Yearly Closing Dates
NONE

CONTACT DETAILS
REGINA HOTEL
VIA VENETO 72
I-00187 ROME
ITALY
TEL +39 06 421111
FAX +39 06 42012130
REGINA.ROMA@BAGLIONIHOTELS.COM
WWW.BAGLIONIHOTELS.COM

OWNER: BAGLIONI HOTELS SPA
GENERAL MANAGER: MR MICHELE ZANCONATO
DIRECTOR OF SALES: MS ALESSANDRA RUGGERI

AFFILIATIONS
SUMMIT HOTELS & RESORTS

RELAIS LA SUVERA

Pievescola

From medieval castle to renaissance villa, Relais La Suvera has a rich and varied history. In the late 80s, Marchese Ricci and his wife, Princess Massimo decided to convert their glorious private residence in the Tuscan countryside into a unique country retreat.

The accommodations are housed in 3 buildings, the most exclusive accommodations being in the 16th Century Papal Villa and in the Fattoria. Beautiful rooms are situated in the Scuderie. The historical furnishings, many of which have been handed down through the royal family for hundreds of years, or come from the family's art collection, offer a unique environment.

The Oliviera Restaurant, in the ancient olive oil mill, offers a traditional and creative a la carte menu. Superb, organically produced wine carrying La Suvera d.o.c is available to the guests.

On the leisure side, one can relax at the hotel's health centre, which features a steam bath, fitness facilities and a Jacuzzi. Two massage cabins and a heated swimming pool are equally available as are the beautiful surrounding parklands for a leisurely stroll.

FACILITIES

Accommodation
19 ROOMS & 13 SUITES

Recreational facilities
HEATED SWIMMING POOL
FITNESS FACILITIES
STEAM BATH
JACUZZI
MASSAGE TREATMENTS
MOUNTAIN BIKING
TENNIS COURT
RESTAURANT & BAR
EXCURSIONS

Meeting facilities
2 MEETING ROOMS FOR UP TO 40 PEOPLE

International Airports
FLORENCE INTERNATIONAL AIRPORT (FLR)
45 MINUTES DRIVE AWAY

RESERVATIONS

Prices
ROOMS FROM 360 EURO PER NIGHT
SUITES FROM 480 EURO PER NIGHT

Credit cards
AE, DC, MC, V

GDS Reservation Codes
NONE

Yearly Closing Dates
2 NOVEMBER 2004 – 21 APRIL 2005

CONTACT DETAILS

RELAIS LA SUVERA
COMMUNE DI CASOLE D'ELSA
I-53030 PIEVESCOLA (PROVINCIA DI SIENA)
ITALY
TEL +39 0577 960300
FAX +39 0577 960220
LASUVERA@LASUVERA.IT
WWW.LASUVERA.IT

OWNER: MARCHESI RICCI
GENERAL MANAGER: MR GIUSEPPE RICCI
DIRECTOR OF SALES: MRS FRANCESCA DELLA TORRE
RESIDENT MANAGER: MRS CLAUDINE LECHNER

AFFILIATIONS

NONE

VILLA ANTEA
Florence

The boutique hotel Villa Antea with its fine furniture and sumptuous decors, offers a luxurious atmosphere in the quietness of one of the city-center's most elegant areas.

Villa Antea has paid great attention to every detail in the rooms, decorated with splendid tapestries and important antique furniture dating back to Empire and Charles X times, and featuring en-suite bathrooms entirely decorated with Carrara marble. The rooms also offer all the amenities demanded by today's discerning travelers.

The restaurant's One Star Michelin-Chef Denny Bruci prepares exclusively on clients' request specialities from the delicious Tuscan cuisines as well as own creations, along with a fine selection of fabulous Italian wines. The hotel's staff guarantees the highest standards of service and the very finest Florentine hospitality. A stay in hotel Villa Antea will be an unforgettable one.

FACILITIES

Accommodation
3 SUPERIOR ROOMS,
2 DELUXE ROOMS & 1 SUITE

Recreational facilities
LOUNGE
GARDEN
RESTAURANT (ONE STAR MICHELIN)
AMAZINGLY CENTRAL LOCATION
CULTURAL VISITS
EXCURSIONS

Meeting facilities
MEETING ROOM FOR UP TO 20 PEOPLE

International Airports
FLORENCE INTERNATIONAL AIRPORT (FLR)
15 MINUTES DRIVE AWAY

RESERVATIONS

Prices
SUPERIOR ROOMS FROM 340 EURO PER NIGHT
DELUXE ROOMS FROM 390 EURO PER NIGHT
SUITE FROM 440 EURO PER NIGHT

Credit cards
AE, DC, MC, V

GDS Reservation Codes
AMADEUS UZ FLR74
GALILEO UZ 67502
SABRE UZ 25233
WORLDSPAN UZ 747

Yearly Closing Dates
NONE

CONTACT DETAILS

VILLA ANTEA
VIA FRANCESCO PUCCINOTTI, 44-46-48
I-50129 FIRENZE
ITALY
TEL +39 055 484106
FAX +39 055 484539
INFO@VILLAANTEA.COM
WWW.VILLAANTEA.COM

OWNER: C.C.S. INVESTMENTS SRL
GENERAL MANAGER: MR CHRISTOPH DOELZ
DIRECTOR OF SALES: MR CHRISTOPH DOELZ

AFFILIATIONS
NONE

VILLA LA VEDETTA
Florence

The exclusive hotel Villa La Vedetta, situated beside Piazzale Michelangelo, with a unique and sublime view of Florence was once a patrician villa. The surrounding Italian garden and beautiful park that slopes toward the Arno river provide a perfect setting for a long romantic walk.

Each room is a different colour, which is repeated in the fine marble in the bathroom and patinated walls, creating a very soft and elegant environment. All spacious and luxurious rooms feature a bathroom with Jacuzzi and boast glorious views over Florence or the hotel's private garden.

La villa provides a glamorous and sophisticated ambiance, with lounge bar, gourmet restaurant, pool and American bar, fitness and sauna. The swimming pool, looking out over Florence, features aquatic plants and an unusual large Jacuzzi for 20 people. Guests can enjoy a of magical moment of relaxation and admire the panorama from the magnificent terrace.

FACILITIES
Accommodation
10 ROOMS & 8 SUITES
Recreational facilities
HEATED SWIMMING POOL
JACUZZI
SAUNA
PRIVATE GARDEN & PARK
JOGGING PATH
LIBRARY
POOL BAR
AMERICAN BAR
ONICE LOUNGE & RESTAURANT
CENTRAL LOCATION
Meeting facilities
MEETING ROOM FOR UP TO 40 PEOPLE
International Airports
FLORENCE INTERNATIONAL AIRPORT (FLR)
15 MINUTES DRIVE AWAY

RESERVATIONS
Prices
ROOMS FROM 561 EURO PER NIGHT
SUITES FROM 957 EURO PER NIGHT
Credit cards
AE, DC, MC, V
GDS Reservation Codes
AMADEUS GW FLR464
GALILEO GW 68207
SABRE GW 35444
WORLDSPAN GW 35444
Yearly Closing Dates
NONE

CONTACT DETAILS
VILLA LA VEDETTA
VIALE MICHELANGIOLO 78
I-50125 FIRENZE
ITALY
TEL +39 055 681631
FAX +39 055 6582544
INFO@VILLALAVEDETTAHOTEL.COM
WWW.VILLALAVEDETTAHOTEL.COM
OWNER: CLASSIFIED
DIRECTOR OF SALES: MRS CHIARA ROSATI

AFFILIATIONS
NONE

VIGILIUS MOUNTAIN RESORT

Lana Südtirol

At a height of 1,500 m, woods, flowers, pure air and the silence of the mountain surround the Vigilius Mountain Resort. Minimalism was chosen by the architect Matteo Thun to enhance the process of mind regeneration and search for oneself by opening to the guest a new dimension outlined by physical activities, wellbeing and beauty.

Guests will spend their holidays resting and relaxing at the tranquil spa, where the unique Vigilius Feedback Method has been invented for the individual wellbeing. Curiosity will take travellers outside to experience the mountain world. The Vigilius Sports Team is available for personal tailored programs with paragliding, archery, hiking, mountain biking, yoga, skiing or snow shoeing.

The cuisine is evocative of the areas two cultures, Alpine and Italian. The Restaurant offers delicious local food specialties, whereas at the Gourmet restaurant 1,500 a local chef with international experience and with a specialisation in Mediterranean-style 'Amuse Bouche Menus' will prepare exquisite meals.

FACILITIES

Accommodation
35 DOUBLE ROOMS & 6 SUITES

Recreational facilities
SHISEIDO QI SPA
INDOOR AND OUTDOOR POOL WITH JACUZZI
3 SUN-TERRACES
MOUNTAIN LOUNGE AND
PIAZZA WITH FIREPLACE
MOVEMENT ROOM FOR YOGA & MEDITATION
LIBRARY AND CINEMA
50 KM HIKING TRAILS
PERSONAL TRAINING
SPORT PROGRAMS WITH TREKKING, BIKING,
HIKING, PARAGLIDING, NORDIC WALKING,
YOGA, STRETCHING, ARCHERY
2 RESTAURANTS

Meeting facilities
MEETING ROOM FOR UP TO 40 PEOPLE

International Airports
VERONA INTERNATIONAL AIRPORT (VRN)
120 MINUTES DRIVE AWAY
INNSBRUCK AIRPORT (INN)
120 MINUTES DRIVE AWAY

RESERVATIONS

Prices
ROOMS FROM 310 EURO PER NIGHT

Credit cards
AE, DC, MC, V

GDS Reservation Codes
AMADEUS DS BZ OVMR
GALILEO DS 63018
SABRE DS 61449
WORLDSPAN DS VIGL

Yearly Closing Dates
MID NOVEMBER – MID DECEMBER

CONTACT DETAILS

VIGILIUS MOUNTAIN RESORT
VIGILJOCH
I-39011 LANA
SÜDTIROL
ITALY
TEL +39 0473 556600
FAX + 39 0473 556699
INFO@VIGILIUS.IT
WWW.VIGILIUS.IT

OWNER: MR ULRICH LADURNER
GENERAL MANAGER: MRS DOROTHEA SCHUSTER
DIRECTOR OF SALES: MRS BARBARA ASTER

AFFILIATIONS

a member of
design hotels™

GRAND PALACE HOTEL
Riga

On pushing open the massive door of the Grand Palace Hotel, you may get the strange feeling that you are finally back home. The Grand Palace Hotel offers travellers a place of warmth and comfort, accompanied by attentiveness and impeccable service. The intimate atmosphere, a blend of Old Russian and European influences, echo the romantic cultures of the past.

All 56 deluxe rooms and suites are exquisitely decorated in a European neoclassical décor and offer luxury en-suite bathrooms, direct dial telephones, ISDN lines, voicemail, modem facilities and mini bar.

The Health Club Bleu Marin offers a traditional sauna, steam bath, solarium and massage as well as a gymnasium.

Heaven for the senses, the glow of candles reflect off large gilt mirrors in the dining rooms bronze hued intimacy. The famous Seasons Restaurant provides guests with the best culinary creations in the Baltic region. Enjoy imaginative local and international dishes while contemplating the dancing flames of the log fire.

FACILITIES

Accommodation
50 ROOMS AND 6 SUITES

Recreational facilities
CITY CENTRE LOCATION
GYMNASIUM
SAUNA & STEAM ROOM
SOLARIUM & MASSAGE
RESTAURANT SEASONS
RESTAURANT ORANGERIE
PILS BAR

Meeting facilities
MEETING ROOM FOR UP TO 12 PEOPLE

International Airports
RIGA INTERNATIONAL AIRPORT (RIX)
15 MINUTES DRIVE AWAY

RESERVATIONS

Prices
ROOMS FROM 201 EURO PER NIGHT

Credit cards
AE, MC, V

GDS Reservation Codes
AMADEUS XL RIXGRP
GALILEO XL 28550
SABRE XL 54086
WORLDSPAN XL 41581

Yearly Closing Dates
NONE

CONTACT DETAILS
GRAND PALACE HOTEL
PILS 12
LV-1050 RIGA
LATVIA
TEL +371 704 40 00
FAX +371 704 40 01
GRANDPALACE.RESERVATIONS@
SCHLOSSLE-HOTELS.COM
WWW.SCHLOSSLE-HOTELS.COM

OWNER: SCHLÖSSLE HOTEL GROUP
GENERAL MANAGER: MR BERNHARD LOEW
DIRECTOR OF SALES: MRS IVETA LININA

AFFILIATIONS
SUMMIT HOTELS AND RESORTS

COLUMBUS MONACO
Fontvieille

Ideal for those who value the combination of stylish and relaxed surroundings, Columbus Monaco was designed by enthusiasts, for people to enjoy, slow down and feel good about themselves.

Located in the picturesque Fontvieille Marine and only five minutes away from the centre of Monte-Carlo, the Columbus Monaco is ideally suited for those seeking a venue away from the city's hubbub, yet close enough to enjoy the excitement it has to offer.

The 153 rooms and 28 suites feature a classic contemporary style. True comfort in crisp, cool and calm décor combined with the subtle hues reflects the Riviera lifestyle. All rooms are equipped with the latest amenities.

As the Columbus Monaco is all about pleasure, the restaurant and cocktail bar areas have been created for complete relaxation in attractive surroundings. The Brasserie and Terrace are the life and soul of the hotel. The Bar has great ambience with music and comfortable furnishings, and is the place to relax after a day's sunbathing by the outdoor pool.

FACILITIES

Accommodation
181 ROOMS, INCLUDING 28 SUITES

Recreational facilities
OUTDOOR SWIMMING POOL
GYM WITH TECHNOGYM EQUIPMENT
COLUMBUS BRASSERIE
COCKTAIL BAR
SCREENING ROOM
PRIVATE BEACH NEARBY
TENNIS & GOLF NEARBY

Meeting facilities
AUDITORIUM FOR UP TO 90 PEOPLE
2 MEETING ROOMS FOR UP TO 20 PEOPLE

International Airports
NICE INTERNATIONAL AIRPORT (NCE)
6 MINUTES HELICOPTER FLIGHT AWAY
30 MINUTES DRIVE AWAY

RESERVATIONS

Prices
ROOMS FROM 220 EURO PER NIGHT

Credit cards
AE, DC, MC, V

GDS Reservation Codes
NONE

Yearly Closing Dates
NONE

CONTACT DETAILS

COLUMBUS MONACO
23 AVENUE DES PAPALINS
MC-98000 MONACO
PRINCIPALITY OF MONACO
TEL +377 92 05 9000
FAX +377 92 05 9167
INFO@COLUMBUSHOTELS.COM
WWW.COLUMBUSHOTELS.COM

OWNER: MR KEN MCCULLOCH
DIRECTOR OF SALES: MRS PAOLA PARRIGO

AFFILIATIONS

NONE

LE RÉGINA
Warsaw

The elegant and intimate hotel Le Régina is situated in a historic building, faithfully restored to the style of an 18th century palace. It happens to be the first, and only hotel in the most prestigious part of Warsaw – The Old Town. Close by are historical landmarks, including The Royal Castle, The National Opera House and the Umschlagplatz.

The hotel offers stylish spacious rooms in pleasant natural shades of brown and vanilla, uniquely adorned with hand-painted frescos. All guest rooms are decorated with custom-made wood furniture of fine Italian artisanship and equipped with all the modern amenities. Luxurious bathrooms are designed in a contemporary style, outfitted in pale sandstone and Venetian mosaic.

The hotel has a quiet, lovely courtyard garden with a splashing water fountain. Guests can relax in a Spa area, which features a sauna, fitness equipment and a heated swimming pool. 'La Rotisserie' restaurant offers the best international gourmet delights in town.

FACILITIES

Accommodation
58 ROOMS & 3 SUITES

Recreational facilities
FITNESS CENTRE
INDOOR HEATED SWIMMING POOL
SAUNA
PATIO WITH SUMMER RESTAURANT
BAR
RESTAURANT

Meeting facilities
2 MEETING ROOMS FOR UP TO 150 PEOPLE

International Airports
WARSAW INTERNATIONAL AIRPORT (WAW)
20 MINUTES DRIVE AWAY

RESERVATIONS

Prices
ROOMS FROM 220 EURO PER NIGHT

Credit cards
AE, DC, MC, V

GDS Reservation Codes
AMADEUS LX WAWLRE
GALILEO LX 68668
SABRE LX 64009
WORLDSPAN LX WAWLR

Yearly Closing Dates
NONE

CONTACT DETAILS

LE RÉGINA
UL. KOSCIELNA 12
00-218 WARSAW
POLAND
TEL +48 22 531 6000
FAX + 48 22 531 6001
INFO@LEREGINA.COM
WWW.LEREGINA.COM

OWNER: ORCO HOTEL COLLECTION
GENERAL MANAGER: MR STEFAN RADSTROM
DIRECTOR OF SALES: MRS AGNIESZKA TUCHARZ

AFFILIATIONS

BAIRRO ALTO
Lisbon

Having opened its doors recently in Lisbon, and named after the fashionable district where it is located, the Bairro Alto hotel is not to be missed.

Reflecting its Portuguese heritage in hues of ochre, amber and red, the hotel incorporates a more modern-day feeling. The 55 rooms and suites feature custom-designed wood and wicker furniture exclusively designed for the hotel, as well as copper coloured wood panelling, flat LCD TVs and sumptuous bathrooms in Alpenina marble.

As well as a Portuguese inspired restaurant, the ground floor houses a bar with 2 levels, one of which, raised on a mezzanine, looks out over the Camões Square. Situated on the top floor, a fully equipped meeting room welcomes business guests, whilst the fitness room and the beautiful panoramic terrace provide a dramatic view over the Tage river and the rooftops of Lisbon.

FACILITIES

Accommodation
55 ROOMS & SUITES

Recreational facilities
SAUNA
FITNESS CENTRE OVERLOOKING THE TAGE
RESTAURANT & BAR

Meeting facilities
MEETING ROOM FOR UP TO 20 PEOPLE

International Airports
LISBON INTERNATIONAL AIRPORT (LIS)
20 MINUTES DRIVE AWAY

RESERVATIONS

Prices
ROOMS FROM 330 EURO PER NIGHT

Credit cards
AE, DC, MC, V

GDS Reservation Codes
TBA

Yearly Closing Dates
NONE

CONTACT DETAILS

BAIRRO ALTO
8 PRAÇA LUIS DE CAMÕES
BAIRRO ALTO
1200-243 LISBON
PORTUGAL
TEL +351 21 340 82 88
FAX +351 21 340 82 99
HOTELBAIRROALTO@VIANW.PT
WWW.BAIRROALTO.COM

OWNER: MR PEDRO MENDES LEAL
GENERAL MANAGER: MRS ADÉLIA CARVALHO
DIRECTOR OF SALES: MRS MARIA JOÃO ROCHA

AFFILIATIONS
TBA

CHOUPANA HILLS RESORT & SPA
Madeira

Choupana Hills, nestled on the verdant hillside of Funchal, is comprised of 34 bungalow-style units built on pillars, revealing African and Asian influences in its unique decoration as well as in other antique pieces sourced from various Portuguese discoveries.

The spacious rooms and suites are decorated in a contemporary style with an exotic touch. All rooms have large verandas with views of the Atlantic Ocean or the sub-tropical gardens. The suites offer also heated outdoor Jacuzzis on the verandas, DVD, internet access and Hi-Fi system.

The Xôpana Restaurant offers its guests' exotic and innovative "fusion" cuisine. Whilst enjoying your day at the pool or SPA, try the isotonic drinks at the Pool Bar. "High afternoon tea" is a must and is served in the Lounge.

Comforts here are extremely pleasant, with the Health and Beauty Spa offering a range of innovative relaxation methods, massages and treatments such as Aromatherapy, Rasul, Algae Wraps, Reflexology, Turkish baths and saunas, outdoor lagoon pool and indoor hydrotherapy pool.

FACILITIES
Accommodation
60 DELUXE ROOMS AND 4 SUITES

Recreational facilities
HEALTH & BEAUTY TREATMENTS
INDOOR HEATED HYDROTHERAPY POOL
OUTDOOR HEATED LAGOON SWIMMING POOL
SAUNA
GYMNASIUM
HAMMAM
LIBRARY WITH INTERNET CONNECTION
LEVADA WALKS
GOLF AND HORSEBACK RIDING NEARBY

Meeting facilities
MEETING ROOM FOR UP TO 40 PEOPLE

International Airports
FUNCHAL INTERNATIONAL AIRPORT (FNC)
20 MINUTES DRIVE AWAY

RESERVATIONS
Prices
ROOMS FROM 251 EURO PER NIGHT

Credit cards
AE, DC, MC, V

GDS Reservation Codes
NONE

Yearly Closing Dates
NONE

CONTACT DETAILS
CHOUPANA HILLS RESORT & SPA
TRAVESSA DO LARGO DA CHOUPANA
P-9060-348 FUNCHAL
MADEIRA
PORTUGAL
TEL +35 1291 20 60 20
FAX +35 1291 20 60 21
INFO@CHOUPANAHILLS.COM
WWW.CHOUPANAHILLS.COM

OWNER: CHOUPANA HILLS RESORTS –
EMPREENDIMENTOS TURÍSTICOS SA
GENERAL MANAGER: MR PHILIPPE MOREAU
DIRECTOR OF SALES: MRS KATJA HEKKALA

AFFILIATIONS
– a member of
 design hotels

CA'S XORC

Mallorca

Tucked away in the Soller Valley, overlooked by the jagged mountains of the Sierra Tramuntana, is the delightful Hotel Agroturismo Ca's Xorc.

The hotel is charmingly intimate, with only 12 rooms, most of which have their own terrace. Each one is individually and exclusively designed and furnished, blending modern with regional, classical touches. The stylish comfort, panoramic views and subtle mix of traditional and contemporary design offers the utmost in luxury. An exclusive hideaway for private gatherings.

Dining in the restaurant is a memorable gastronomic experience. Indulge in delicious, international and local dishes whilst you take in dramatic vistas over olive groves and the sea beyond.

The grounds are extensive with quiet, secluded corners to explore. The bubbling Jacuzzi and adjacent heated infinity pool offer indulgent relaxation, whilst you drink in the glorious view.

Ca's Xorc is a beautiful sanctuary of peace and quiet, a sublime place in which to relax and unwind.

FACILITIES

Accommodation
12 ROOMS

Recreational facilities
HEATED OUTDOOR 'INFINITY' SWIMMING POOL & JACUZZI
ELEGANT FINCA RESTAURANT
GOLF COURSE
SAILING & BOATING
SCUBA DIVING
FISHING
HIKING TRAILS
MOUNTAIN BIKING
SECLUDED COVES & BAYS NEARBY

Meeting facilities
INDOOR MEETING ROOM
FOR UP TO 14 PEOPLE
OUTDOOR MEETING ROOM
FOR UP TO 35 PEOPLE

International Airports
PALMA DE MALLORCA AIRPORT (PMI)
30 MINUTES DRIVE AWAY

RESERVATIONS

Prices
ROOMS FROM 160 EURO PER NIGHT

Credit cards
AE, DC, MC, V

GDS Reservation Codes
NONE

Yearly Closing Dates
15 NOVEMBER 2004 – 4 MARCH 2005

CONTACT DETAILS

CA'S XORC
CARRETERA DE DÉIA, KM 56.1
E-07100 SÓLLER/MALLORCA
SPAIN
TEL +34 971 63 82 80
FAX +34 971 63 29 49
STAY@CASXORC.COM
WWW.CASXORC.COM

OWNER: CLASSIFIED
DIRECTOR: MRS CARINA CLEIRBAUT
DIRECTOR OF SALES: MRS BRITTA PLOENZKE

AFFILIATIONS

NONE

HOTEL CORTIJO SOTO REAL
Seville

The five star luxury palace, the former residence of an Algerian Prince, is located on 1000 acres of hills and valleys. Blending traditional Andalusian architecture with modern technology, this resort offers 24 uniquely decorated luxury rooms and suites. All the rooms boast a private terrace or garden offering breathtaking views over the hills and valleys.

Being in the full countryside, the Cortijo provides opportunities for 4x4, quad biking, nature walks, horseback riding and mountain biking as well as swimming and tennis. Cultural visits to the magical cities Jerez and Seville are a must. Some of the finest golf courses in Europe are situated close by. Guests wishing to relax and be pampered can enjoy a treatment or massage in the spa.

Typical Andalusian and international cuisine is served in the two dining rooms, in the luxurious lounge and several cosy 'patios' and terraces. Refreshing cocktails or aperitifs await on the attractive entrance terrace or in the beautiful romantic garden.

FACILITIES

Accommodation
24 ROOMS AND SUITES WITH JACUZZI

Recreational facilities
OUTDOOR SWIMMING POOL
QUAD BIKING
HORSEBACK RIDING
MOUNTAIN BIKING
TENNIS & GYM
CLAY- AND PARTRIDGE SHOOTING
SPA FEATURING INDOOR SWIMMING POOL,
JACUZZI, SAUNA & MASSAGE TREATMENTS
EXCURSIONS TO JEREZ

Meeting facilities
MEETING ROOMS FOR UP TO 150 PEOPLE

International Airports
SEVILLE INTERNATIONAL AIRPORT (SVQ)
45 MINUTES DRIVE AWAY
JEREZ AIRPORT (XRY)
30 MINUTES DRIVE AWAY

RESERVATIONS

Prices
ROOMS FROM 290 EURO PER NIGHT

Credit cards
AE, DC, MC, V

GDS Reservation Codes
AMADEUS LX SVQHCS
GALILEO LX 64599
SABRE LX 907
WORLDSPAN LX SVQHC

Yearly Closing Dates
NONE

CONTACT DETAILS

HOTEL CORTIJO SOTO REAL
APT. CORREOS 69
41730 LAS CABEZAS DE SAN JUAN
SEVILLA
SPAIN
TEL +34 955 869 200
FAX +34 955 869 202
INFO@HOTELCORTIJOSOTOREAL.COM
WWW.HOTELCORTIJOSOTOREAL.COM

OWNER: CLASSIFIED
DIRECTOR: MR EDUARDO BLANCO
GUEST RELATIONS: MRS INGE SNOEKS

AFFILIATIONS

ELBA PALACE GOLF
Fuerteventura

Hotel Elba Palace is set on the mostly uninhabited island of Fuerteventura, which has a sunny year-round climate.

The hotel, part of the Club House of Fuerteventura Golf Club, is beautifully situated between the golf course and the gorgeous beach. The elegant hotel has been designed in typical Canarian architectural style, with magnificent wooden balconies and inner patios with palm trees and autochthonous plants.

The spacious, individually decorated rooms feature private terrace or balcony magnificently looking onto the sea and the golf course.

The hotel boasts a large swimming pool and spacious terraces with relaxing sunloungers. Other leisure activities on offer include paddle tennis, sailing, scuba diving, jet ski, mountain biking, a gymnasium, a health centre and of course, the challenging 18-holes golf course for those who want to golf their days away.

The restaurant and wine cellar invite you on a fine culinary journey, while the piano bar provides nightly entertainment.

FACILITIES

Accommodation
51 Rooms & 10 Suites

Recreational facilities
Freshwater Swimming Pool
Gymnasium
Jacuzzi
Health & Beauty Centre
Padle & Tennis Courts
Sailing, Scuba Diving, Jet Ski
Mountain Biking
Children's Pool
18-hole Golf Course
Piano Bar
Excursions

Meeting facilities
2 Meeting Rooms for up to 250 people

International Airports
Fuerteventura Int'l Airport (FUE)
10 minutes drive away

RESERVATIONS

Prices
Rooms from 250 Euro per night

Credit cards
AE, DC, MC, V

GDS Reservation Codes
Amadeus LX FUEPAL
Galileo LX 43592
Sabre LX 20788
Worldspan LX ELBA

Yearly Closing Dates
None

CONTACT DETAILS
Elba Palace Golf
Urbanización Fuerteventura Golf Club
35610 Antigua
Fuerteventura
Canary Islands
Spain
Tel +928 163922
Fax +928 163923
epg@hoteleselba.com
www.hoteleselba.com

Owner: Mr Angel Jove Capellan
General Manager: Mr Fernando de las Heras
Director of sales: Mr Ignacio Susilla

AFFILIATIONS

HACIENDA BENAZUZA - ELBULLIHOTEL

Seville

A 10th century Arab palace was transformed a few years ago to this unique and emblematic grand luxe hotel situated in one of the 'small white villages' of magical Andalusia, just 15 minutes driving distance from Seville.

The rooms and suites are lavishly decorated with works of art and surrounded by beautiful gardens and lovely patios.

The Hacienda Benazuza has wagered on becoming doubly famous by offering not only its enchanting architecture and renowned service, but also an alive and vibrant, contemporary cuisine. The one star Michelin gourmet restaurant 'La Alquería' offers the guests an unforgettable experience to discover the famous creations of Chef Ferran Adrià in an enchanting place. 'La Alberca' restaurant, al-fresco dinning by the pool, serves Mediterranean dishes with Ferran Adrià's touch. 'La Abacería' is a typical tapas-bar with an exclusive selection of Spanish products. At the English bar 'El Guadarnés' guests are treated to original cocktails.

The Hacienda Benazuza, a peaceful and discreet place for a magical gourmet experience.

FACILITIES

Accommodation
44 ROOMS & SUITES

Recreational facilities
SWIMMING POOL
JACUZZI
MASSAGE TREATMENTS
TENNIS COURT
HORSEBACK RIDING, BIKING
TERRACES & GARDENS
EXCURSION SERVICE
HOT AIR BALLOONING
GOLF COURSES NEARBY
PRIVATE HELIPORT
3 GOURMET RESTAURANTS
(ONE STAR MICHELIN)
2 BARS

Meeting facilities
5 MEETING ROOMS FOR UP TO 300 PEOPLE

International Airports
SEVILLE INTERNATIONAL AIRPORT (SVQ)
25 MINUTES DRIVE AWAY

RESERVATIONS

Prices
ROOMS FROM 320 EURO PER NIGHT
SUITES FROM 430 EURO PER NIGHT

Credit cards
AE, DC, MC, V

GDS Reservation Codes
AMADEUS TA SVQ414
GALILEO TA 63557
SABRE TA 64340
WORLDSPAN TV 382

Yearly Closing Dates
NONE

CONTACT DETAILS

ELBULLIHOTEL HACIENDA BENAZUZA
VIRGEN DE LAS NIEVES S/N
SANLUCAR LA MAYOR
E-41800SEVILLE
SPAIN
TEL +34 95 570 33 44
FAX + 34 95 570 34 10
HBENAZUZA@ELBULLIHOTEL.COM
WWW.HBENAZUZA.COM

OWNER: ELBULLI HOTELS & RESORTS
GENERAL MANAGER: MR LUCAS RAMIREZ
DIRECTOR OF SALES: MRS ANA PRIETO

AFFILIATIONS

NONE

HOTEL CLARIS
Barcelona

In the heart of Barcelona, next to the Paseo de Gracia and the buildings of Gaudi, located in a 19th century palace, the Hotel Claris represents one of the best choices for an unforgettable stay in Barcelona.

Hotel Claris cleverly combines traditional and modern with antique and art nouveau in a smart post-modern mansion. It is a unique blend of unexpected contrasts in a hotel that stands in a class of its own.

The hotel, with its unique architectural style, is admired as a work of art in its own right. It is a union between form and function, utility and beauty. The carefully chosen contents and elegant decor lend a special feel to the hotel that you notice as soon as you enter.

The Claris offers 120 luxurious rooms, where you can find unique art works. In addition, there are top-class facilities, including a sauna, Jacuzzi, swimming-pool, fitness room, solarium, business centre, an Egyptian Museum, cocktail bar and 3 restaurants with different styles: East 47, La Terraza del Claris and Claris.

FACILITIES

Accommodation
120 ROOMS & SUITES

Recreational facilities
SWIMMING POOL
SOLARIUM
SAUNA
GYMNASIUM
3 RESTAURANTS
BAR
ANCIENT EGYPT ART COLLECTION
CENTRAL LOCATION

Meeting facilities
6 MEETING ROOMS FOR UP TO 200 PEOPLE

International Airports
BARCELONA INTERNATIONAL AIRPORT (BCN)
30 MINUTES DRIVE AWAY

RESERVATIONS

Prices
ROOM FROM 270 EURO PER NIGHT
SUITES FROM 450 EURO PER NIGHT
DUPLEX SUITES FROM 975 EURO PER NIGHT

Credit cards
AE, DC, MC,V

GDS Reservation Codes
AMADEUS DS BCN010
GALILEO LX 6801
SABRE LX 31003
WORLDSPAN DS 2010

Yearly Closing Dates
NONE

CONTACT DETAILS

HOTEL CLARIS
PAU CLARIS, 150
E-08009 BARCELONA
SPAIN
TEL +34 93 487 62 62
FAX + 34 93 215 79 70
CLARIS@DERBYHOTELS.COM
WWW.DERBYHOTELS.COM

OWNER: DERBY HOTELS COLLECTION
GENERAL MANAGER: MR JOSE LUIS FERNÁNDEZ
DIRECTOR OF SALES: MS ANNA PONS

AFFILIATIONS

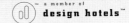

HOTEL URBAN
Madrid

With a stunning outdoor swimming pool, a moonlight restaurant, a spectacular patio adjoining the heart of the city and the last word in architecture in Madrid, the Hotel Urban has come into being. Beyond question, it is a new hotel that will be a reference point for quality.

Art and design, intimacy and silence, comfort and service, and all in the best location in the city, right in real Madrid, in the centre for culture, shopping, politics and finance. The Urban Hotel is a contemporary alternative to the more traditional hotels in this area. The hotel is close to the best Museums of Madrid and the most important sights of the city.

Guests can enjoy the hotel's unique Egyptian and ancient Oriental art collection in the hall, restaurants and even in their rooms.

FACILITIES

Accommodation
96 ROOMS, INCLUDING 7 SUITES

Recreational facilities
SWIMMING POOL
SOLARIUM
SAUNA
GYMNASIUM
EGYPTIAN ART COLLECTION
ANCIENT ART COLLECTION
3 RESTAURANTS
GLASS BAR
CENTRAL LOCATION
CULTURAL VISITS

Meeting facilities
4 MEETING ROOMS FOR UP TO 170 PEOPLE

International Airports
MADRID INTERNATIONAL AIRPORT (MAD)
30 MINUTES DRIVE AWAY

RESERVATIONS

Prices
ROOMS FROM 180 EURO PER NIGHT
SUITES FROM 450 EURO PER NIGHT

Credit cards
AE, DC, MC, V

GDS Reservation Codes
AMADEUS DS MADURB
GALILEO DS 68963
SABRE DS 45801
WORLDSPAN DS MADHU

Yearly Closing Dates
NONE

CONTACT DETAILS

HOTEL URBAN
CARRERA SAN JERÓNIMO, 34
E-28014 MADRID
SPAIN
TEL +34 91 787 77 70
FAX +34 91 787 77 99
URBAN@DERBYHOTELS.COM
WWW.DERBYHOTELS.COM

OWNER: DERBY HOTELS COLLECTION
GENERAL MANAGER: MR FELIX GARCÍA
DIRECTOR OF SALES: MS ANNA PONS

AFFILIATIONS
— a member of
 design hotels™

HOTEL VILLA REAL
Madrid

Once guests have passed through the doors of the Hotel Villa Real, they will find themselves in a warm, comfortable and discreet atmosphere, which makes the hotel an ideal refuge from a day of active entertainment, or from business operations in Madrid.

The Hotel Villa Real is located in the most elegant and emblematic area of Madrid, in the heart of cultural, political, financial and business affairs. The hotel is close to the Prado Museum, Thyssen Bornemisza Museum, The Reina Sofía Contemporary Art Museum and The Opera Theatre.

Although only recently constructed, the hotel reflects the character and charm of 19th century Spanish classical architecture. Frequently defined as a balcony over the Retiro Park, the Villa Real offers breathtaking views from all its rooms. The hotel boasts richly appointed rooms with luxurious bathrooms and some of them have a Jacuzzi.

Culture and art blend together, actually breathe the same air within the hotel. This is apparent in the sculptures and Roman mosaics in the lounge and even in the design of all the small details.

FACILITIES

Accommodation
96 ROOMS & 19 SUITES

Recreational facilities
ANCIENT ART COLLECTION
2 RESTAURANTS
BAR
COFFEE-SHOP
CENTRAL LOCATION
CULTURAL VISITS
EXCURSIONS

Meeting facilities
6 MEETING ROOMS FOR UP TO 220 PEOPLE

International Airports
MADRID INTERNATIONAL AIRPORT (MAD)
30 MINUTES DRIVE AWAY

RESERVATIONS

Prices
ROOMS FROM 246 EURO PER NIGHT
SUITES FROM 450 EURO PER NIGHT
DUPLEX SUITES FROM 975 EURO

Credit cards
AE, DC, MC, V

GDS Reservation Codes
AMADEUS LX MADVIL
GALILEO LX 58968
SABRE LX 23277
WORLDSPAN UI 27026

Yearly Closing Dates
NONE

CONTACT DETAILS

HOTEL VILLA REAL
PLAZA DE LAS CORTES, 10
E-28014 MADRID
SPAIN
TEL +34 91 420 37 67
FAX +34 91 420 25 47
VILLAREAL@DERBYHOTELS.COM
WWW.DERBYHOTELS.COM

OWNER: DERBY HOTELS COLLECTION
GENERAL MANAGER: MR FELIX GARCÍA
DIRECTOR OF SALES: MS ANNA PONS

AFFILIATIONS

THE PRIVATE COLLECTION

MARBELLA CLUB HOTEL · GOLF RESORT & SPA

Marbella

Nearly five decades ago, Prince Alfonso von Hohenlohe, realised a dream and transformed his fine family home into the now world-famous Marbella Club Hotel. Situated in the heart of the 'Golden Mile' between Marbella and Puerto Banus, the Marbella Club is tucked away in lush, subtropical gardens.

This luxurious beachfront resort offers 121 elegant rooms and suites and 16 private villas, all boasting spacious marble bathrooms and a private balcony or terrace. A tempting variety of dinning experiences is available, appealing to all tastes: a Champagne buffet breakfast in the Winter Garden, an opulent buffet lunch at the Beach Club Restaurant, fine Mediterranean cuisine in the candlelit Grill, or a light snack at the poolside bar.

The Marbella Club Hotel, with its spectacular facilities and year-round sunshine, is unique for leisure pursuits. Of particular note are the renowned Beach Club, with its choice of swimming and extensive water sports facilities, the beach front Marbella Club Thalasso Spa and the private 18-hole Marbella Club Golf Resort and adjoining Riding Stables.

FACILITIES

Accommodation
121 ROOMS, SUITES AND 16 PRIVATE VILLAS
WITH 2,3 AND 5 BEDROOMS

Recreational facilities
MARBELLA CLUB THALASSO SPA
MARBELLA CLUB GOLF RESORT
AND RIDING STABLES
BEACH CLUB
2 HEATED OUTDOOR SWIMMING POOLS
SEASONAL WATER SPORTS
MARBELLA CLUB SHOPPING & ART GALLERY
PUENTO ROMANO TENNIS & FITNESS
POLO NEARBY

Meeting facilities
MEETING ROOMS FOR UP TO 120 PEOPLE

International Airports
MALAGA INTERNATIONAL AIRPORT (AGP)
35 MINUTES DRIVE AWAY
GIBRALTAR INTERNATIONAL AIRPORT (GIB)
75 MINUTES DRIVE AWAY

RESERVATIONS

Prices
ROOMS FROM 215 EURO PER NIGHT

Credit cards
AE, DC, MC, V

GDS Reservation Codes
AMADEUS LW QRL109
GALILEO LW 8397
SABRE LW 04759
WORLDSPAN LW 1409

Yearly Closing Dates
NONE

CONTACT DETAILS

MARBELLA CLUB HOTEL · GOLF RESORT & SPA
BLV PRINCIPE ALFONSO VON HOHENLOHE, S/N
E-29600 MARBELLA, MALAGA
SPAIN
TEL +34 952 82 22 11
FAX +34 952 82 98 84
HOTEL@MARBELLACLUB.COM
WWW.MARBELLACLUB.COM

OWNER: CLASSIFIED
DIRECTOR OF SALES: MS KATJA GOTTWIK

AFFILIATIONS

The Leading Small Hotels
of the World

THE PRIVATE COLLECTION

BEAU-RIVAGE PALACE

Lausanne

Located in 10 acres of of private gardens on the banks of the Lake Geneva, only a few steps from the Olympic Museum, the elegant belle époque buildings of the Beau-Rivage Palace command breathtaking views across the lake to the majestic Swiss and French Alps beyond.

The guest rooms and suites are richly appointed and offer the utmost in elegance and comfort. 7 Executive suites were created to be different and unique in style.   Most of the luxurious bathrooms are equipped with Jacuzzi-style systems.

The hotel's new Spa, opening in September 2005 with 1500 sqm, will be a haven for relaxation and pampering, offering a variety of massages and treatments and an indoor and outdoor swimming pool. At the end of the day, the hotel's bars and 2 restaurants provide ample choice for excellent dining. A sumptuous ballroom and other 11 major banquet and meeting rooms are ideal for all sorts of events. The Beau Rivage Palace also caters on the oldest and most beautiful steamboat on Lake Geneva, the 'Montreux'.

FACILITIES

Accommodation
140 GUEST ROOMS, 22 JUNIOR SUITES
& 7 EXECUTIVE SUITES

Recreational facilities
IN AND OUTDOOR SWIMMING POOL
FITNESS CENTRE
MASSAGE & BEAUTY TREATMENTS
SAUNA, SOLARIUM & STEAM BATH
2 TENNIS COURTS & TABLE TENNIS
SURROUNDED BY 10 ACRES
OF PRIVATE GARDENS
PLAYGROUND FOR CHILDREN
GOLF COURSES NEARBY
RESTAURANTS & BARS

Meeting facilities
12 MEETING ROOMS FOR UP TO 600 PEOPLE

International Airports
GENEVA INTERNATIONAL AIRPORT (GVA)
35 MINUTES DRIVE AWAY

RESERVATIONS

Prices
ROOMS FROM 315 EURO PER NIGHT
SUITES FROM 660 EURO PER NIGHT

Credit cards
AE, DC, MC, V

GDS Reservation Codes
AMADEUS LW QLS608
GALILEO LW 8464
SABRE LW 4717
WORLDSPAN LW 1608

Yearly Closing Dates
NONE

CONTACT DETAILS

BEAU-RIVAGE PALACE
PLACE DU PORT 17-19
CH-1006 LAUSANNE
SWITZERLAND
TEL +41 21 613 33 33
FAX +41 21 613 33 34
RESERVATION@BRP.CH
WWW.BRP.CH

OWNER: CLASSIFIED
GENERAL MANAGER: MR FRANÇOIS DUSSART
DIRECTOR OF SALES: MS ODILE VOGEL

AFFILIATIONS
The Leading Hotels
of the World®

THE PRIVATE COLLECTION

HOTEL PALAFITTE
Neuchâtel

The Hotel Palafitte is situated on the outskirts of Neuchâtel town, midway between Geneva and Zurich Airport on one of the most prized sites of the Three Lakes Region with breathtaking views of the lake and the Alps.

Its state-of-the-art technology makes the Hotel Palafitte a vision of what a hotel should be while still meeting the rigorous requirements of a five-star establishment.

With its dependencies, built on stilts in the open countryside, The Palafitte is unique in Europe and provides well-being in a quiet and relaxing lakeside setting. The Hotel boasts 40 junior suites in a spacious area of 68m?. The Pavilions with their office nook, design bathroom featuring a Jacuzzi and private outside terrace, have all Lakeview. 24 Pavilions are built directly on the lake.

The "Le Colvert" restaurant invites you on a marvelous culinary journey whilst "Le Bar" is the elegant and cosy area where intimate conversations take over in a magic atmosphere around the fire.

FACILITIES

Accommodation
40 PAVILIONS OF WHICH 24 ARE ON THE LAKE

Recreational facilities
LAKE ACCESS FROM YOUR ROOM
GOURMET RESTAURANT & BAR
GOLF COURSE NEARBY
JOGGING, BIKING AND SKATING POSSIBILITIES
SWIMMING POOL NEARBY
MASSAGE TREATMENTS ON REQUEST

Meeting facilities
2 MEETING ROOMS FOR UP TO 50 PEOPLE

International Airports
GENEVA INTERNATIONAL AIRPORT (GVA)
70 MINUTES DRIVE AWAY
ZURICH INTERNATIONAL AIRPORT (ZRH)
105 MINUTES DRIVE AWAY

RESERVATIONS

Prices
PAVILIONS FROM 260 EURO PER NIGHT

Credit cards
AE, DC, MC, V

GDS Reservation Codes
AMADEUS LM BRN369
GALILEO LM 56673
SABRE LM 51296
WORLDSPAN LM 09369

Yearly Closing Dates
NONE

CONTACT DETAILS

HOTEL PALAFITTE
ROUTE DES GOUTTES D'OR 2
CH-2000 NEUCHÂTEL
SWITZERLAND
TEL +41 32 723 02 02
FAX +41 32 723 02 03
RESERVATION@PALAFITTE.CH
WWW.PALAFITTE.CH

OWNER: CLASSIFIED
GENERAL MANAGER: MR ANTOINE CHAUMERON
DIRECTOR OF SALES: MRS GÉRALDINE FERUGLIO

AFFILIATIONS
NONE

KULM HOTEL
St. Moritz

As the first hotel in world-famous St. Moritz, the Kulm Hotel has been setting the standard since 1856. The hotel is perfectly located in a quiet, sunny setting with a view of the Upper Engadine valley, lakes and mountains.

The Kulm Hotel has undergone continuous renovation that reflects a combination of tradition, elegance and modern comfort. The 183 spacious bedrooms and suites enjoy luxury amenities and offer a variety of mountain and lake views.

For dining, the elegant Le Grand Restaurant offers an intriguing selection of Swiss and international dishes. In addition, guests may choose to dine at "La Rôtisserie des Chevaliers", an exclusive grill; the Pizzeria or Chesa Al Parc, situated at the entrance to the Kulm Park. Visitors enjoy the hotel's lounge that run the gamut from an inviting après-ski ambiance to a sophisticated piano bar scene.

The Panorama Spa & Health Club with its 1400 m^2 surface allows guests to enjoy the spectacular views over the lake and mountain scenery during their relaxation.

FACILITIES

Accommodation
183 ROOMS, INCLUDING 40 SUITES

Recreational facilities
1,400 M^2 PANORAMA SPA & HEALTH CLUB FEATURING A 25M SWIMMING POOL, WHIRLPOOL, STEAM BATH, SALTWATER GROTTO, CALDARIUM, SAUNAS, GYMNASIUM, MASSAGE & BEAUTY TREATMENTS, CHAMP HEALTH&FITNESS®
3 TENNIS COURTS
9-HOLE GOLF COURSE WITH GOLF ACADEMY, PUTTING GREEN AND DRIVING RANGE
ICE RINK, CURLING CENTRE AND OLYMPIC BOB & CRESTA RUN IN WINTER
MOUNTAIN BIKING, HORSEBACK RIDING, WINDSURFING, MOUNTAINEERING NEARBY.
SHUTTLE FROM HOTEL TO CORVIGLIA MOUNTAIN RAILWAY

Meeting facilities
10 MEETING ROOMS FOR UP TO 450 PEOPLE

International Airports
ZURICH INTERNATIONAL AIRPORT (ZRH)
120 MINUTES DRIVE AWAY

RESERVATIONS

Prices
ROOMS FROM 275 EURO PER NIGHT

Credit cards
AE, DC, MC, V

GDS Reservation Codes
AMADEUS LW SMV614
GALILEO LW 87863
SABRE LW 12175
WORLDSPAN LW 1614

Yearly Closing Dates
3 APRIL 2005 – 24 JUNE 2005
11 SEPTEMBER 2005 – 9 DECEMBER 2005

CONTACT DETAILS

KULM HOTEL
VIA VEGLIA 18
CH-7500 ST. MORITZ
SWITZERLAND
TEL +41 81 836 8000
FAX +41 81 836 8001
INFO@KULMHOTEL-STMORITZ.CH
WWW.KULMHOTEL-STMORITZ.CH

OWNER: CLASSIFIED
GENERAL MANAGER: MR DOMINIQUE GODAT
DIRECTOR OF SALES: MS FLURINA CAVIEZEL

AFFILIATIONS
The Leading Hotels of the World®

LA RESERVE GENEVE HOTEL & SPA
Geneva

This unique property has reopened in 2003 following a complete makeover by Parisian interior designer Jacques Garcia. The talented designer has visualized an exquisitely refined and totally new concept for La Réserve on the shores of Lake Geneva.

Built amongst 4 hectares of beautifully landscaped grounds, overlooking Lake Geneva and its surrounding Alps, la Réserve Genève boasts 85 rooms and 17 suites, all luxuriously decorated and virtually all rooms and suites have a private terrace or balcony.

The magnificent Spa and wellness centre "Une Autre Histoire" offers an indoor and outdoor pool, sauna, steam bath, a hair salon, two tennis courts, 17 private massage and treatment rooms as well as the most up-to-date cardiovascular equipment. As for recreation time, the hotel has a private beach offering windsurfing, water-skiing and sailing boats.

Style and elegance as well as attention to detail and service will ensure guests a memorable and unique experience whilst in Geneva.

FACILITIES

Accommodation
85 ROOMS & 17 SUITES

Recreational facilities
2,000 SQ M SPA & WELLNESS CENTRE
FEATURING
INDOOR SWIMMING POOL, SAUNAS, STEAM BATHS, SOLARIUM,
17 MASSAGE AND TREATMENT ROOMS, GYMNASIUM, HEALTHY RESTAURANT AND RELAXATION AREA
2 TENNIS COURTS
OUTDOOR SWIMMING POOL
PRIVATE BEACH AND MOORING FACILITIES WINDSURFING, SAILING, WATERSKIING
VENETIAN TAXI BOAT
RESTAURANTS & LOUNGE BAR

Meeting facilities
MEETING ROOM FOR UP TO 25 PEOPLE

International Airports
GENEVA INTERNATIONAL AIRPORT (GVA)
15 MINUTES DRIVE AWAY

RESERVATIONS

Prices
ROOMS FROM 250 EURO PER NIGHT
SUITES FROM 1,350 EURO PER NIGHT

Credit cards
AE, DC, MC, V

GDS Reservation Codes
AMADEUS LW 1A GVARES
GALILEO LW UA 22244
SABRE LW AA 21668
WORLDSPAN LW 1P13606

Yearly Closing Dates
NONE

CONTACT DETAILS

LA RÉSERVE GENÈVE HOTEL AND SPA
301, ROUTE DE LAUSANNE
CH-1293 GENEVA BELLEVUE
SWITZERLAND
TEL +41 22 959 59 59
FAX +41 22 959 59 60
INFO@LARESERVE.CH
WWW.LARESERVE.CH

OWNER: MR MICHEL REYBIER
GENERAL MANAGER: MR RAOUF FINAN
SALES MANAGER: MS ALEXIA BEUGNON

AFFILIATIONS
The Leading Hotels of the World

PARK HOTEL VITZNAU

Lake Lucerne

The Park Hotel Vitznau is located in a magnificent setting in the heart of Switzerland, direct on the shore of Lake Lucerne and at the foot of Mount Rigi.

Offering the utmost in quality, the hotel features 103 luxuriously appointed rooms. The 'Quatre Cantons' à la carte restaurant, with a beautiful terrace is widely considered the finest French fare in Switzerland. The elegant 'Panorama Restaurant', with a breathtaking view over the Alps and the lake, features international cuisine. At the poolside restaurant are served Mediterranean charcoal-grilled specialities and refreshing snacks.

Different traditional and Far Eastern treatments can be enjoyed in the unique Beauty & Wellness Centre. For all treatments are used only exquisite products from the collections of Clarins, Kanebo and Phytomer.

The hotel is renowned for the excellent and discreet personalised service and sophisticated gastronomy. Whatever the guest's favourite luxury, they will find it at the lakeside haven Park Hotel Vitznau.

FACILITIES

Accommodation
103 ROOMS, INCLUDING 7 SUITES AND 25 JUNIOR SUITES

Recreational facilities
HEATED INDOOR-OUTDOOR SWIMMING POOL
FITNESS CENTRE
2 TENNIS COURTS
MOTORBOATS FOR WATERSKIING AND LAKE CRUISING
BEAUTY & WELLNESS TREATMENTS
SOLARIUM, SAUNA AND STEAM BATH
GOLF COURSES NEARBY
HIKING AND BIKING
WINDSURFING AND SNORKELLING
HORSEBACK RIDING
PARAGLIDING
2 RESTAURANTS & BAR

Meeting facilities
8 MEETING ROOMS FOR UP TO 130 PEOPLE

International Airports
ZURICH INTERNATIONAL AIRPORT (ZRH)
60 MINUTES DRIVE AWAY

RESERVATIONS

Prices
ROOMS FROM 253 EURO PER NIGHT
SUITES FROM 567 EURO PER NIGHT

Credit cards
AE, DC, MC, V

GDS Reservation Codes
AMADEUS PH ZRH147
GALILEO PH 21692
SABRE PH 8241
WORLDSPAN PH 6979

Yearly Closing Dates
7 NOVEMBER 2004 – 13 APRIL 2005
30 OCTOBER 2005 – 15 APRIL 2006

CONTACT DETAILS

PARK HOTEL VITZNAU
SEESTRASSE
CH-6354 VITZNAU
SWITZERLAND
TEL +41 (0)41 399 60 60
FAX +41 (0)41 399 60 70
INFO@PHV.CH
WWW.PARKHOTEL-VITZNAU.CH

OWNER: CLASSIFIED
MANAGING DIRECTOR: MR THOMAS KLEBER
SALES MANAGER: MRS JULIA WASSERMANN

AFFILIATIONS

DYLAN
Amsterdam

Created by international renowned British Designer, Anouska Hempel, Dylan is now established as totally unique, the model for the 'fashionable small hotel' around the world.

Besides Blakes London and The Hempel in London, the celebrated hotelier opened Dylan in Amsterdam in 1999 in an exceptional 17th century landmark, in the old days used as theatre, on 'Keizersgracht', one of the city's famous canals.

Each of the rooms and suites has been individually designed to provide the ideal blend of colour, texture and atmosphere. Daring and dramatic, offering style, elegance, efficiency and sensational service.

Dylan offers a haven, protecting the privacy of its guests.

THE PRIVATE COLLECTION

BAGLIONI HOTEL
London

The latest gem to join the Baglioni group carries a most prestigious address as it is situated in the residential area of South Kensington and boasts enchanting views over Hyde Park.

Baglioni Hotel London provides its guests with an elegant synthesis of international luxury hospitality and Italian lifestyle in an exclusive way. Everything, from the cuisine to the high service levels and details of the rich furnishings, creates the hotel's distinguished identity which offers guests a warm exclusive atmosphere and surroundings, marked by the most prestigious traits of Italian elegance and charm.

Complementing the exquisite accommodation are the authentic Italian restaurant 'Brunello' and an exclusive club specialising in famous Italian and international liqueurs. For the discerning leisure or business traveller alike, a special beauty centre offers a wide range of wellness treatments and a professional business centre is at hand.

FACILITIES

Accommodation
68 ROOMS AND 50 SUITES

Recreational facilities
BRUNELLO RESTAURANT
COCKTAIL LOUNGE & BAR
BEAUTY CENTRE
SAUNA
JACUZZI
EXCURSIONS

Meeting facilities
MEETING ROOM FOR UP TO 80 PEOPLE

International Airports
LONDON HEATHROW INT'L AIRPORT (LHR)
40 MINUTES DRIVE AWAY

RESERVATIONS

Prices
ROOMS FROM 447 EURO PER NIGHT
JUNIOR SUITES FROM 745 EURO PER NIGHT

Credit cards
AE, DC, MC, V

GDS Reservation Codes
AMADEUS GW LON017
GALILEO GW 64335
SABRE GW 3551
WORLDSPAN GW 3551

Yearly Closing Dates
NONE

CONTACT DETAILS

BAGLIONI HOTEL LONDON
60 HYDE PARK GATE
KENSINGTON
LONDON SW7 5BB
UNITED KINGDOM
TEL +44(0) 2073685700
FAX +44(0) 2073685701
INFO@BAGLIONIHOTELLONDON.COM
WWW.BAGLIONIHOTELLONDON.COM

OWNER: BAGLIONI HOTELS SPA
GENERAL MANAGER: MR FABIO GALLO
DIRECTOR OF SALES: MS ALESSANDRA RUGGERI

AFFILIATIONS

NONE

DURLEY HOUSE
London

Durley House is an "all suite hotel" in London's Sloane Street in the heart of Knightsbridge Situated opposite the private Cadogan Gardens to which guests have access and can spend an enjoyable time strolling among the gardens or playing tennis. Durley House also offers complimentary access to a Private Health Club just 2 minutes walk from the hotel.

All the 11 suites are individually designed and elegantly furnished with antiques, exclusive fabrics and carefully chosen materials and colours that combine to make the guest feel relaxed and comfortable. The view of Cadogan Gardens and the original fireplace in the living room also act to make the guest feel at home. The antique furniture lends warmth to the suites and contributes immensely to the luxurious atmosphere.

Although Durley House has no restaurant, it offers 24-hour room service with a variety of sumptuous dishes served in the intimacy of the suites. Durley House also offers the exciting opportunity to have a Celebrity Chef cater for the guests and their friends and family.

FACILITIES
Accommodation
11 Suites
Recreational facilities
Private Gardens
Private Tennis Courts
Offsite Luxury Health Club
Excursions & Guided Tours
A few steps away from Sloane Square,
Harvey Nichols and Harrods
Guest Service Assistants
Meeting facilities
Meeting Room for up to 25 people
Functions for up to 60 people
International Airports
London Heathrow Int'l Airport (LHR)
30 minutes drive away

RESERVATIONS
Prices
Suites from 500 Euro per night
Credit cards
AE, MC, V
GDS Reservation Codes
Amadeus YX LON 478
Galileo YX 40882
Sabre YX 33478
Worldspan YX 33478
Yearly Closing Dates
None

CONTACT DETAILS
Durley House
Sloane Street 115
London SW1X 9PJ
United Kingdom
Tel +44 20 72 35 55 37
Fax +44 20 72 54 69 77
info@durleyhouse.com
www.durleyhouse.com

Owner: The Stein Group
General Manager: Ms Stella Amor
Director of sales: Mr Borja Ochoa

AFFILIATIONS

The Stein Group

THE PRIVATE COLLECTION

THE MILESTONE HOTEL & APARTMENTS
London

The Milestone Hotel & Apartments provides a select clientele with unrivalled, panoramic views of Kensington Palace, Gardens and Hyde Park. Built in the late 19th Century as two gracious townhouses and splendidly restored retaining many of the period details and original architectural features, the Milestone offers the ultimate in style and elegance.

All guest rooms are beautifully, individually designed with antique furnishings, marble baths, and the latest technology – including wireless broadband Internet access. A 24-hour butler service is available to the guests residing in the sumptuous suites. For longer stays, The Milestone has six stunning apartments available.

Experience the finest in European cuisine and personal service at the intimate Cheneston's restaurant, relax with casual dining in the Conservatory, take the afternoon tea in the Park Lounge and unwind in the Stables Bar.

Whilst for the more energetic souls, a health club with cardiovascular equipment, free weights, a sauna and a resistance swimming pool are on hand.

FACILITIES

Accommodation
45 ROOMS, 12 SUITES & 6 APARTMENTS

Recreational facilities
HEALTH SUITE WITH 'RESISTANCE' SWIMMING POOL, SAUNA, FULLY EQUIPPED GYM, FREE WEIGHTS, AND CARDIOVASCULAR EQUIPMENT
RESTAURANTS & BARS
OVERLOOKING KENSINGTON PALACE & GARDENS

Meeting facilities
2 MEETING ROOMS FOR UP TO 32 PEOPLE

International Airports
LONDON HEATHROW INT'L AIRPORT (LHR) 45 MINUTES DRIVE AWAY

RESERVATIONS

Prices
ROOMS FROM 400 EURO PER NIGHT

Credit cards
AE, DC, MC, V

GDS Reservation Codes
AMADEUS LW LONMIL
GALILEO LW 48252
SABRE LW 30954
WORLDSPAN LW LONMI

Yearly Closing Dates
NONE

CONTACT DETAILS

THE MILESTONE HOTEL & APARTMENTS
1 KENSINGTON COURT
LONDON W8 5DL
UNITED KINGDOM
TEL +44 20 7917 1000
FAX +44 20 7917 1010
BOOKMS@RCHMAIL.COM
WWW.MILESTONEHOTEL.COM

OWNER: RED CARNATION HOTELS
MANAGING DIRECTOR: MR JONATHAN RAGGETT
DIRECTOR OF SALES: MRS JUSTINE CULLEN

AFFILIATIONS

The Leading Small Hotels
of the World

THE PRIVATE COLLECTION

THE RITZ
London

Perfectly located in a landmark position on Piccadilly in the heart of London's West End, the luxury hotel is ideally placed to suit both business and leisure visitors alike. The elegant rooms combine the original Louis XVI style interiors with modern day technology.

The Ritz Restaurant features a magnificent frescoed ceiling with west facing windows overlooking the Terrace, the Italian Garden and Green Park beyond. The Restaurant is open daily, with a Dinner Dance on Fridays and Saturdays. The Palm Court restaurant is famous for its daily Afternoon Tea service.

The most recent addition to The Ritz includes the stylishly updated Rivoli Bar. Designed by Tessa Kennedy, the early Art Deco interiors are a recreation of the original bar. Private dining facilities at The Ritz include the Marie Antoinette Suite – a replica of a room at the Palace of Versailles.

The Ritz, London is a Grade II listed building and received the Royal Warrant from his Royal Highness The Prince of Wales for banqueting and catering services.

FACILITIES

Accommodation
133 ROOMS, INCLUDING 38 SUITES

Recreational facilities
FITNESS ROOM
RESTAURANT
BAR
HIGH TEA
HAIRDRESSER
EXCURSIONS AND SIGHTSEEING

Meeting facilities
2 MEETING ROOMS FOR UP TO 55 PEOPLE

International Airports
LONDON HEATHROW INT'L AIRPORT (LHR)
45 MINUTES DRIVE AWAY

RESERVATIONS

Prices
ROOMS FROM 548 EURO PER NIGHT

Credit cards
AE, DC, MC, V

GDS Reservation Codes
AMADEUS LW LON999
GALILEO LW 55523
SABRE LW 10629
WORLDSPAN LW LONTR

Yearly Closing Dates
NONE

CONTACT DETAILS

UNITED KINGDOM
THE RITZ, LONDON
150 PICCADILLY
LONDON W1J 9BR
UNITED KINGDOM
TEL +44 (0)20 7493 8181
FAX + 44 (0)20 7493 2687
ENQUIRE@THERITZLONDON.COM
WWW.THERITZLONDON.COM

OWNER: CLASSIFIED
GENERAL MANAGER: MR STEPHEN BOXALL
DIRECTOR OF SALES: MR UMBERTO SCHIOPPA

AFFILIATIONS
The Leading Hotels of the World®

XO PRIVATE THE PRIVATE COLLECTION

Heritage Craftsmanship
Design Performance Exclusivity

AFRICA

Africa has something for everyone: from the most hard bitten adventurer to the most discerning connoisseur of food and wine.

It is inherently a wild and adventurous area that has only been partly tamed by man, its sophistication apparent in its fashionable cities and charming towns, its primitive origins still evident in its rugged peaks and sprawling savannah and desert lands.

JNANE TAMSNA
Marrakech

Jnane Tamsna, in the heart of Marrakech's famed palm grove, is the latest creation of designer Meryanne Loum-Martin. With the help of her husband Dr. Gary J. Martin – an American ethnobotanist – she designed a Moorish country house which celebrates vernacular architecture and the rural landscapes of the Palmeraie.

Date palms, olive trees and grapevines create an oasis atmosphere in the midst of spontaneous vegetation on vast plains and rolling hills surrounding the estate. Extensive fruit orchards and vegetable gardens provide fresh produce for Jnane Tamsna's Moroccan-Mediterranean cuisine. Inside the architecture is structured around two courtyard gardens filled with fragrant white flowered plants.

Jnane Tamsna has 17 double rooms to rent individually or in exclusivity, a heated pool and clay tennis court. A stay at Jnane Tamsna offers you cultural experiences to satiate your spirit, healthy living to restore your body, and intellectual discoveries to stimulate your mind.

FACILITIES

Accommodation
17 ROOMS

Recreational facilities
3 HEATED SWIMMING POOLS
GARDENS & TERRACES
CLAY TENNIS COURT
MASSAGE & HAMMAM
BIKING & CAMEL RIDES
HORSE CARRIAGE TOURS
EXCURSIONS
GOLF COURSES NEARBY
RESTAURANT & BAR
LIBRARY

Meeting facilities
MEETING ROOMS FOR UP TO 10 PEOPLE

International Airports
MARRAKECH INTERNATIONAL AIRPORT (RAK)
25 MINUTES DRIVE AWAY

RESERVATIONS

Prices
ROOMS FROM 300 EURO PER NIGHT

Credit cards
MC, V

GDS Reservation Codes
NONE

Yearly Closing Dates
15 JULY – 20 AUGUST 2005

CONTACT DETAILS

JNANE TAMSNA
P.O. BOX 1337
MARRAKECH HAY MOHAMMADI
MOROCCO
TEL +212 44 32 94 23
FAX +212 44 32 98 84
MERYANNE@JNANETAMSNA.COM
WWW.JNANETAMSNA.COM

OWNER: MRS MERYANNE LOUM-MARTIN
GENERAL MANAGER: MRS MERYANNE LOUM-MARTIN
DIRECTOR OF SALES: MRS MERYANNE LOUM-MARTIN

AFFILIATIONS
NONE

XO PRIVATE   THE PRIVATE COLLECTION

KASBAH DU TOUBKAL

Imlil

The Kasbah du Toubkal is an extraordinary venture, the product of an imaginative Berber and European partnership. There is a shared belief that the beauty of the Toubkal National Park should be accessible to all who respect it. To this end the Kasbah has been transformed using traditional methods, from the home of a Feudal Caid into an unprecedented haven. As Condé Nast Traveller stated "... with the best rooftop views in North Africa...this is the country's first and foremost mountain retreat ...".

Situated above the village of Imlil and in view of the highest mountain in North Africa the setting is exceptional - Martin Scorsese used it as a set for his film on the Dalai Lama.

The Kasbah is a welcoming environment for those seeking superb rooms in a stunning setting and for those who are searching for a venue that inspires providing peace in a spectacular and rural location.

FACILITIES

Accommodation
8 Rooms, 1 Private House (3 Rooms) and 3 Berber Salons

Recreational facilities
Gardens
Hammam
Country Picnics
Guided Trekking
Ascents of Mt Toubkal
Events by prior Arrangements

Meeting facilities
Meeting Room for up to 60 people

International Airports
Marrakech International Airport (RAK)
75 minutes drive away

RESERVATIONS

Prices
Rooms from 130 Euro per night

Credit cards
MC, V

GDS Reservation Codes
None

Yearly Closing Dates
None

CONTACT DETAILS

Kasbah du Toubkal
BP 31
Imlil, Asni
Marrakech
Morocco
Tel +33 4 66 45 83 95 (reservations)
Fax +33 4 66 45 84 73 (reservations)
kasbah@discover.ltd.uk
www.kasbahdutoubkal.com

Owner: Discover Ltd. UK
General Manager: Mr Hajj Maurice
Director of sales: Mr Mike McHugo

AFFILIATIONS

None

LA MAMOUNIA
Marrakech

La Mamounia lies sheltered within the walls of the old city of Marrakech, its Art deco design in perfect harmony with its Moroccan architecture and magnificent centuries-old gardens. Ornamented columns and splashing fountains combine with marble floors and graceful archways to create a suitable opulent haven from which to explore this fascinating city.

The rooms and suites reflect the warmth and style of the 1920's, their large windows overlooking either the picturesque central courtyard or the splendid Koutoubia Minaret. Several of the suites are individually themed. The pool, with its buffet grill, is usually the daytime centre of attention, although other recreational facilities include a Spa, tennis courts, as well as two nearby 18-hole golf courses.

A distinctly cosmopolitan choice awaits when it comes to dining, pampered guests are able to decide between the gourmet fare of the Marrakech L'Imperiale, the traditional favourites of Le Marocain, the Venetian dishes of L'Italien and the French cuisine of L'Orangerie.

FACILITIES

Accommodation
171 ROOMS, 57 SUITES AND 3 VILLAS

Recreational facilities
SWIMMING POOL
2 TENNIS COURTS
SPA CENTRE & HAIRDRESSER
FRENCH BILLIARD SALON
GOLF DRIVING RANGE
CASINO & BOUTIQUES
JEU DE BOULES
HORSEBACK RIDING
HIKING & TREKKING
SKIING NEARBY
5 RESTAURANTS & BARS

Meeting facilities
MEETING ROOMS FOR UP TO 350 PEOPLE

International Airports
MARRAKECH INTERNATIONAL AIRPORT (RAK)
15 MINUTES DRIVE AWAY

RESERVATIONS

Prices
ROOMS FROM 235 EURO PER NIGHT
SUITES FROM 364 EURO PER NIGHT

Credit cards
AE, DC, MC, V

GDS Reservation Codes
AMADEUS LW RAK333
GALILEO LW 8507
SABRE LW 4738
WORLDSPAN LW 6003

Yearly Closing Dates
NONE

CONTACT DETAILS

LA MAMOUNIA
AVENUE BAB JDID
MARRAKECH 40000
MOROCCO
TEL +212 44 38 86 00
FAX +212 44 44 46 60
RESA@MAMOUNIA.COM
WWW.MAMOUNIA.COM

OWNER: SOCIÉTÉ LA MAMOUNIA
GENERAL MANAGER: MR ROBERT JEAN BERGÉ
DIRECTOR OF SALES: MS HANANE BEKKALI

AFFILIATIONS

The Leading Hotels of the World®

CONCORDE
HOTELS

LA SULTANA
Marrakech

La Sultana's privileged guests can experience the exclusivity of the secluded retreats that they may rent in their entirety or per room to enjoy treasures housed within 4 Riads stepped in history. The 21 luxury rooms and suites lure discerning travelers by the fairytale atmosphere and beautiful surroundings they offer.

Choose panoramic terraces boasting a 360° dazzling view, flowered patios, refreshingly creative cuisine under vaulted ceilings, heated pools or so many other glamorous amenities promising hours of lounging to take pleasure in a personalized stay with a unique cultural slant.

The prestigious Spa of La Sultana evokes 2000 years of different cultural influences from Orient to Occident. A star-domed marble Jacuzzi and hammam, ancient Indian doors and antic marble columns create a unique atmosphere.

Nearby Marrakech, one can enjoy playing at the 18-hole golf courses, horse riding in the legendary Palmeraie, hiking in the pink-tinted Oukaimeden mountains and picnic by the bizarre desert countryside of lake Takerkoust.

FACILITIES

Accommodation
21 ROOMS, SUITES & APARTMENTS

Recreational facilities
OUTDOOR HEATED SWIMMING POOL
SPA FEATURING MASSAGES,
BEAUTY TREATMENTS,
HAMMAM, SAUNA, JACUZZI
FITNESS CENTRE
1,200 M² ROOF-GARDEN TERRACES
MISTED SOLARIUM
KAIDAL TENTS
LIBRARY & DVD'S
ART COLLECTION
RESTAURANT & BAR
3 18-HOLE GOLF COURSES NEARBY
4X4 AND QUAD BIKING EXCURSIONS
HORSEBACK RIDING
TENNIS

Meeting facilities
MEETING ROOM FOR UP TO 400 PEOPLE

International Airports
MARRAKECH INT'L AIRPORT (RAK)
10 MINUTES DRIVE AWAY

RESERVATIONS

Prices
ROOMS FROM 210 EURO PER NIGHT
SUITES FROM 295 EURO PER NIGHT
APARTMENTS FROM 515 EURO PER NIGHT

Credit cards
AE, MC, V

GDS Reservation Codes
AMADEUS GW RAK229
GALILEO GW 68607
SABRE GW 40890
WORLDSPAN GW 5229

Yearly Closing Dates
NONE

CONTACT DETAILS
LA SULTANA
RUE DE LA KASBAH
40 000 MARRAKECH
MOROCCO
TEL +212 44 38 80 08
FAX +212 44 38 77 77
CONTACT@LASULTANAMARRAKECH.COM
WWW.LASULTANAMARRAKECH.COM

OWNER: CLASSIFIED
GENERAL MANAGER: MRS ISABELLE NICLOT
DIRECTOR OF SALES: MRS MARIE GIRODET

AFFILIATIONS
NONE

ELEPHANT BACK SAFARIS

Okavango Delta

Elephant Back Safaris are based at Abu Camp on the western side of the Okavango Delta and are set in an amazing half a million acres of private concession.

Guests are accommodation in luxurious, custom-designed tents which are raised on teak decking and overlook a beautiful lagoon. All the tents are richly and individually furnished and boast a luxury en-suite bathroom complete with copper or porcelain bath tubs and showers. The sumptuous dining, bar and relaxation area is set on tiered teak decking sculpted around specimens of the magnificent giant trees of the Okavango.

On safari, guests are seated in large paddle saddles, which are mounted behind experienced and knowledgeable elephant-handlers. The elephant back safaris offer the possibility to come very close to other game, which is unconcerned by the approach of the elephant herd of which guests are a privileged part.

The Abu camp is named after Randall Moore's legendary elephant 'Abu', the star of many motion pictures. Abu is an Arabic word meaning 'everything to do with elephants'.

FACILITIES

Accommodation
6 LUXURY TENTED CHALETS

Recreational facilities
SWIMMING POOL
ELEPHANT BACK SAFARIS
MOKORO CANOENING
MOTOR BOAT EXCURSIONS
GAME DRIVES
FISHING
LIBRARY
RESTAURANT & BAR

Meeting facilities
NONE

International Airports
MAUN INT'L AIRPORT (MUB)
30 MINUTES FLIGHT AWAY

RESERVATIONS

Prices
TENTED CHALETS FROM 1,528 EURO PP
PER NIGHT (ALL INCLUSIVE)

Credit cards
NONE

GDS Reservation Codes
NONE

Yearly Closing Dates
NONE

CONTACT DETAILS

ELEPHANT BACK SAFARIS
PRIVATE BAG 332
MAUN
BOTSWANA
TEL +267 6861260
FAX +267 6861005
EBS@INFO.BW
WWW.ELEPHANTBACKSAFARIS.COM

OWNER: CLASSIFIED
GENERAL MANAGER: MR ALISTAIR RANKIN

AFFILIATIONS

NONE

DUGONG BEACH LODGE

San Sebastian Peninsula

Dugong Beach Lodge, situated within the boundaries of "The Vilanculos Coastal Wildlife Sanctuary" on 30 000 hectares of pristine marine and wildlife territory, provides a unique "Beach and Wilderness" experience.

10 Luxuriously appointed rooms with hardwood floors and jekka thatched grass roofs offer elegant en-suite bathrooms, huge feature baths and outside showers. Water sport enthusiasts can look forward to an array of water sports, salt water fly fishing, deep sea fishing, scuba diving, snorkelling, kayaking, and for the not so energetic, quite simply relaxation.

This diverse eco-system of wilderness and wetland, with its powder white beaches and crystal clear water is host to a magnificent array of fish. Shallow and deepwater reefs reveal beautiful creatures such as the leatherback turtles, sailfish, dolphin, manta ray and the nearly extinct Dugong. Discover the tranquility and un-spoilt paradise of Dugong Lodge, set right on the edge of the beach.

FACILITIES

Accommodation
10 LUXURIOUS ROOMS

Recreational facilities
DEEP SEA FISHING
FLY FISHING
FRESHWATER SWIMMING POOL
SCUBA DIVING
SNORKELLING
PEDAL BOATS
KAYAKING

Meeting facilities
NONE

International Airports
VILANCULOS AIRPORT (VNX)
35 MINUTES BY BOAT

RESERVATIONS

Prices
ROOMS FROM 206 EURO PP PER NIGHT

Credit cards
MC, V

GDS Reservation Codes
NONE

Yearly Closing Dates
NONE

CONTACT DETAILS

DUGONG BEACH LODGE
ADMINISTRATIVE OFFICES
29 HOMESTEAD ROAD, RIVONIA, 2128
P O BOX 781549
SANDTON 2146
SOUTH AFRICA
TEL + 27 11 234 1584
FAX + 27 11 234 4951
RESERVATIONS@DUGONGLODGE.CO.ZA
WWW.DUGONGLODGE.CO.ZA

OWNER: MERCURY INVESTMENTS LIMITADA
GENERAL MANAGER: MR GAVIN LA MARQUE
DIRECTOR OF SALES: MRS BEVERLEY FERGUSON

AFFILIATIONS

NONE

QUILÁLEA
Quilálea Island

Quilálea is an idyllic Mozambique island resort nestling in a forgotten corner of Mozambique's Quirimbas Archipelago in the Indian Ocean. The 9 charming, air-conditioned villas offer enviable panoramic sea views and provide a malaria-free haven of luxury and natural beauty, with the highest degree of seclusion on an entirely private and uninhabited tropical island.

Quilálea is a water-lovers delight with activities ranging from superb scuba diving, snorkeling, fly fishing, sport fishing, canoeing, sailing, swimming and bird watching. Quilálea Island is one of the most biodiverse marine sanctuaries in the world.

Indulge the flavours and spices of Mozambican cuisine influenced by Portugal and Goa, prepared by the gourmet chef.

Journey to Quilálea and find romance and adventure, and share the dream of rediscovery of this forgotten part of Africa.

FACILITIES

Accommodation
9 LUXURY VILLAS

Recreational facilities
SALT WATER SWIMMING POOL
SCUBA DIVING (PADI)
SNORKELLING
SEA KAYAKING
DHOW SAILING
DEEP SEA FISHING
FLY FISHING
MASSAGE ROOMS
ISLAND EXPLORATION AND TRAILS
HISTORICAL AND CULTURAL VISITS
TO QUIRIMBA ISLANDS

Meeting facilities
NONE

International Airports
PEMBA AIRPORT (POL)
20 MINUTES FLIGHT AWAY
20 MINUTES BY BOAT

RESERVATIONS

Prices
VILLAS FROM 618 EURO PER NIGHT

Credit cards
MC, V

GDS Reservation Codes
NONE

Yearly Closing Dates
NONE

CONTACT DETAILS

QUILÁLEA ISLAND
C.P. 323, PEMBA
CABO DELGADO
MOZAMBIQUE
TEL +258 72 21808
FAX +258 72 21808
QUIRIMBAS@PLEXUSMOZ.COM
WWW.QUILALEA.COM

OWNER: ARQUIPELAGOS DAS QUIRIMBAS LDA.
CHAIRMAN: MR JOHN HEWLETT
DIRECTOR: MRS MARJOLAINE HEWLETT

AFFILIATIONS
NONE

EPACHA GAME LODGE & SPA
Etosha National Park

Epacha Game Lodge and Spa is situated on the magnificent 27 000 hectares Epacha Game Reserve.

Each of the individually decorated luxury en-suite chalets has its own private balcony with a breathtaking view across the bush. All air-conditioned chalets are equipped with all the amenities discerning travelers expect. In keeping with the Victorian era in Africa, all chalets are furnished with antiques and decorated in subtle, relaxing colors.

Besides daily game drives throughout the beautiful park and the nearby Etosha National Park you can also partake in activities such as guided walks, quad biking and horse trails, or simply relax by the pool, in the cosy lounge overlooking a waterhole, in the billiard room or at the inviting pool bar. Be rejuvenated by stress relieving therapies in the spa, which features sauna, Jacuzzi, steam room, treatment rooms and outdoor treatment areas.

The Epacha Game Reserve is home to 21 antelope species as well as endangered species such as the black rhino and sable antelope.

FACILITIES

Accommodation
18 LUXURY CHALETS &
1 PRESIDENTIAL SUITE WITH 5 ROOMS

Recreational facilities
FRESHWATER SWIMMING POOL
HIKING TRAILS
SPA & HEALTH CENTRE
EXTENSIVE LIBRARY
GYMNASIUM
QUAD BIKING
HORSEBACK RIDING
CLAY PIGEON SHOOTING
GAME DRIVES

Meeting facilities
MEETING ROOM FOR UP TO 50 PEOPLE

International Airports
WINDHOEK INTERNATIONAL AIRPORT (WDH)
70 MINUTES FLIGHT AWAY

RESERVATIONS

Prices
ROOMS FROM 130 EURO PP PER NIGHT

Credit cards
AE, DC, MC, V

GDS Reservation Codes
NONE

Yearly Closing Dates
NONE

CONTACT DETAILS

LEADING LODGES OF AFRICA
P O BOX 90538
CHATEAUSTREET 37
WINDHOEK
NAMIBIA
TEL +264 61 375 300
FAX +264 61 375 333
RES@LEADINGLODGES.COM
WWW.LEADINGLODGES.COM

OWNER: VDV HOLDINGS
GENERAL MANAGER: MR LAURENCE MC GRATH

AFFILIATIONS
NONE

HOTEL HEINITZBURG
Windhoek

Originally built by Count von Schwerin as a gorgeous castle for his fiancé Margarethe von Heinitzburg in 1914, Heinitzburg today is the home of a lovely hotel. It is built on a hill, with splendid views across Windhoek and the surrounding mountains.

The hotel complements traditional African friendliness and beauty with excellent European culinary and a world-class wine cellar. 'Leo's' top gourmet restaurant offers spectacular views of the beautiful city lights below and the romantic terrace is very popular for sundowner drinks.

You will find yourself in touch with your soul, in the 16 tastefully decorated spacious en-suite rooms, each with superb views and offering the ideal space to relax, reminisce and dream. Your host, Beate Raith, pays wonderful attention to detail. Hotel Heinitzburg will make your stay in Windhoek a memorable experience.

FACILITIES

Accommodation
16 ROOMS

Recreational facilities
HEATED OUTDOOR SWIMMING POOL
RESTAURANT
SIGHTSEEING & EXCURSIONS

Meeting facilities
NONE

International Airports
WINDHOEK INTERNATIONAL AIRPORT (WDH)
20 MINUTES DRIVE AWAY

RESERVATIONS

Prices
ROOMS FROM 190 EURO PER NIGHT

Credit cards
AE, DC, MC, V

GDS Reservation Codes
NONE

Yearly Closing Dates
24 DECEMBER 2004 - 02 JANUARY 2005

CONTACT DETAILS

HOTEL HEINITZBURG
HEINITZBURGSTREET 22
WINDHOEK
NAMIBIA
TEL +264 61 249597
FAX +264 61 249598
HEINITZ@MWEB.COM.NA
WWW.HEINITZBURG.COM

OWNER: MRS BEATE RAITH
GENERAL MANAGER: MRS BEATE RAITH
DIRECTOR OF SALES: MRS BEATE RAITH

AFFILIATIONS

RELAIS &
CHATEAUX

THE PRIVATE COLLECTION

MOWANI MOUNTAIN CAMP
Twyfelfontein

Between the Ugab and Huab rivers in southern Damaraland lies a vast, beautiful and unspoilt wilderness area of unsurpassed desert scenery, unusual geological formations, archaeological sites and a unique variety of desert fauna and flora.

The harshness of the countryside contrasts with the luxurious softness and pure comfort of the camp's interior. Inside and out blend together as the dining and lounge area open to the outside, capturing the cooling breeze and ensuring that guests are never too far from breathtaking scenery. An enormous flat boulder serves as the camp's sundowner spot, affording guest's spectacular views. Guests are housed in luxury tents that have their own en-suite shower, washbasin and toilet. Individual verandas encourage guests to linger while admiring the unspoilt wilderness of the area.

Activities on offer include guided game drives, hot air ballooning at dawn, flights in a micro-light, excursions to the ancient Twyfelfontein rock engravings, the Organ Pipes and Burnt Mountain.

FACILITIES

Accommodation
4 VIEW TENTS, 8 STANDARD TENTS,
1 LUXURY ROOM & 1 SUITE

Recreational facilities
SWIMMING
NATURE WALKS
GAME AND NATURE DRIVES
HOT AIR BALLOONING
MICRO-LIGHT FLIGHTS
AEROPLANE FLIGHTS

Meeting facilities
NONE

International Airports
WINDHOEK INTERNATIONAL AIRPORT (WDH)
90 MINUTES FLIGHT AWAY

RESERVATIONS

Prices
TENTS FROM 161 EURO PP PER NIGHT

Credit cards
AE, DC, MC, V

GDS Reservation Codes
NONE

Yearly Closing Dates
FEBRUARY

CONTACT DETAILS

MOWANI MOUNTAIN CAMP
TWYFELFONTEIN
DAMARALAND
KUNENE REGION
NAMIBIA
TEL +264 61 221 994
FAX +264 61 222 574
MOWANI@VISIONSOFAFRICA.COM.NA
WWW.MOWANI.COM

OWNER: MR ANDRE LOUW
GENERAL MANAGER: MR RIAAN LIEBENBERG

AFFILIATIONS

NONE

WOLWEDANS DUNES LODGE
NamibRand Nature Reserve

Situated in the heart of NamibRand, a private nature reserve measuring some 185.000 hectares on the doorstep of Sossusvlei – the Dunes Lodge aims at providing a unique experience close to nature, yet without compromising comfort and style. The entire lodge is constructed on wooden platforms and overlooks panoramic vistas in all directions.

The building style is a combination of wooden poles, large canvas blinds and windows that open up to the desert beyond. The lodge reflects the ambience of a tented camp, but provides the comfort and protection of a permanent building. Each of the 8 spacious chalets with en-suite bathrooms leads onto a private veranda and vast stretches of untouched sand. The reception complex consists of 2 lounges, a library, a fireplace under the stars, a tea deck, 2 dining rooms, a wine cellar and a pool.

Wolwedans is the perfect destination for nature lovers seeking tranquillity to clear the mind, beauty to feed the soul and space for the imagination to fly. Wolwedans should be integrated into any holiday to Namibian, be it as a self-drive or a fly-in safari.

BIRKENHEAD HOUSE

Hermanus

Only one hour and a half from Cape Town, Birkenhead House is named after a British troop ship that sank in Walker Bay in 1852. Decorated to reflect the beauty of its coastal setting, it is adorned with exquisite antiques. No expense has been spared in making this the ultimate coastal retreat.

Most of the opulently appointed sea-facing suites offer expansive vistas of Walker Bay. From the comfort of the residence, guests can look forward to sighting the majestic Southern Right whales that enter the sheltered waters of Walker Bay every year to calve. Other attractions include a gym, treatment centre and a dual-level swimming pool located in a sheltered courtyard. Not forgetting, of course, Hermanus' two best swimming beaches which are just a stone's throw away.

Spectacular mountain trails and breathtaking cliff path walks are also in easy reach from Birkenhead House. Guests can explore the thriving floral kingdom, which has a higher diversity of species than anywhere else in the world.

FACILITIES

Accommodation
11 LUXURY SUITES

Recreational facilities
STUNNING BEACHES
3 SWIMMING POOLS
MOUNTAIN & CLIFF TRAILS
SEASIDE WALKS
WHALE WATCHING
FITNESS CENTRE
SPA & TREATMENT ROOM
SHARK CAGE DIVING, GOLF, DEEP SEA FISHING
QUAD BIKING, HORSEBACK RIDING,
SEA KAYAKING
AND LOCAL WINE TOURS CAN BE ARRANGED

Meeting facilities
NONE

International Airports
CAPE TOWN INTERNATIONAL AIRPORT (CPT)
90 MINUTES DRIVE AWAY

RESERVATIONS

Prices
SUITES FROM 476 EURO PER NIGHT

Credit cards
AE, MC, V

GDS Reservation Codes
NONE

Yearly Closing Dates
NONE

CONTACT DETAILS

BIRKENHEAD HOUSE
7TH AVENUE
VOELKLIP
HERMANUS
7200
SOUTH AFRICA
TEL +27 15 793 0150
FAX +27 15 793 2879
INFO@BIRKENHEADHOUSE.COM
WWW.BIRKENHEADHOUSE.COM

OWNER: MRS LIZ BIDEN
GENERAL MANAGER: MR GARTH ROUX
DIRECTOR OF SALES: MRS LIZ BIDEN

AFFILIATIONS

NONE

EARTH LODGE

Sabi Sabi Private Game Reserve

This magnificent eco-lodge has been sensitively landscaped deep into the earth until almost invisible, inspired by the textures, colours and shapes of nature with an emphasis on space and freedom throughout.

Each of the 13 stunning suites is attended by a private butler. Created in spacious open-plan style with a termite mound-shaped roof, the décor is minimalist but subtly elegant with natural colours and seating carved from tree trunks. The enormous glass-fronted bathrooms have a granite feature bath, double basins and a large indoor and outdoor shower. Both the living area and the bathroom open on to a fully furnished covered terrace overlooking a private plunge pool and the bushveld beyond, where a watering hole directly opposite the Lodge ensures regular animal sightings.

Along with its legendary Sabi Sabi safaris, the lodge's purpose is to let nothing stand in your way in re-kindling your bonds with earth. Truly, to return to nature is to return to yourself…

FACILITIES

Accommodation
12 Luxury Suites &
1 Amber Presidential Suite

Recreational facilities
13 Private Plunge Pools
Earth Nature Spa
Non-smoking Lounge & Library
Art Gallery
Zen / Meditation Garden
Wine Cellar
Open Landrover Safaris
Boutique Curio Shop

Meeting facilities
Meeting Room for up to 120 people

International Airports
Kruger Mpumalanga Int'l Airport (KMI)
90 minutes drive away
Sabi Sabi Private Airstrip
10 minutes drive away

RESERVATIONS

Prices
Suites from 695 Euro per person per night
(all inclusive)

Credit cards
AE, DC, MC, V

GDS Reservation Codes
None

Yearly Closing Dates
None

CONTACT DETAILS
Sabi Sabi Head Office
P.O. Box 52665
Saxonwold
2132
South Africa
Tel +27 (011) 483 3939
Fax +27 (011) 483 3799
res@sabisabi.com
www.sabisabi.com

Owner: Mr & Mrs Hilton and Jacqui Loon
Managing Director: Mr Patrick Shorten
Operations Director: Mr Rod Wyndham
Director of sales: Mrs Desiree Thomas

AFFILIATIONS
None

IVORY LODGE – LION SANDS PRIVATE GAME RESERVE

Sabi Sand Game Reserve

Lion Sands is situated in the Southern part of the world famous Sabi Sand Game Reserve, an area well known for its spectacular predator viewing.

The uniqueness of the Lion Sands reserve lies in both its diverse selection of safari based activities allowing you to tailor-make your stay, and its position, bordering the perennial Sabie River. Being family owned since 1932, the reserve retains both its soul and tradition.

Combining Afro-European elegance and exotic flair with exquisite taste, the 6 air-conditioned suites of Ivory lodge offer amenities that include luxury en-suite bathrooms, outdoor and indoor shower, elegant courtyard, lounge with romantic fireplace, internet access, maxi-bar, telephone, private plunge pool and wooden viewing deck with breathtaking views over the river. A health spa, world-class wine cellar and indoor and outdoor dining areas for the ultimate culinary delights, make Ivory Lodge a leader in its field.

A Senior Ecologist and her team of professional rangers and tracking teams ensure that your personal safari experience not only meets, but exceeds your highest expectations.

FACILITIES

Accommodation
6 Ultra Luxurious Suites

Recreational facilities
Game Drives in open Land Rovers
Bush Walks & Wildlife Lectures
Astronomy
Bush Breakfasts and Dinners
Hippopotomus Tour
Picnic Lunch
Ballooning in Hazyview
Helicopter Trips over Blyde River Canyon
Clay Pigeon Shooting
Golf Courses nearby
Health Spa
Private Plunge Pools

Meeting facilities
Meeting Rooms for up to 12 people

International Airports
Mala Mala Airfield (AAM)
60 minutes direct flight from
Johannesburg International Airport
45 minutes open Land Rover transfer

RESERVATIONS

Prices
Suites from 877 Euro pp per night

Credit cards
AE, DC, MC, V

GDS Reservation Codes
None

Yearly Closing Dates
None

CONTACT DETAILS

Lion Sands Private Game Reserve
Sabi Sand Game Reserve
Skukuza
Kruger National Park, 1350
South Africa
Tel +27 11 484 9911
Fax + 27 11 484 9916
res@lionsands.com
www.lionsands.com

Owner: Mr Nicholas More & Mr Robert More
General Manager: Mr Nicholas More
Director of Sales: Mr Robert More

AFFILIATIONS

None

KURLAND

Plettenberg Bay

Baroness Dianne and Baron Peter Behr have created a luxurious boutique hotel on their age-old magnificent family estate of 700 hectares, near the finest beaches of Natures Valley and Plettenberg Bay, along the famous Garden Route. Each room is uniquely decorated and exudes understated elegance, and an easy-going atmosphere of a private country home mixed with South African charm and friendliness. At Kurland you are at home from the moment you arrive.

With just 12 rooms, exclusivity and personalised service are guaranteed. Families adore Kurland, as 10 rooms have separate en-suite loft rooms for children of all ages, nannies and the extended family-friends.

The world-class Kurland Polo Estate has five polo fields and a fully equipped Polo school. The polo pavilion is in a unique setting to relax and enjoy this magnificent sport. International Polo tournaments are hosted here annually.

For gourmets, Kurland is an epicure's delight. Kurland is designed to provide an all-encompassing sense of comfort and graciousness.

FACILITIES

Accommodation
12 ROOMS, 10 WITH CHILDREN'S LOFT

Recreational facilities
700 HA POLO ESTATE & CLUB HOUSE
SPA, GYM, SAUNA & STEAM ROOM
PLAYROOM & CHILDREN SWIMMING POOLS
TENNIS, HORSEBACK RIDING
MOUNTAIN BIKING
QUAD BIKING, HIKING
GOLF COURSE NEARBY
PRISTINE BEACH NEARBY
WHALE AND DOLPHIN WATCHING

Meeting facilities
MEETING ROOM FOR UP TO 20 PEOPLE

International Airports
PLETTENBERG BAY AIRPORT (PBZ)
20 MINUTES DRIVE AWAY
GEORGE AIRPORT (GRJ)
90 MINUTES DRIVE AWAY

RESERVATIONS

Prices
ROOMS FROM 450 EURO PER NIGHT

Credit cards
AE, DC, MC, V

GDS Reservation Codes
NONE

Yearly Closing Dates
JUNE 2005

CONTACT DETAILS

KURLAND HOTEL
PO BOX 209
THE CRAGS, PLETTENBERG BAY
6602
SOUTH AFRICA
TEL +27 44 534 8082
FAX + 27 44 534 8699
INFO@KURLAND.CO.ZA
WWW.KURLAND.CO.ZA

OWNER: BEHR FAMILY
GENERAL MANAGER: MR THOMAS WEBER
DIRECTOR OF SALES: MRS BRENDA WALL

AFFILIATIONS

NONE

LA COURONNE HOTEL
Franschhoek

La Couronne, the crown, is situated in the centre of a working wine farm, overlooking the magnificent Franschhoek valley.

La Couronne has 24 individually decorated bedrooms, most of which offer glorious views of mountains, vineyards and valleys. Air-conditioning, under-floor heating, safes and satellite television are standard features in the rooms. Luxurious suites offer plunge pools on private terraces overlooking the valley. Details such as toweling robes, percale linen, romantic turndowns, fresh fruit and flowers in the rooms, all enhance the personal touch.

Fine dining is the hallmark of La Couronne's a la carte restaurant. Private lounges, with fireplaces are the perfect place to curl up on a couch with a glass of local wine.

The hotel offers guests use of the swimming pool, massage facilities, sauna, mountain bikes, vineyard picnics and the Colonial-style Cigar bar. The surroundings offer guests a game of golf, fly fishing, mountain walks and hikes, cellar tours and horseback riding.

FACILITIES

Accommodation
24 ROOMS & 3 EXCLUSIVE SUITES

Recreational facilities
SWIMMING & GYMNASIUM
HIKING & WALKING
MOUNTAIN BIKING
HORSEBACK RIDING, FLY FISHING
GOLF COURSES NEARBY
HEALTH AND BEAUTY CENTRE
RESTAURANT & BAR
WINE TASTING
CHOCOLATE TASTING
CHEESE TASTING

Meeting facilities
MEETING ROOM FOR UP TO 20 PEOPLE

International Airports
CAPE TOWN INTERNATIONAL AIRPORT (CPT)
50 MINUTES DRIVE AWAY

RESERVATIONS

Prices
ROOMS FROM 226 EURO PER NIGHT
SUITES FROM 370 EURO PER NIGHT

Credit cards
AE, DC, MC, V

GDS Reservation Codes
NONE

Yearly Closing Dates
NONE

CONTACT DETAILS

LA COURONNE HOTEL
DASSENBERG ROAD
FRANSCHHOEK
7690
CAPE TOWN
SOUTH AFRICA
TEL +27 21 876 2770
FAX +27 21 876 3788
RESERVATIONS@LACOURONNEHOTEL.CO.ZA
WWW.LACOURONNEHOTEL.CO.ZA

OWNER: MR ERWIN SCHNITZLER &
MIKO RWAYITARE
MANAGING DIRECTOR: MR ERWIN SCHNITZLER
DIRECTOR OF SALES: MS KERRIN TITMAS

AFFILIATIONS
NONE

ROYAL MALEWANE
Thornybush Game Reserve

Royal Malewane is situated in the renowned Thornybush Game Reserve on the western fringe of the Kruger National Park, in the heart of South Africa's 'Big Five' (lion, leopard, elephant, rhino and buffalo) territory.

The lodge accommodates just 20 guests in utmost splendour, amidst breath-taking scenery. Each of the private suites has its own spectacular outdoor terrace with secluded pool and gazebo. Boasting panoramic views, the Royal and the Malewane Suites are the pinnacles of refinement and opulence. Fine dining is the order of the day at Royal Malewane. Dinner is a very special occasion served under the African stars, or with crystal and silver in the dining area. Indulge in the finest cuisine while your every whim is expertly catered for.

Enjoy game viewing, with an expert ranger and master tracker, either by open Land Rover or on foot. Your senses will be seduced and your skin will prickle with awe at this beautiful, savage, unspoilt land and the incredible wildlife it supports.

FACILITIES

Accommodation
6 LUXURY SUITES, 1 ROYAL SUITE AND 1 MALEWANE SUITE

Recreational facilities
GAME DRIVES
GAME WALKS
BIRD WATCHING
PRIVATE SWIMMING POOLS
FITNESS CENTRE
SPA AND TREATMENT CENTRE
LIBRARY
HORSE RIDING, HOT AIR BALLOON FLIGHTS, GOLF, ELEPHANT BACK SAFARIS AND WHITE WATER RAFTING CAN BE ARRANGED AT NEARBY LOCATIONS

Meeting facilities
NONE

International Airports
JOHANNESBURG INTERNATIONAL AIRPORT (JNB)
80 MINUTES FLIGHT AWAY

RESERVATIONS

Prices
LUXURY SUITES FROM 685 EURO PP PER NIGHT

Credit cards
AE, DC, MC, V

GDS Reservation Codes
NONE

Yearly Closing Dates
NONE

CONTACT DETAILS

ROYAL MALEWANE
P.O. BOX 1542
HOEDSPRUIT
1380
SOUTH AFRICA
TEL + 2715 793 0150
FAX + 2715 793 2879
INFO@ROYALMALEWANE.COM
WWW.ROYALMALEWANE.COM

Owner: MRS LIZ BIDEN
General Manager: MR JOHN JACKSON
Director of sales: MRS LIZ BIDEN

AFFILIATIONS
NONE

SINGITA LEBOMBO & SWENI LODGES
Kruger National Park

Singita Lebombo Lodge and Sweni Lodge form the heart of an exclusive 15,000-hectare private concession situated on a spectacular site, on the southern edge of the Nwanetsi River. Here, wildlife is dominated by large herds of animals and interpretive game drives are led by game rangers in open Landrovers.

Striking floor to ceiling glass walls ensure that guests have a 360° view when relaxing under the slatted roof of woven branches. The tastefully appointed, exclusive suites are set into a clifftop overlooking the river and both intimate lodges are located in such way to take full advantage of the sweeping views of the Lebombo mountains and surrounding bush.

Singita Lebombo Lodge and Sweni Lodge consist of various exquisite dining and living areas, a unique wine cellar and a fully equipped gymnasium and health Spa. Guests will encounter an original cuisine inspired by African flavours yet guided by the Western culinary tradition.

FACILITIES

Accommodation
15 SUITES AT SINGITA LEBOMBO LODGE
6 SUITES AT SWENI LODGE

Recreational facilities
SWIMMING POOL
GAME DRIVES
BUSH WALKS
SPA
GYMNASIUM
LIBRARY
AFRICAN TRADING STORE
WINE CELLAR
RESTAURANTS

Meeting facilities
NONE

International Airports
KRUGER MPUMALANGA INT'L AIRPORT (KMI)
40 MINUTES FLIGHT AWAY

RESERVATIONS

Prices
SUITES FROM 853 EURO PP PER NIGHT

Credit cards
AE, DC, MC, V

GDS Reservation Codes
NONE

Yearly Closing Dates
NONE

CONTACT DETAILS

SINGITA LEBOMBO LODGE
P.O. BOX 23367
CLAREMONT
7735
SOUTH AFRICA
TEL +27 21 683 3424
FAX +27 21 683 3502
SINGITA@SINGITA.CO.ZA
WWW.SINGITA.COM

OWNER: CLASSIFIED
GENERAL MANAGER: MR JASON TROLLIP
DIRECTOR OF SALES: MR LEW ROOD

AFFILIATIONS

RELAIS &
CHATEAUX

THE PRIVATE COLLECTION

THE TWELVE APOSTLES HOTEL & SPA

Camps Bay

Situated on the rim of the Atlantic Ocean in Camps Bay, just 15 minutes from the V&A Waterfront and near to Cape Town's finest beaches, the Twelve Apostles Hotel and Spa offers the warmth and service of a small hotel, enhanced by the restorative properties of a private health spa.

The elegant luxury bedrooms have a variety of decor styles, from beach house chic to a mix of African indigenous woods, leather and woven fabrics, all offering the latest business technology.

Guests can relax at the pool, surrounded by rocks and fynbos while watching whales at play in the ocean below, or hike up Table Mountain's unspoiled walking trails behind the hotel.

The Sanctuary Spa situated in an underground cavern is the ideal escape for gently restoring harmony and tranquility while soothing the soul.

The Twelve Apostles Hotel and Spa is sheer indulgence in a natural secure paradise offering endless seductive views.

FACILITIES

Accommodation
55 DELUXE ROOMS &
15 LUXURY SUITES

Recreational facilities
THE SANCTUARY SPA & GYM
16-SEATER CINEMA
2 HEATED OUTDOOR POOLS
2 RESTAURANTS & BAR
WHALE & DOLPHIN WATCHING
DEEP SEA DIVING & FISHING
MOUNTAIN WALKS
PICNIC SITES
EXCURSIONS TO TABLE MOUNTAIN,
V&A WATERFRONT,
ROBBEN ISLAND, THE CAPE CASTLE,
CAPE PENINSULA,
CAPE WINELANDS,
KIRSTENBOSCH BOTANICAL GARDENS,
GOLF COURSES NEARBY

Meeting facilities
MEETING ROOMS FOR UP TO 90 PEOPLE

International Airports
CAPE TOWN INTERNATIONAL AIRPORT (CPT)
40 MINUTES DRIVE AWAY
HELICOPTER TRANSFERS BY PRIOR ARRANGEMENT

RESERVATIONS

Prices
ROOMS FROM 385 EURO PER NIGHT

Credit cards
AE, MC, V

GDS Reservation Codes
AMADEUS LW CPT057
GALILEO LW 30404
SABRE LW 55288
WORLDSPAN LW 6057

Yearly Closing Dates
NONE

CONTACT DETAILS

THE TWELVE APOSTLES HOTEL & SPA
VICTORIA ROAD
CAMPS BAY
8040
CAPE TOWN
SOUTH AFRICA
TEL +27 21 437 9000
FAX +27 21 437 9055
BOOKTA@RCHMAIL.COM
WWW.12APOSTLESHOTEL.COM

OWNER: RED CARNATION HOTELS
GENERAL MANAGER: MR CLIVE BENNETT
DIRECTOR OF SALES: MS TRACY MARTIN

AFFILIATIONS

The Leading Small Hotels
of the World

THE PALMS

Zanzibar

On the South Eastern coast of the exotic island of Zanzibar, lies an exclusive property, which combines effortless elegance with Zanzibari sophistication.

This collection of beautifully designed villas offers luxurious comfort in an intimate setting. On the veranda, a silk draped four poster Zanzibar Bed accents a sunken, midnight blue Jacuzzi concealed by billowing curtains which reveal long views of the Indian Ocean.

The Palms provides a range of beautifully appointed facilities reflecting the warmth and character of the local architecture. Overlooking the beach, private palm thatched "bandas" provide intimate beachfront privacy. The Spa offers a variety of treatments and massages while listening to the lapping of the waves of the Indian Ocean. The colonnaded terrace of The Plantation House leads into the Spice inspired bar, and onto the elegant antique dining room, which serves exotic cuisine.

The Palms is a sanctuary for those in search of tranquillity...a place to stimulate the senses and experience the magic of Zanzibar.

FACILITIES

Accommodation
6 LUXURY VILLAS

Recreational facilities
PRIVATE OUTDOOR JACUZZI
SWIMMING POOL
PRIVATE BEACH
SCUBA DIVING
FITNESS CENTRE
TENNIS COURT
WATER SPORTS
SPA
RESTAURANT & BARS
INTERNET FACILITIES

Meeting facilities
NONE

International Airports
ZANZIBAR INTERNATIONAL AIRPORT (ZNZ)
50 MINUTES DRIVE AWAY

RESERVATIONS

Prices
LUXURY VILLA FROM 320 EURO PP PER NIGHT

Credit cards
AE, MC, V

GDS Reservation Codes
NONE

Yearly Closing Dates
NONE

CONTACT DETAILS

THE PALMS RESERVATIONS OFFICE
C/O TOUR AFRICA SAFARIS LTD
P.O. BOX 48728
NAIROBI
KENYA
TEL +254 20 272 9333
FAX +254 20 272 3513
INFO@PALMS-ZANZIBAR.COM
WWW.PALMS-ZANZIBAR.COM

OWNER: CLASSIFIED
DIRECTOR OF SALES: MS PAULINA RAGUZ

AFFILIATIONS

NONE

STANLEY SAFARI LODGE
Livingstone

Stanley Safari Lodge is located on a hill overlooking the spray of the Victoria Falls, the Zambezi river and the elephants drinking place.

Accommodation ranges from double suites, to the honeymoon cottage – with both its own fireplace and plunge pool. The open-sided design affords a unique, magical view across the National Park to the mighty Zambezi River and the magnificent Victoria Falls – one of the Seven Natural Wonders of the World.

The main house provides the romantic setting for the French style cuisine; alternatively dine under the stars on the lawn, at the pool or in the privacy of your own cottage, whilst enjoying the personal service of the Zambian staff, all with in-depth knowledge of Livingstone and its environs.

The Victoria Falls area boasts a wealth of activities such as safaris to Chobe National Park, horseback riding, golf, elephant back safaris, micro light or helicopter flights and visits to a real African village, as well as canoeing, sunset cruises, rafting, fishing on the Zambezi river.

FACILITIES

Accommodation
3 AFRICAN COTTAGES
2 OPEN SUITES
WITH PRIVATE PLUNGE POOL
2 AIR-CONDITIONED SUITES
WITH PRIVATE PLUNGE POOL

Recreational facilities
SWIMMING POOL
SUNSET CRUISE, CANOEING,
RAFTING AND RIVER SAFARIS ON ZAMBEZI
FISHING
HELICOPTER OR MICROLIGHT FLIGHTS
HORSEBACK RIDING
ELEPHANT BACK SAFARIS
QUAD BIKING
GOLF NEARBY
BUNGEE JUMPING
CULTURAL VISITS

Meeting facilities
NONE

International Airports
LIVINGSTONE AIRPORT (LVI)
25 MINUTES DRIVE AWAY
VICTORIA FALLS AIRPORT (VFA)
60 MINUTES DRIVE AWAY

RESERVATIONS

Prices
ROOMS FROM 150 EURO PP PER NIGHT

Credit cards
MC, V

GDS Reservation Codes
NONE

Yearly Closing Dates
NONE

CONTACT DETAILS

STANLEY SAFARIS
RESERVATIONS OFFICE
KON. ASTRIDLAAN 37 B BUS 9
B-2950 KAPELLEN
BELGIUM
TEL +32 496 67 20 40
FAX +1 206 350 0259
INFO@STANLEYSAFARIS.COM
WWW.STANLEYSAFARIS.COM

OWNER: CLASSIFIED
GENERAL MANAGER: MR R. DE GRUIJTER
DIRECTOR OF SALES: MR R. DE GRUIJTER

AFFILIATIONS

NONE

PAMUSHANA

Malilangwe Private Wildlife Reserve

Perched on top of an escarpment in the south-east corner of Zimbabwe, with panoramic views of the surrounding hills and the hippo filled dam far below, Pamushana is an opulent, luxurious and unrivalled celebration of the glory of the African bush. This superb lodge is perched on top of an escarpment in the south-east corner of Zimbabwe, and has the ultimate panoramic views of the Malilangwe Private Wildlife Reserve.

Each air-conditioned villa is completely private and has its own individual view of the Conservancy - in fact the whole lodge is designed so as not to miss whats happening in the wild bush or lake below. With full-length glass windows even in the bathrooms this would be hard. One of the favorite features, however, is the teak deck outside the main bedroom. Not only does this run the whole width of the villa but along with sun-loungers, the guest's own Swarovski telescope, an outside shower and a private spill-over swimming pool, which appears to be part of the lake below.

Other features of Pamushana are the gym, the health centre, the Jacuzzi set in the indigenous gardens, the spectacular swimming pool, the comfortable lounge full of exotic African works of art, the library, exciting game drives, game walks and the dining room with the most amazing mural and fabulous food.

FACILITIES

Accommodation
7 LUXURY VILLAS

Recreational facilities
SWIMMING POOL
GAME DRIVES
WALKING SAFARIS
CANADIAN CANOEING
SUNDOWNER LAKE CRUISES
FISHING
GOLF NEARBY
YOGA
HEALTH CENTRE & AROMATHERAPY
RESTAURANT & BAR

Meeting facilities
MEETING ROOM FOR UP TO 16 PEOPLE

International Airports
HARARE INT'L AIRPORT (HRE)
270 MINUTES DRIVE AWAY
BUFFALO RANGE INT'L AIRPORT (BFO)
30 MINUTES DRIVE AWAY

RESERVATIONS

Prices
VILLAS FROM 536 EURO PP PER NIGHT
(ALL INCLUSIVE)

Credit cards
MC, V

GDS Reservation Codes
NONE

Yearly Closing Dates
LATE JUNE – EARLY JULY 2005

CONTACT DETAILS

PAMUSHANA HEAD OFFICE
P.O. BOX MP845
MOUNT PLEASANT
HARARE
ZIMBABWE
TEL +263 4 369136
FAX +263 4 369523
MCTSALES@AFRICAONLINE.CO.ZW
WWW.MALILANGWE.COM

OWNER: MALILANGWE TRUST
GENERAL MANAGER: MR LAWRENCE MATTOCK
SALES MANAGER: MS DEBORAH O'BRIEN

AFFILIATIONS

The individual way to travel.

www.proair.de

M I D D L E E A S T & I N D I A N O C E A N

The Sheikhdoms of deserts and stunning beaches boast a sophisticated lifestyle and plenty of exotic elements to make it truly exciting …
This part of the world is a spectacular East-meets-West phenomenon, where white beaches, azure blue waters and endless deserts stand cheek-to-cheek with towering skyscrapers, domed mosques and haute-couture shops.

Idyllic islands adrift in the Indian Ocean are just waiting for the chance to seduce elegant travellers with their warm waters, spice markets and a unique style of barefoot luxury … In general, the style of the Indian Ocean is that of relaxed simplicity with several, truly stylish hotels built from nothing but palm, wood and thatch. Where shoes can be forgotten and computers are a myth.

THE PRIVATE COLLECTION

AL MAHA DESERT RESORT & SPA
Dubai Desert Conservation Reserve

An exclusive oasis styled after a traditional Bedouin encampment, the Al Maha Desert Resort & Spa introduces its guests to all the customs, wildlife and dramatic beauty of the Arabian desert.

The new Jamilah Spa overlooks the resort's oasis-style pool, with views across sweeping dunes, providing a natural, tranquil backdrop to the Spa's impressive array of relaxation and beauty therapies using the exclusively produced Al Maha 'Timeless' products. Camel-trekking, horse-riding, guided nature walks and four-wheel drive safaris all bring the surrounding 3,500 acres of desert plains up close and personal. Oryx, gazelle and fox are just a sample of the wildlife that can be spotted, whilst falconry exhibitions display a traditional art long forgotten elsewhere.

Guests are accommodated in an intimate collection of 40 luxurious Bedouin Suites, each one a combination of tented ceilings, Arabian antiques, hedonistic bathrooms and individual temperature controlled pools. The wrap-around verandas are ideal for enjoying the Arabian or Mediterranean cuisine.
Winner of the World Legacy Award 2004 (Nature Travel) by National Geographic & Conservation International.

FACILITIES

Accommodation
40 SUITES, EACH WITH PRIVATE TEMPERATURE CONTROLLED POOL (7,5 x 6,5M)

Recreational facilities
EXCLUSIVE 'JAMILAH SPA'
MAIN POOL IN ADDITION TO PRIVATE POOLS
ARCHERY
CAMEL TREKKING
GUIDED NATURAL WALKS
HORSE RIDING
FALCONRY
FOUR WHEEL DRIVE SAFARIS

Meeting facilities
MEETING ROOM FOR UP TO 120 PEOPLE, BUSINESS CENTRE

International Airports
DUBAI INTERNATIONAL AIRPORT (DXB)
45 MINUTES DRIVE AWAY

RESERVATIONS

Prices
SUITES FROM 740 EURO PER NIGHT
INCLUSIVE OF FULL BOARD AND ACTIVITIES

Credit cards
AE, DC, MC, V

GDS Reservation Codes
AMADEUS LW DXB202
GALILEO LW 28316
SABRE LW 53804
WORLDSPAN LW 6202

Yearly Closing Dates
NONE

CONTACT DETAILS

AL MAHA DESERT RESORT & SPA
CENTRAL RESERVATIONS OFFICE
SHEIKH ZAYED ROAD
EMIRATES HOLIDAYS BUILDING – 3RD FLOOR
P.O. BOX 7631
DUBAI, UNITED ARAB EMIRATES
TEL + 971 4 303 42 22
FAX + 971 4 343 96 96
ALMAHA@EMIRATES.COM
WWW.AL-MAHA.COM

OWNER: EMIRATES AIRLINES
GENERAL MANAGER: MR TONY WILLIAMS
DIRECTOR OF SALES: MRS MARY BISHARA

AFFILIATIONS

The Leading Small Hotels
of the World

ONE&ONLY ROYAL MIRAGE
Dubai

One&Only Royal Mirage is considered Dubai's most stylish beach resort where genuine care and hospitality blend with fantasy and tradition, creating an ambiance of Arabian influenced refinement and majesty.

The resort offers understated elegance and exclusive charm, overlooking the Arabian Gulf with a kilometre of private coastline and 65 acres of lush landscaped gardens, ensuring an abundance of space.

One&Only Royal Mirage comprises three equally distinctive properties, The Palace, Arabian Court and Residence & Spa. The resort offers an outstanding array of dining outlets and rich leisure facilities such as oasis-like pools, water sports centre, tennis courts as well as an exclusive Givenchy Spa and a traditional Oriental Hammam.

One&Only Royal Mirage invites guests to discover the magic of Arabia.

FACILITIES

Accommodation
250 ROOMS & SUITES AT THE PALACE
172 ROOMS & SUITES AT THE ARABIAN COURT
50 ROOMS & SUITES AT THE RESIDENCE & SPA

Recreational facilities
TEMPERATURE CONTROLLED SWIMMING POOLS
WATER SPORT CENTRE
TENNIS COURTS
GOLF PUTTING GREEN
CHILDREN'S FACILITIES
HEALTH & BEAUTY INSTITUTE FEATURING SPA, HAMMAM AND FITNESS CENTRE
RESTAURANTS

Meeting facilities
MEETING ROOMS FOR UP TO 350 PEOPLE AT THE PALACE
MEETING ROOMS FOR UP TO 300 PEOPLE AT THE ARABIAN COURT

International Airports
DUBAI INTERNATIONAL AIRPORT (DXB)
20 MINUTES DRIVE AWAY

RESERVATIONS

Prices
ROOMS FROM 500 EURO PER NIGHT

Credit cards
AE, DC, MC, V

GDS Reservation Codes
NONE

Yearly Closing Dates
NONE

CONTACT DETAILS
ONE&ONLY ROYAL MIRAGE
JUMEIRA ROAD
PO BOX 37252
DUBAI, UAE
TEL +971 4 399 9999
FAX +971 4 399 9998
ROYALMIRAGE@ONEANDONLYRESORT.AE
WWW.ONEANDONLYROYALMIRAGE.COM

OWNER: KERZNER INTERNATIONAL
GENERAL MANAGER: MR OLIVIER LOUIS
DIRECTOR OF SALES: MRS ANITA CREMER

AFFILIATIONS
The Leading Small Hotels
of the World

XO PRIVATE — THE PRIVATE COLLECTION

THE CHEDI MUSCAT
Muscat

Flanked by azure ocean waters at the heart of Oman, The Chedi Muscat pampers its guests offering access to 2 turqoise pools, a serene +water garden, lush poolside cabanas, a popular spa and a private stretch of beach.

Established around original Omani structures and architectural design, the hotel reflects a modern view of Eastern opulence. Understated and sleek, the emphasis is on exclusive sophistication; a theme that is consisted throughout the Chedi Muscat's spacious rooms and suites with breathtaking views of the Gulf of Oman and the mysterious mountain ranges of Muscat.

Located adjacent to the elegant lobby lounge overlooking the water garden, the restaurant boasts a blend of contemporary Mediterranean and Asian influenced cuisine. Houseguests can cool off at either The Chedi or The Serai poolside cabana; both serve an extensive range of snacks, delicious desserts and assorted refreshments.

FACILITIES

Accommodation
151 ROOMS & SUITES

Recreational facilities
PRIVATE BEACH
FRESHWATER SWIMMING POOLS
SPA
HEALTH & BEAUTY CENTRE
LIBRARY
CLUB LOUNGE
GYMNASIUM
2 TENNIS COURTS

Meeting facilities
MEETING ROOM FOR UP TO 40 PEOPLE

International Airports
SEEB INTERNATIONAL AIRPORT (MCT)
15 MINUTES DRIVE AWAY

RESERVATIONS

Prices
ROOMS FROM 220 EURO PER NIGHT

Credit cards
AE, DC, MC, V

GDS Reservation Codes
AMADEUS DS MCTMUS
GALILEO DS 58695
SABRE DS 51483
WORLDSPAN DS CHMUS

Yearly Closing Dates
NONE

CONTACT DETAILS

THE CHEDI MUSCAT
PO BOX 964
POSTAL CODE 133, AL KHUWAIR
MUSCAT
SULTANATE OF OMAN
TEL +968 24524400
FAX +968 24493485
THECHEDI@OMANTEL.NET.OM
WWW.GHMHOTELS.COM

OWNER: BOARD OF DIRECTORS
GENERAL MANAGER: MR YORK BRANDES
DIRECTOR OF SALES: MS LORE KOENIG

AFFILIATIONS

GHM
A STYLE TO REMEMBER

a member of
design hotels

DHONI MIGHILI
North Ari Atoll

Transcend. Explore the Ari Atoll aboard your handcrafted Maldivian sailboat. Relish a room with a view as the ivory sail flickers in the sun.

Your very own Dhoni is a living metaphor of the sublime - a harmony of natural materials, century-old tradition married with modern design, the cabin enhanced with air-conditioning, king-sized bed, LCD screen and surround sound. Its shape and grace is part of the romance of the Maldives.

Should you wish to take a break from the sea, indulge in the ecstasy of a private plunge pool, open-air waterfall shower, thatched bungalow, walled courtyard or undholi, a traditional Maldivian swing.

A personal Thakuru, a Maldivian butler, pampers your every whim, while your chef fulfills your culinary desires. Savour unsurpassed levels of service at the restaurant, bar, diving base and spa.

Move with ease and insouciance between your private sailboat, luxury island and stunning surroundings. Dhoni Mighili, a very private affair.

FACILITIES

Accommodation
6 Luxury Dhoni, each partnered with a Beach Bungalow

Recreational facilities
Sen Spa
Non-motorized Water Sports
Big Game Fishing
Night Fishing
Scuba Diving
Snorkelling
Library
Bar & Restaurant
Boutique

Meeting facilities
None

International Airports
Malé International Airport (MLE)
30 minutes Flight away by seaplane or 240 minutes by Dhoni

RESERVATIONS

Prices
Dhoni & Beach Bungalow
from 554 Euro pp per night

Credit cards
AE, DC, MC, V

GDS Reservation Codes
None

Yearly Closing Dates
None

CONTACT DETAILS

Dhoni Mighili
North Ari Atoll
PO Box 2017
Republic of Maldives
Tel +960 450 751
Fax +960 450 727
INFO@DHONIMIGHILI.COM
WWW.DHONIMIGHILI.COM

Owner: Universal Enterprises
General Manager: Mr and Mrs Scot and Donna Toon
Director of sales: Mrs Asma Rasheed

AFFILIATIONS
None

HUVAFEN FUSHI
North Malé Atoll

Huvafen Fushi is set within its very own private lagoon amongst mesmeric settings of transparent ocean. Showcasing the world's first underwater spa guests will grasp the true meaning of imagination, devotion and natural harmony.

The resort comprises of 43 bungalows, all of which are fully equipped with private pool, private dining area, air-conditioning, bar, open-air bathroom, relaxing daybed and plasma screen with DVD.

Enjoy the seductive cuisine from lush Mediterranean to vibrant South East Asian, truly superb and extremely intimate in the 3 elegant restaurants: 'Salt' over water, the main bar 'UMbar' offering designer cocktails and 'Vinum' the cavernous underground wine cellar.

The pavilions are pure escapism, situated on prime locations of the land and sea, featuring two rooms, expansive private pools, split level decks, glass floor and Jacuzzi.

Additional services include Yoga Island, over water gym, Padi scuba diving, water sports and a full range of daily excursions such as sand bank snorkelling.

FACILITIES

Accommodation
43 BUNGALOWS & PAVILIONS

Recreational facilities
AQUUM SPA FEATURING UNDERWATER SPA
INFINITY SWIMMING POOL
OVER WATER YOGA PAVILION
OVER WATER GYMNASIUM
SALT WATER FLOATATION POOL
WATER SPORTS
BIG GAME FISHING
NIGHT FISHING
SCUBA DIVING
SNORKELLING
LIBRARY
THEATRETTE
BAR & RESTAURANT
BOUTIQUE

Meeting facilities
NONE

International Airports
MALÉ INTERNATIONAL AIRPORT (MLE)
30 MINUTES BY SPEEDBOAT

RESERVATIONS

Prices
ROOMS FROM 550 EURO PER NIGHT

Credit cards
AE, DC, MC, V

GDS Reservation Codes
NONE

Yearly Closing Dates
NONE

CONTACT DETAILS

HUVAFEN FUSHI
NORTH MALE' ATOLL
PO BOX 2017
REPUBLIC OF MALDIVES
TEL +960 444 222
FAX +960 444 333
INFO@HUVAFENFUSHI.COM
WWW.HUVAFENFUSHI.COM

OWNER: UNIVERSAL ENTERPRISES
GENERAL MANAGER: MR TOM MCLOUGHLIN
DIRECTOR OF SALES: MRS ASMA RASHEED

AFFILIATIONS

SONEVA FUSHI RESORT & SIX SENSES SPA

Kunfunadhoo Island

Surrounded by white sand beaches that shelve gently into an azure blue sea, the exclusive Soneva Fushi on the privately owned island of Kunfunadhoo in The Maldives offers the ultimate in barefoot sophistication.

All 65 rooms and villas – some equipped with private pool - are set back into vegetation. The trees and the plants separate each of the villas ensuring the utmost in privacy. It also means that the trees and natural vegetation of the island are kept intact. So designer marble entrance lobbies and motorized golf carts are banished in favour of a more natural environment. Guests are encouraged to go barefoot throughout the course of their stay, or ride bicycles to get around the island, from their villa to the library, the dive school or the relaxing Six Senses Spa.

Soneva Fushi also presents a variety of gourmet dining options in settings as memorable as the food itself, such as a seaside moonlit barbecue, a desert island picnic, a lunch under a canopy of trees, or an intimate meal by lantern on a private beach.

FACILITIES

Accommodation
65 ROOMS AND VILLAS

Recreational facilities
PADI DIVING SCHOOL
DEEP SEA FISHING BY DHONI
SIX SENSES SPA & FITNESS
WATERSKIING
CULTURAL EXCURSIONS
TREETOP LIBRARY AND INTERNET ACCESS
WINDSURFING, HOBIE CAT SAILING
AND CANOEING
TENNIS COURT, BADMINTON, VOLLEYBALL,
TABLE TENNIS
SNORKELLING, BICYCLE RIDING
BOULES & JOGGING
TUESDAY SANDBANK PARTY

Meeting facilities
SMALL GROUPS ON REQUEST

International Airports
MALÉ INTERNATIONAL AIRPORT (MLE)
25 MINUTES BY SEAPLANE

RESERVATIONS

Prices
ROOMS FROM 275 EURO PER NIGHT

Credit cards
AE, DC, MC, V

GDS Reservation Codes
AMADEUS LX MLESFR
GALILEO LX 74090
SABRE LX 22048
WORLDSPAN LX MLESF

Yearly Closing Dates
NONE

CONTACT DETAILS

SONEVA FUSHI MALÉ OFFICE
4/3 BUILDING, FAAMUDHEYRI MAGU
MALE
REPUBLIC OF MALDIVES
TEL + 960 230 304 / 5
FAX + 960 230 374
RESERVATIONS-FUSHI@SONEVARESORTS.COM
WWW.SIXSENSES.COM

OWNER: MR SONU SHIVDASANI
GENERAL MANAGER: MR STEPHEN ANTRAM
DIRECTOR OF SALES: MR JAMES SULLIVAN-TAILYOUR

AFFILIATIONS

SONEVA GILI RESORT & SIX SENSES SPA
Lankanfushi Island

Soneva Gili is The Maldives' first resort located entirely over water, the beautiful turquoise blue waters of Lankanfushi, one of the largest resort lagoons in the Maldives.

The 44 villas and residences are extremely spacious. The bathrooms have been designed with a separate shower, accessed along an open-air walkway, along its own private water garden. The roof sundeck is a private oasis of luxury – some of the villas also have an open-air Jacuzzi – and there is also a lower level sundeck just above the water level.

Open air dining at Soneva Gili is romantic, private and unique. A moonlit dinner on the sun deck of the villa, or on the floating deck moored on the sunset side of the island, breakfast in the living room of a private residence, or lunch over the water in the over water restaurant – the settings are as memorable as the cuisine.

Soneva Gili shares the Six Senses philosophy so there is naturally a tantalizing over water Six Senses Spa, offering an extensive menu of pampering and healthy therapies.

FACILITIES

Accommodation
44 OVER WATER VILLAS

Recreational facilities
DIVING SCHOOL
DEEP SEA FISHING BY DHONI
SIX SENSES SPA
WATERSKIING
CULTURAL EXCURSIONS
LIBRARY AND INTERNET ACCESS
WINDSURFING, SNORKELLING, HOBIE CAT
SAILING AND CANOEING
TENNIS COURT, BADMINTON
VOLLEYBALL, TABLE TENNIS
BOULES & JOGGING

Meeting facilities
SMALL GROUPS ON REQUEST

International Airports
MALÉ INTERNATIONAL AIRPORT (MLE)
20 MINUTES BY SPEEDBOAT

RESERVATIONS

Prices
VILLA SUITES FROM 615 EURO PER NIGHT

Credit cards
AE, DC, MC, V

GDS Reservation Codes
AMADEUS LX MLESGR
GALILEO LX 39968
SABRE LX 61151
WORLDSPAN LX MLESG

Yearly Closing Dates
NONE

CONTACT DETAILS

SONEVA GILI MALÉ OFFICE
4/3, FAAMUDHEYRI MAGU
MALE
REPUBLIC OF MALDIVES
TEL + 960 440 304
FAX + 960 440 305
RESERVATIONS-GILI@SONEVARESORTS.COM
WWW.SIXSENSES.COM

Owner: CLASSIFIED
General Manager: MR GARRY SNODGRASS
Director of sales: MR JAMES SULLIVAN-TAILYOUR

AFFILIATIONS

LE PRINCE MAURICE
Poste de Flacq

Le Prince Maurice enjoys an idyllic location in a secluded and sheltered spot on the splendid east coast of Mauritius. Named after Prince Maurice of Nassau, a pioneer of the island ancient spice trade, the hotel nestles on a lagoon-lapped beach, screened by lush tropical vegetation and blends naturally with the beauty and simplicity of the environment.

Elegant and natural building materials such as marble, wood and stone as well as an architecture allowing nature, water, space and light to create an atmosphere of comfort. An all-suite hotel, some of the 89 colonial-style suites are built on stilts over a natural fish reserve, while the large senior suites face the sea and have private plunge pools and sunken Jacuzzis in the gardens.

The hotel features 4 sheltered coral sand beaches, a Guerlain Spa, a kid's club, a fitness centre, water sports, as well as a unique floating restaurant, Le Barachois and for golfers, two 18-holes championship golf courses of international standard.

FACILITIES

Accommodation
76 JUNIOR SUITES,
12 SENIOR SUITES &
1 PRINCELY SUITE

Recreational facilities
TENNIS COURTS
2 CHAMPIONSHIP GOLF COURSES
KAYAK & PEDALO
WATERSKIING & WINDSURFING
HOBBY CAT & LASER
GLASS BOTTOM BOAT EXCURSIONS
BICYCLES
KID'S CLUB
GUERLAIN BEAUTY CENTRE
FITNESS & HEALTH CENTRE
SCUBA DIVING & SNORKELLING
BOAT TRIPS
DEEP SEA FISHING
FLY FISHING

Meeting facilities
MEETING ROOM FOR UP TO 16 PEOPLE

International Airports
MAURITIUS INTERNATIONAL AIRPORT (MRU)
60 MINUTES DRIVE AWAY
15 MINUTES BY HELICOPTER

RESERVATIONS

Prices
JUNIOR SUITES FROM 266 EURO PP PER NIGHT
SENIOR SUITES FROM 557 EURO PP PER NIGHT
PRINCELY SUITE FROM 5,250 EURO PP PER NIGHT

Credit cards
AE, DC, MC, V

GDS Reservation Codes
NONE

Yearly Closing Dates
NONE

CONTACT DETAILS

LE PRINCE MAURICE
CHOISY ROAD
POSTE DE FLACQ
MAURITIUS
TEL +230 413 9100
FAX +9230 413 9130
RESA@PRINCEMAURICE.COM
WWW.PRINCEMAURICE.COM

OWNER: CONSTANCE HOTELS SERVICES LTD
GENERAL MANAGER: MR ANDREW MILTON
DIRECTOR OF SALES: MR SIEGFRIED ESPITALIER NOEL
& MRS BRIGITTE DE FONTENAY

AFFILIATIONS

RELAIS &
CHATEAUX®

FRÉGATE ISLAND PRIVATE
Frégate Island

A tropical island paradise that was originally a secret hideaway for pirates is now a stylish refuge for those in need of privacy and comfort.

The 16 villas are designed for privacy, featuring a living room, large bedroom and 2 bathrooms with both inside and outdoor showers. Amenities include air-conditioning, satellite TVs, DVD and CD players and furnished sundecks leading down to Jacuzzis where guests can revel in the ocean views in complete privacy.

Dining here is also a feast for the senses, international gourmet cuisine presented in the Frégate House restaurant alternating with Creole delicacies served in the carefully-restored Plantation House.

Recreational possibilities include 7 stunning beaches, 2 infinity-edge swimming pools, a PADI dive centre and a gymnasium, as well as a 'Castaway Kid's Club' and a marina with a fleet of boats and motor yachts for big game fishing and day cruises. The top-class "The Rock Spa" nestles on one of the peaks of the island and is the first indigenous spa in Seychelles incorporating nature's element whilst offering outstanding signature treatments.

FACILITIES

Accommodation
16 Luxury Villas

Recreational facilities
Sunfish and Hobby Sailboats
Big Game Fishing
Scuba Diving (PADI)
The Rock Spa featuring Products by Li'Tya
2 Freshwater Swimming Pools
Guided Nature Walks
Gymnasium
Mountain Biking
Extensive Library
Castaway Kid's Club

Meeting facilities
Meeting Room for up to 12 people

International Airports
Seychelles International Airport (SEZ)
20 minutes flight away
(small aircraft or helicopter)

RESERVATIONS

Prices
Villas from 2,185 Euro per night

Credit cards
None

GDS Reservation Codes
None

Yearly Closing Dates
None

CONTACT DETAILS

Frégate Island Private
Worldwide Reservations,
Sales & Marketing Office
Schwalbenstrasse 15
63263 Neu-Isenburg
Germany
Tel + (49) 6102-501 321
Fax + (49) 6102-501 322
unique.experiences@debitel.net
www.fregate.com

Owner: Classified
General Manager: Mr Patrick V. Brizio
Director of sales: Mrs Astrid Oberhummer

AFFILIATIONS
None

LEMURIA RESORT OF PRASLIN
Praslin

A luxury Spa resort in idyllic surroundings in the Seychelles to unwind and relax. The architecture of the resort and its interior design were created using natural materials such as wood, stone, pink granite and thatch to create a resort in harmony with the outstanding beauty of the surrounding landscapes. The quality and design of the hotel meet the expectations of guests who want the highest standard of luxury and comfort.

The hotel has a relaxed ambience and features top class facilities including a Guerlain institute, an indoor and outdoor swimming pool, a dive centre, a kid's club, tennis courts, a fitness centre and a wide range of water sports. A unique attraction is The Lemuria 18-hole golf course, which offers a great challenge to all levels of players and borders the enchanting beaches of both the small Kerlan Cove and the Grand Kerlan Cove.

Dining at Lemuria is a gourmet treat with the 3 sumptuous restaurants. The 4 elegant bars offer music entertainment in the evening.

FACILITIES
Accommodation
88 JUNIOR SUITES,
8 SENIOR SUITES,
8 LUXURY VILLAS &
1 PRESIDENTIAL VILLA

Recreational facilities
SWIMMING POOL
TENNIS COURTS
SNORKELLING
HOBBY CAT & LASER
18-HOLE GOLF COURSE
KAYAK & PEDALO
KID'S CLUB
GUERLAIN BEAUTY CENTRE
FITNESS & HEALTH CENTRE
SCUBA DIVING (PADI)
DEEP SEA FISHING
MOUNTAIN BIKING

Meeting facilities
NONE

International Airports
SEYCHELLES INTERNATIONAL AIRPORT (SEZ)
10 MINUTES DRIVE AWAY

RESERVATIONS
Prices
JUNIOR SUITES FROM 323 EURO PP PER NIGHT
SENIOR SUITES FROM 645 EURO PP PER NIGHT
VILLAS FROM 2,475 EURO PP PER NIGHT
PRES. VILLA FROM 10,800 EURO PP PER NIGHT

Credit cards
AE, DC, MC, V

GDS Reservation Codes
NONE

Yearly Closing Dates
NONE

CONTACT DETAILS
LEMURIA RESORT OF PRASLIN
ANSE KERLAN
PRASLIN
SEYCHELLES
TEL +248 281 281
FAX +248 281 001
RESA@LEMURIARESORT.COM
WWW.LEMURIARESORT.COM

OWNER: CONSTANCE HOTELS SERVICES LTD
GENERAL MANAGER: MR ANDREW SPEARMAN
DIRECTOR OF SALES: MR SIEGFRIED ESPITALIER NOEL
& MRS BRIGITTE DE FONTENAY

AFFILIATIONS

RELAIS &
CHATEAUX

NORTH ISLAND
North Island

Here on the private island sanctuary of North Island – a luxurious new Robinson Crusoe retreat has been created which fuses local Seychellois culture with those of Zanzibar and Bali. North Island remains a sustainable, ecologically sensitive utilisation of a precious natural treasure.

Only 9 Presidential Villas, 1 Villa Royale and 1 Villa North Island, all handcrafted from wood, local stone and glass provide the amazingly luxurious accommodation. Each villa is over 450m^2 and is completely self-contained all with private plunge pools. High-level hosting caters for your every need including in-villa meals or delicious champagne picnics on a secluded beach. Each villa is allocated one private buggy and mountain bikes with which to explore the island. All the villas have spectacular views from every living area and have direct access onto East Beach.

Such a private paradise is North Island that many endangered Seychelles' species are being re-introduced in this tropical paradise.

Welcome to barefoot paradise!

FACILITIES

Accommodation
11 LUXURY VILLAS

Recreational facilities
SNORKELLING
SCUBA DIVING CENTRE (REEF & WALL DIVING)
DEEP SEA & FLY FISHING
HEALTH SPA & IN VILLA TREATMENTS
FITNESS CENTRE
NATURE WALKS WITH RESIDENT ECOLOGIST
GUIDED & SUPPORTED SEA KAYAKING
MOUNTAIN BIKING
4 PRIVATE BEACHES
HOBIE CAT SAILING
YACHT CHARTER

Meeting facilities
NONE

International Airports
SEYCHELLES INTERNATIONAL AIRPORT (SEZ)
15 MIN HELICOPTER FLIGHT TO ISLAND

RESERVATIONS

Prices
LUXURY VILLAS FROM 2,470 EURO PER NIGHT

Credit cards
MC, V

GDS Reservation Codes
NONE

Yearly Closing Dates
NONE

CONTACT DETAILS

PRIVATE OCEAN ISLANDS
RESERVATIONS OFFICE
P.O. BOX 68954, BRYANSTON, 2021
GAUTENG
SOUTH AFRICA
TEL + 27 11 781 9210
FAX + 27 11 781 9211
SAMANTHA.STANGE@PRIVATEOCEANISLANDS.COM
WWW.PRIVATEOCEANISLANDS.COM

OWNER: CLASSIFIED
GENERAL MANAGER: MR BRUCE SIMPSON
DIRECTOR OF SALES: MR STEVE ELLIS

AFFILIATIONS

NONE

FAR AWAY FROM MASS AND SERIES PRODUCTION, CARAT KEEPS THE ACCURATE SENSE OF THE INDIVIDUAL AND DEVELOPS PRESTIGE LIMOUSINES WHERE THE HIGHEST SECURITY GOES WITH A UNIQUE ATMOSPHERE OF LUXURY, COMFORT, BEAUTY, TECHNICAL BRILLIANCE AND CRAFTMANSHIP AS WELL AS AN EXTREME DEGREE OF EXCLUSIVITY.

.... BECAUSE YOU'RE UNIQUE AND YOU DESERVE THE BEST.

ARMOURED AND STRETCHED LIMOUSINES

WWW. CARATDUCHATELET. COM
TEL : + 32 43 49 55 56

FAR EAST & PACIFIC

The Far East is synonymous with fragrant spices and ancient temples, gentle smiles and exotic culture. To stay in a luxury hideaway in the Far East is like to experience a little slice of paradise. It's all there whilst the rest of the world strives to emulate its exemplary service levels, rejuvenating health spas and architectural designs that seem to define either contemporary or traditional style.

These magical Pacific islands are a seductive blend of enthralling legends, smiling people and superb natural scenery. The Pacific is almost a mythical place. Rupert Booke, James Michener and Paul Gauguin are just a handful of the artists and writers who found their inspiration in these islands and who tried to do justice to their azure lagoons, volcanic peaks and idyllic way of life.

THE PRIVATE COLLECTION

ANANDA - IN THE HIMALAYAS
Rishikesh

Nestling in the foothills of the Himalayas and overlooking the sacred River Ganges, lies the state-of-the-art lifestyle destination spa, Ananda – In The Himalayas.

Located near to the spiritual town of Rishikesh, Ananda specialises in the traditional Indian sciences of holistic well-being, which rejuvenate the whole system, tone the body and relax the mind. Ananda is dedicated to providing its guests with a total immersion in discovering a well-being oriented lifestyle.

Accommodation is provided in 75 charming rooms and suites set amidst beautifully landscaped gardens. Each one features air-conditioning and heating and open air balconies offering breathtaking views of the Himalayan Valley and the river Ganges or the Maharaja's Palace.

The cuisine at Ananda is a pleasurable and delectable mix of spa and gourmet culled from Ayurvedic, Asian and European cuisine's that can be enjoyed in unique dining venues.

Travel into the world of harmony and discover the Ananda … you are sure to return with total rejuvenation of both body and soul.

FACILITIES

Accommodation
75 Rooms, including 5 Suites

Recreational facilities
Spa & Health Centre
Golf
Swimming Pool
Hiking Trails
Fitness Centre
Squash Court
White Water Rafting
Kayaking
Angling
Visit to Rajaji National Park –
Wild Elephants

Meeting facilities
Meeting Rooms for up to 100 people

International Airports
New Delhi International Airport (DEL)
240 minutes drive away

RESERVATIONS

Prices
Rooms from 300 Euro per night
Suites from 664 Euro per night

Credit cards
AE, DC, MC, V

GDS Reservation Codes
Amadeus NT DELANA
Galileo NT 33012
Sabre NT 51930
Worldspan NT AITH

Yearly Closing Dates
None

CONTACT DETAILS

Ananda - In The Himalayas
The Palace Estate
Narendra Nagar
Dist. Tehri-Garhwal
Uttaranchal, 249175
India
Tel +91 11 2689 9999
Fax +91 11 2613 1066
sales@anandaspa.com
www.anandaspa.com

Owner: IHHR Hospitality
General Manager: Mr Andrew Saldanha
Director of sales: Mr Naresh Chandnani

AFFILIATIONS
None

DEVI GARH
Udaipur

Set in the Aravalli hills of Rajasthan, the 18th century palace, Devi Garh casts a mighty profile against the Indian horizon. It is an eclectic mix of the traditional and the modern.

30 suites adorned with details in semi-precious stones, with separate dining and sitting areas, feature seamless white marble furniture and bedrooms with terrazzo-tiled floors. A wide range of facilities, include heated swimming pools, a gymnasium and riding. Alternatively, traditional ayurvedic massages, yoga and meditation are on hand for those who prefer something a little more reflective.

The restaurant at Devi Garh features authentic, home-cooked Asian cuisine and innovative continental dishes. Guests who choose not to leave the luxury of their room can make use of the 24-hour in-room dining facilities, but for something really special, one can dine in the other private venues available.

This spectacular heritage property, complemented by personalised and intimate service, creates a new image of India for the 21st century.

FACILITIES

Accommodation
30 SUITES

Recreational facilities
HEATED SWIMMING POOL
AYURVEDIC SPA
YOGA & MEDITATION
FITNESS CENTRE
SAUNA, JACUZZI & STEAM
BEAUTY PARLOUR
BICYCLE TRIPS
KITE FLYING
TREKKING
TABLE TENNIS & POOL TABLE
CROQUET & PUTTING GREENS
IN-HOUSE MUSEUM
SHOPPING ARCADE

Meeting facilities
MEETING ROOM FOR UP TO 50 PEOPLE

International Airports
UDAIPUR MAHARANA PRATAP AIRPORT (UDR)
40 MINUTES DRIVE AWAY

RESERVATIONS

Prices
SUITES FROM 350 EURO PER NIGHT

Credit cards
AE, DC, MC, V

GDS Reservation Codes
NONE

Yearly Closing Dates
NONE

CONTACT DETAILS

DEVI GARH
VILLAGE DELWARA, TEHSIL NATHDWARA
DISTRICT RAJSAMAND
RAJASTHAN
INDIA
TEL +91 2953 289211
FAX +91 2953 289357
DEVIGARH@DEVIRESORT.COM
WWW.DEVIRESORT.COM

OWNER: BOUTIQUE HOTELS INDIA LIMITED
GENERAL MANAGER: MR RAJNISH SABHARWAL
DIRECTOR OF SALES: MR B. VENKATESH

AFFILIATIONS

NONE

INDONESIA CRUISES
Ombak Putih

The luxury traditional wooden schooner, Ombak Putih, sets sail for the East of Bali islands for unforgettable getaways.

Sail to seas holding a wealth of treasures and secrets, all waiting to be discovered. Isolated island cultures, almost untouched by the passing of time, offer a glimpse of a unique and fascinating world while providing ample opportunities to collect artifacts and handicrafts unavailable elsewhere in the world. Your chance to discover the unspoiled beauty of the chain of volcanic islands East of Bali. In only one week, you will visit enchanting islands, swim around pristine beaches, explore traditional villages, snorkel above colorful coral gardens, and encounter the Jurassic Komodo dragons of Komodo.

Take your time and feel nature's rhythm. Laze in the shade of sails on your way to another adventure. Get up close to traditional cultures, smoldering volcanoes, tropical beaches, colorful coral reefs, and the famous Komodo dragon. Sail, dive, explore... Never forget!

FACILITIES

Accommodation
36 METER WOODEN SCHOONER,
12 DOUBLE CABINS

Recreational facilities
SAILING
DIVING
SNORKELLING
HIKING
CULTURAL VISITS OF EASTERN BALI ISLANDS
VISITS TO KOMODO NATIONAL PARK
LIBRARY
CHILDREN GAMES
MOVIES
LOUNGING DECKS

Meeting facilities
MEETING ROOM FOR UP TO 18 PEOPLE

International Airports
BALI DENPASAR INT'L AIRPORT (DPS)
15 MINUTES DRIVE AWAY

RESERVATIONS

Prices
7-DAY CRUISES PROGRAMS
FROM 1060 EURO PP
PRIVATE CHARTER PRICES
FROM 1975 EURO PER DAY

Credit cards
MC, V

GDS Reservation Codes
NONE

Yearly Closing Dates
FEBRUARY

CONTACT DETAILS

INDONESIA CRUISES
KUTA POLENG D-7
JL. SETIABUDI
KUTA, BALI, 80361
INDONESIA
TEL 62-361-766-269
FAX 62-361-766-546
INFO@INDONESIACRUISES.COM
WWW.INDONESIACRUISES.COM

OWNER: PT. OMBAK PUTIH
MANAGING DIRECTOR: MR GUIDO BRINK
MARKETING & BDM: MRS MARYSE LAROCQUE

AFFILIATIONS

PETER HUGHES DIVING

MAYA UBUD RESORT & SPA
Ubud

Perched majestically between the Petanu River valley and the rice terraces of Peliatan is a landmark of luxury and design: Maya Ubud Resort & Spa. An outstanding blend of form and function; unique in concept, scope and location. Within minutes from the heart of the bustling artist's village of Ubud, yet far away from the everyday world. Rooms and villas with all the comfort, facilities and conveniences you would expect.

Dining alternatives include, informal riverside dining or sophisticated a la carte European and Asian cuisine. Classical interpretations, as well as innovative fusion cooking.

Beside the swirling waters of the Petanu River, amidst the lushness of the rainforest, nestles the Spa at Maya. Private treatment pavilions provide an individual oasis in which refreshing and aromatic oils, sooth and relax. Enjoy light healthy cuisine in the adjacent River Café after a leisurely morning rice field walk, a village bicycle tour or in the after glow of a memorable massage.

FACILITIES

Accommodation
48 SUPERIOR & DELUXE ROOMS,
23 SUPERIOR GARDEN VILLAS,
34 DELUXE POOL VILLAS,
2 DUPLEX POOL VILLAS
& 1 PRESIDENTIAL VILLA

Recreational facilities
TENNIS COURT
YOGA
PITCH & PUTT GOLF GREEN
VILLAGE & COUNTRYSIDE TREKKING
MOUNTAIN BIKING
LIBRARY & INTERNET SERVICE
2 SWIMMING POOLS
CHILDREN'S POOL
RIVERSIDE SPA

Meeting facilities
MEETING ROOM FOR UP TO 60 PEOPLE

International Airports
BALI DENPASAR INT'L AIRPORT (DPS)
50 MINUTES DRIVE AWAY

RESERVATIONS

Prices
ROOMS FROM 200 EURO PER NIGHT
VILLAS FROM 300 EURO PER NIGHT

Credit cards
AE, DC, MC, V

GDS Reservation Codes
NONE

Yearly Closing Dates
NONE

CONTACT DETAILS

MAYA UBUD RESORT & SPA
JL. GUNUNG SARI PELIATAN
PO BOX 1001, UBUD
BALI 80571
INDONESIA
TEL +62 361 977 888
FAX +62 361 977 555
INFO@MAYAUBUD.COM
WWW.MAYAUBUD.COM

OWNER: CLASSIFIED
GENERAL MANAGER: MR PAUL A. BLAKE
DIRECTOR OF SALES: MR TAUFIK JUNIANTO

AFFILIATIONS
NONE

PURI WULANDARI

Ubud

Each Puri Wulandari private villa nestles on a series of steep downhill embankments with breathtaking views over the Ayung River. They feature elegant furnishings and artefacts in reverence to the surrounding natural beauty. Thatched grass roofs, traditional Balinese doors, and the sweet smell of fresh tropical flowers welcome you to your open aired luxurious living with your own private swimming pool. A traditional bale bengong lies beside the pool, perfect to relish the surrounding views or just relax in quiet while contemplating the refined butler services.

The Lila Ulangun Spa facility offers a wide range of customized therapeutic treatments using traditional natural healing remedies passed down from old generations of Balinese healers. Equally available are Jacuzzis, a sauna and traditional outdoor showers, boasting views of the surrounding rice paddies.

Puri Wulandari furthermore offers its guests a choice of two fine 'global fusion' dining establishments using only the freshest of ingredients.

FACILITIES

Accommodation
34 LUXURY VILLAS

Recreational facilities
PRIVATE SWIMMING POOL
INFINITY SWIMMING POOL
SPA & BEAUTY CENTRE
MEDITATION & REIKI SERVICES
JOGGING TRACK
GALLERY & LIBRARY
GAME ROOM
GOLF COURSE nearby
RAFTING & BIKING nearby

Meeting facilities
NONE

International Airports
BALI DENPASAR INT'L AIRPORT (DPS)
50 MINUTES DRIVE AWAY

RESERVATIONS

Prices
VILLAS FROM 430 EURO PER NIGHT

Credit cards
MC,V

GDS Reservation Codes
AMADEUS LX DPSPUR
GALILEO LX 30091
SABRE LX 55136
WORLDSPAN LX DPSPW

Yearly Closing Dates
NONE

CONTACT DETAILS

PURI WULANDARI
DS. KEDEWATAN
UBUD
BALI
INDONESIA
TEL +62 361 980 252
FAX +62 361 980 253
RESERVATION@PURIWULANDARI.NET
WWW.PURIWULANDARI.NET

OWNER: MR RUDY NOORYALDIE
DIRECTOR: MS RAE WOELANDARI

AFFILIATIONS

THE BALÉ
Bali

The Balé is an intimate boutique resort in modern minimalist yet elegant attitude, perched on Nusa Dua's breezy hill overlooking the Indian Ocean

The Balé boasts 20 stylish luxury pavilions featuring private pool, charming relaxation day beds and luxury bedroom with candlelit bathroom offering indoor & outdoor shower in secluded garden

Faces, the gourmet restaurant by the main pool, serves balanced menu with exquisite light contemporary cuisine, rich in detail & flavor. The Bar is complemented by a casual Lounge: a perfect place to relax with a pre-dinner drink or late night cocktail

The Sanctuary Spa offers pampering treatments by using natural products in stylish rooms with private sauna and Jacuzzi surrounded by garden & water features. It also encompasses gym and Bliss Restaurant, which offers a wide range of healthy spa cuisine using organic produce.

The Balé is an absolute sanctuary to rejuvenate your body, expand your mind and spend quality time with partner

FACILITIES

Accommodation
20 PAVILIONS WITH PRIVATE POOL

Recreational facilities
SWIMMING POOL
SPA
BEACH CLUB
GYMNASIUM
MOUNTAIN HIKING
CRUISES
WATER SPORTS
LIBRARY WITH INTERNET ACCESS
BOUTIQUE

Meeting facilities
MEETING ROOM FOR UP TO 16 PEOPLE

International Airports
BALI DENPASAR INT'L AIRPORT (DPS)
20 MINUTES DRIVE AWAY

RESERVATIONS

Prices
SINGLE PAVILION FROM 400 EURO PER NIGHT
DOUBLE PAVILION FROM 665 EURO PER NIGHT

Credit cards
AE, DC, MC, V

GDS Reservation Codes
AMADEUS LX DPSTBR
GALILEO LX 27467
SABRE LX 27467
WORLDSPAN LX DPSTB

Yearly Closing Dates
NONE

CONTACT DETAILS

THE BALÉ
JL. RAYA NUSA DUA SELATAN
PO BOX 76
NUSA DUA 80363 BALI
INDONESIA
TEL +62 361 775 111
FAX +62 361 775 222
BLISS@THEBALE.COM
WWW.SANCTUARYRESORTS.COM

OWNERS: KIKI SUHERLAN & DAVID AGUSTINO
GENERAL MANAGER: MR JOSE LUIS CALLE
DIRECTOR OF SALES: MR AGUS SUARDANA

AFFILIATIONS

THE PRIVATE COLLECTION

THE LEGIAN BALI
Bali

Set in landscaped tropical gardens with unrivalled views of the Indian Ocean and Seminyak Beach, the exclusive all-suite The Legian Bali is a unique and relaxing hideaway to experience the magical island of Bali.

Decorated in rich woods and cool marble, each suite is designed with comfortable living and dining areas and a spacious bedroom that soothe the senses. From the balcony, take in an endless view of the magnificent ocean while a split-level swimming pool bridges the pool bar and the boutique in the gardens.

The neighbouring Club at The Legian offers the ultimate in holiday luxury with a choice of 10 one-bedroom villas and 1 three-bedroom villa, in individual compounds, each with a private 10-metre swimming pool and butler service. Guests can also enjoy the facilities of The Club Lounge with its own 35-metre lap pool, offering breakfasts, lunches, dinners and cocktails to villa guests.

FACILITIES

Accommodation
67 SUITES & 11 POOL VILLAS

Recreational facilities
SWIMMING POOL
SPA, YOGA
GYMNASIUM
WHITE SAND BEACH
JOGGING
LIBRARY
BOUTIQUE
POOL BAR
RESTAURANT
GOLF COURSE NEARBY
TENNIS COURT NEARBY

Meeting facilities
2 MEETING ROOMS FOR UP TO 50 PEOPLE

International Airports
BALI DENPASAR INTERN'L AIRPORT (DPS)
20 MINUTES DRIVE AWAY

RESERVATIONS

Prices
SUITES FROM 300 EURO PER NIGHT
POOL VILLAS FROM 700 EURO PER NIGHT

Credit cards
AE, DC, MC, V

GDS Reservation Codes
AMADEUS LW DPS897
GALILEO LW 25642
SABRE LW 23451
WORLDSPAN LW 1897

Yearly Closing Dates
NONE

CONTACT DETAILS

THE LEGIAN BALI
JALAN LAKSMANA
SEMINYAK BEACH
BALI 80361
INDONESIA
TEL +62 361 730 622
FAX +62 561 730 623
LEGIAN@GHMHOTELS.COM
WWW.GHMHOTELS.COM

OWNER: CLASSIFIED
GENERAL MANAGER: MR HANSJÖRG MEIER
DIRECTOR OF SALES: MR YANI WONGSOWINOTO

AFFILIATIONS

The Leading Small Hotels
of the World

a member of
design hotels

A STYLE TO REMEMBER

CHIVA-SOM LUXURY HEALTH RESORT

Hua Hin

Chiva-Som which in Thai means 'Heaven of Life', is a pioneer in combining traditional Asian therapies with western health and wellness. The luxury health resort is set in 7 acres of secluded landscaped gardens, located in Hua Hin on the Gulf of Thailand.

Chiva-Som remains unique in its dedication to total wellness, as evidence by its comprehensive and extensive services ranging from nurturing spa to high-tech medical and the world-class calibre of its practitioners and therapists. Grounded firmly in belief that it is the combined health of the mind, body and spirit that leads to personal fulfilment, Chiva-Som is truly holistic in approach.

A highlight of any stay at Chiva-Som is the delicious cuisine. With many of the ingredients grown in the resort's own organic gardens, the plentiful, low-calorie nutritious food has received international acclaim for its creativity and flavour. Chiva-Som has been recently voted World's Best Destination Spa 2004 by Condé Nast Traveller UK readers.

FACILITIES

Accommodation
33 ROOMS, 7 SUITES
AND 17 THAI PAVILIONS

Recreational facilities
120 HOLISTIC MEDICAL HEALTH PROGRAMMES
INCLUDING
NATUROPATHY, STRESS MANAGEMENT,
ACCUPRESSURE, WEIGHT MANAGEMENT,
HERBALIST, MEDITATION AND MANY MORE
42 TREATMENT ROOMS
SPA & FITNESS CENTRE
PILATES STUDIO
INDOOR SWIMMING POOL
OUTDOOR SWIMMING POOL
2 SPA CUISINE RESTAURANTS
COOKING CLASS

Meeting facilities
NONE

International Airports
BANGKOK INTERNATIONAL AIRPORT (BKK)
150 MINUTES DRIVE AWAY
30 MINUTES FLIGHT AWAY

RESERVATIONS

Prices
ROOMS FROM 300 EURO PP PER NIGHT

Credit cards
AE, DC, MC, V

GDS Reservation Codes
AMADEUS LX HHQCHI
GALILEO LX 92692
SABRE LX 19678
WORLDSPAN LX HHQCH

Yearly Closing Dates
NONE

CONTACT DETAILS

CHIVA-SOM LUXURY HEALTH RESORT
73/4 PETCHKASEM ROAD
HUA HIN
PRACHUAB KHIRIKHAN 77110
THAILAND
TEL +66 32 536 536
FAX +66 32 511 154
RESERV@CHIVASOM.COM
WWW.CHIVASOM.COM

OWNER: KHUN BOONCHU ROJANASTIEN
GENERAL MANAGER: MS JOY MENZIES
DIRECTOR OF SALES: MS CHRISTINE GALLE

AFFILIATIONS

EVASON HIDEAWAY HUA HIN & SIX SENSES SPA

Pranburi

Attention to detail and focus on the reality of the destination is the driving force of Evason Hideaway Hua Hin, together with a focused commitment to environment.

Each romantic villa is surrounded by a stone wall for privacy and has its own private pool, outdoor bath, indoor and outdoor showers and beautifully landscaped garden, offering both spacious and luxurious living conditions.

The open air dining experience itself is romantic, private and unique at the resort. Private sunrise breakfast in the living room of the cosy villa, desert beach picnic or lunch al fresco at the Chef's own herb and vegetable garden - the settings are as memorable as the cuisine.

The luxuriously appointed Six Senses Spa presents creative décor and top standards in spa design for an unforgettable experience. Guests may choose to have treatments in the treatments rooms, within the air-conditioned villa or in the poolside sala.

FACILITIES

Accommodation
55 VILLAS

Recreational facilities
SIX SENSES SPA
WATER SPORTS
BAR & RESTAURANT
WINE CELLAR
BOUTIQUE
LIBRARY WITH INTERNET ACCESS

Meeting facilities
NONE

International Airports
BANGKOK INTERNATIONAL AIRPORT (BKK)
180 MINUTES DRIVE AWAY

RESERVATIONS

Prices
ROOMS FROM 255 EURO PER NIGHT

Credit cards
AE, DC, MC, V

GDS Reservation Codes
AMADEUS LX HHQEHS
GALILEO LX 13880
SABRE LX 62071
WORLDSPAN LX HHQEH

Yearly Closing Dates
NONE

CONTACT DETAILS

EVASON HIDEAWAY HUA HIN & SIX SENSES SPA
9 PAKNAMPARN BEACH
PRACHUAB KHIRI KHAN 77120
THAILAND
TEL +66 32 632 111
FAX +66 32 632 112
RESERVATIONS-HUAHIN@EVASONHIDEAWAYS.COM
WWW.SIXSENSES.COM

OWNER: CLASSIFIED
GENERAL MANAGER: MR CHRISTOPHER OAKES
DIRECTOR OF SALES: MR BJORN COURAGE

AFFILIATIONS

THE EVASON HUA HIN POOL VILLAS

Hua Hin

The Evason Hua Hin Resort and Spa is located at Pranburi approximately 30 kilometres south of Hua Hin and 230 kilometres from Bangkok. It is set amongst 20 acres of beautifully landscaped tropical gardens filled with lotus ponds and waterways, facing the Gulf of Siam.

The Evason Hua Hin Resort and Spa embodies the Evason philosophy of redifining experiences, and as such presents a refreshing reinterpretation of a five star resort designed to appeal to today's more sophisticated travellers.

The luxurious accommodations are spread out within separate low-rise buildings in a tropical garden setting, complemented by 40 oversized stand-alone private Evason Pool Villas. The villas are the first of their kind in Hua Hin. Each villa is secluded by a wall for privacy and has its own private plunge pool, plus an outdoor bathtub in a rustic garden setting surrounded by a lotus pond. A totally new approach to materials, finishes and colours contribute to a refreshing new holiday experience.

Evason service standards ensure great attention to detail and a welcoming and friendly atmosphere. It is the delivery of the service that differentiates The Evason approach from other top resorts.

FACILITIES

Accommodation
185 ROOMS, INCLUDING 40 POOL VILLAS

Recreational facilities
SIX SENSES SPA
WATER SPORTS
TENNIS COURT
SWIMMING POOL
LIBRARY WITH INTERNET ACCESS
RESTAURANTS & BAR
EXCURSIONS
GOLF COURSES NEARBY

Meeting facilities
3 MEETING ROOMS FOR UP TO 250 PERSONS

International Airports
BANGKOK INTERNATIONAL AIRPORT (BKK)
180 MINUTES DRIVE AWAY

RESERVATIONS

Prices
ROOMS FROM 78 EURO PER NIGHT
POOL VILLAS FROM 212 EURO PER NIGHT

Credit cards
AE, DC, MC, V

GDS Reservation Codes
AMADEUS UZ HHQ144
GALILEO UZ 71221
SABRE UZ 55748
WORLDSPAN UZ 6144

Yearly Closing Dates
NONE

CONTACT DETAILS

THE EVASON HUA HIN POOL VILLAS
9 PAKNAMPARN BEACH
PRACHUAB KHIRI KHAN 77120
THAILAND
TEL +66 32 632 111
FAX +66 32 632 112
RESERVATIONS-HUAHIN@EVASONRESORTS.COM
WWW.SIXSENSES.COM

OWNER: CLASSIFIED
GENERAL MANAGER: MR CHRISTOPHER OAKES
DIRECTOR OF SALES: MR BJORN COURAGE

AFFILIATIONS
NONE

THE EVASON PHUKET POOL VILLAS
Phuket

The Evason Phuket Resort and Spa is ideally located on the Rawai Beach on the south eastern side of Phuket Island. The property is nestled amongst 64 acres of beautifully landscaped tropical gardens, facing the Andaman Sea.

The resort embodies the Evason philosophy of redefining experiences, and as such presents a refreshing reinterpretation of a five star resort designed to appeal to today's more sophisticated travellers.

A part of its fresh and unconventionally designed rooms and suites, The Evason Phuket Resort & Spa features also deluxe Evason Pool Villas. Each of the villas boasts a minimum of 110 square metres of pure indulgence consisting of a private plunge pool and garden, open style bathroom, floating outdoor bathtub in the lotus pond, semi-outdoor separate shower and all amenities that can be expected from a five star resort.

Evason service standards ensure great attention to detail and a welcoming and friendly atmosphere. It is the delivery of the service that differentiates The Evason approach from other top resorts.

FACILITIES

Accommodation
260 ROOMS, INCLUDING 7 POOL VILLAS & 21 POOL SUITES

Recreational facilities
SIX SENSES SPA
3 SWIMMING POOLS
TENNIS COURTS
WATER SPORTS
DIVE SCHOOL
EXCURSIONS
LIBRARY WITH INTERNET ACCESS
PRIVATE ISLAND FOR BEACH
RESTAURANTS & BARS
WINE CELLAR

Meeting facilities
5 MEETING ROOMS FOR UP TO 430 PEOPLE

International Airports
PHUKET INTERNATIONAL AIRPORT (HKT)
45 MINUTES DRIVE AWAY

RESERVATIONS

Prices
ROOMS FROM 90 EURO PER NIGHT
POOL VILLAS FROM 440 EURO PER NIGHT

Credit cards
AE, DC, MC, V

GDS Reservation Codes
AMADEUS UZ HKTEPH
GALILEO UZ 71206
SABRE UZ 55147
WORLDSPAN UZ 6143

Yearly Closing Dates
NONE

CONTACT DETAILS
THE EVASON PHUKET RESORT POOL VILLAS
100 VISED ROAD
RAWAI
MUANG DISTRICT
PHUKET 83100
THAILAND
TEL +66 76 381010
FAX +66 76 381018
RESERVATIONS-PHUKET@EVASONRESORTS.COM
WWW.SIXSENSES.COM

OWNER: CLASSIFIED
GENERAL MANAGER: MR ALASDAIR JUNOR
DIRECTOR OF SALES: MR GREG SEDDON

AFFILIATIONS
NONE

SILA EVASON HIDEAWAY & SPA

Samui

The 66 uniquely designed villas are nestled on the northern tip of Samui Island amongst natural vegetation around a sloping headland offering unsurpassed panoramic sea views.

Most of the villas have a private pool and all the villas feature a sun deck with sun loungers and an open-style bathroom, which creates an atmosphere of space and light in the room maintaining superb views of the surrounding sea and islands from almost every location in the villa.

The stunning restaurant located close to the wine cellar offers tasteful Thai and modern Mediterranean Cuisines, along with other popular dishes, which guarantees the best culinary experience on Koh Samui. After having enjoyed relaxing treatments in the Spa, guests can contemplate the fantastic sunsets from the elegant bar that serves a fine selection of frozen margueritas and cocktails, beers and wines, while the wine cellar boasts labels from many of the world's most respected regions.

FACILITIES

Accommodation
66 VILLAS

Recreational facilities
INFINITY SWIMMING POOL
SPA
SAUNA
STEAM ROOMS
GYMNASIUM
NON-MOTORIZED WATER SPORTS
POOL BAR & RESTAURANT
WINE CELLAR
BOUTIQUE

Meeting facilities
MEETING ROOM FOR UP TO 16 PEOPLE

International Airports
BANGKOK INTERNATIONAL AIRPORT (BKK)
60 MINUTES FLIGHT AWAY
KOH SAMUI AIRPORT (USM)
10 MINUTES DRIVE AWAY

RESERVATIONS

Prices
ROOMS FROM 273 EURO PER NIGHT

Credit cards
AE, DC, MC, V

GDS Reservation Codes
AMADEUS LX USMEHR
GALILEO LX 13874
SABRE LX 62049
WORLDSPAN LX USMEH

Yearly Closing Dates
NONE

CONTACT DETAILS

SILA EVASON HIDEAWAY
9/10 MOO5 – BAAN PLAI LAEM BOPHUT
KOH SAMUI SURATTHANI 84320
THAILAND
TEL +66 77 245678
FAX +66 77 245671
RESERVATIONS-SAMUI@EVASONHIDEAWAYS.COM
WWW.SIXSENSES.COM

OWNER: CLASSIFIED
DIRECTOR OF SALES: MR BJORN COURAGE

AFFILIATIONS

THE PRIVATE COLLECTION

EVASON ANA MANDARA RESORT & SPA

Nha Trang

Ana Mandara means "beautiful home for the guests". Reminiscent of an old Vietnamese village, and furnished with native woods and rattan, the Resort reflects the real image of Vietnam, with its warm hospitality, rice culture and unique tastes.

The Ana Mandara Resort comprises of 17 villas containing 74 well-appointed guest rooms. Rooms are either situated in the plush tropical gardens or with spectacular views of Nha Trang Bay. All rooms have their own private terrace along with all amenities and comforts of a five star resort.

Located directly on the beach off the most famous thoroughfare, Tran Phu Boulevard, the resort rests comfortably on 26,000 square metres of private tropical gardens overlooking the sea. The delicate blend of graceful architecture and gracious service, peaceful atmosphere and captivating scenery, Ana Mandara offers a unique experience in simplicity, serenity and refinement. It is an escape to paradise.

FACILITIES

Accommodation
74 Rooms

Recreational facilities
Six Senses Spa
2 Swimming Pools
Tennis Courts
Volleyball
Dive School
Water Sports
Excursions
Library with Internet Access
Bars & Restaurants
Wine Cellar

Meeting facilities
Meeting Room for up to 35 people

International Airports
Ton San Nhat Int'l Airport (SGN)
50 minutes flight away
Cam Ranh Int'l Airport (CXR)
40 minutes drive away

RESERVATIONS

Prices
Rooms from 170 Euro per night

Credit cards
AE, DC, MC, V

GDS Reservation Codes
Amadeus DS NHA606
Galileo DS 31539
Sabre DS 56173
Worldspan DS 07606

Yearly Closing Dates
None

CONTACT DETAILS

Evason Ana Mandara Resort & Spa
Beachside Tran Phu Blvd,
Nha Trang
Vietnam
Tel + 8458 829829
Fax +8458 829629
Reservations-anamandara@
evasonresorts.com
www.sixsenses.com

Owner: Classified
Area General Manager: Mr TJ Grundl-Hong
Area Sales Manager: Ms Do Thi Thu

AFFILIATIONS

a member of
design hotels

EVASON HIDEAWAY AT ANA MANDARA

Nha Trang

The site of Evason Hideaway at Ana Mandara on dramatic Ninh Van Bay is quite unique, taking full advantage of the setting. Impressive rocks formations, the coral reef, white sand beach, a playful stream and the towering mountains behind; all add to the sense of being luxuriously at one with nature.

The resort also presents the true essence of the destination, with an architectural style reflecting the traditions of Vietnam. The tastefully appointed villas have inspired touches like sun decks and plunge pools, as well as unusual additions such as wine cellars.

The hotel's intimate restaurant serves an 'East meets West' menu whith fusion specialities. Blending with rocks beside a gentle waterfall, the Six Senses Spa provides signature treatments together with individual rejuvenation specialities of the region and the international therapists.

FACILITIES

Accommodation
54 VILLAS

Recreational facilities
SWIMMING POOL
SIX SENSES SPA
FITNESS CENTRE
DIVE CENTRE
WATER SPORTS
TENNIS
HIKING & MOUNTAIN BIKING
BAR & RESTAURANT
WINE CELLAR

Meeting facilities
NONE

International Airports
TON SAN NHAT INT'L AIRPORT (SGN)
50 MINUTES FLIGHT AWAY &
20 MINUTES BY SPEEDBOAT
CAM RANH INT'L AIRPORT (CXR)
40 MINUTES DRIVE AWAY
20 MINUTES BY SPEEDBOAT

RESERVATIONS

Prices
ROOMS FROM 332 EURO PER NIGHT

Credit cards
AE, DC, MC, V

GDS Reservation Codes
AMADEUS LX NHAEHS
GALILEO LX 13864
SABRE LX 62024
WORLDSPAN LX NHAEH

Yearly Closing Dates
NONE

CONTACT DETAILS

EVASON HIDEAWAY AT ANA MANDARA
C/O ANA MANDARA RESORT
BEACHSIDE TRAN PHU BLVD,
NHA TRANG
VIETNAM
TEL + 8458 524702
FAX +8458 524701
RESERVATIONS-VIETNAM@
EVASONHIDEAWAYS.COM
WWW.SIXSENSES.COM

OWNER: CLASSIFIED
AREA GENERAL MANAGER: MR TJ GRUNDL-HONG
AREA SALES MANAGER: MS DO THI THU

AFFILIATIONS

THE PRIVATE COLLECTION

DOLPHIN ISLAND
Viti Levu

Dolphin Island is an 8-acre private retreat sitting just off the north-east coast of Viti Levu and is a 10-minute boat journey from shore. It is designed to offer total peace, quiet and privacy for a maximum of just four guests.

There are only two dwellings on the island, both built utilising elements of traditional Fijian architecture and design. The two air-conditioned bures are elevated and enclosed by wide spacious verandas and they catch the sea breezes while facing the spectacular tropical sunsets. One bure has been created for dining, relaxing and entertaining whilst the adjacent bure contains two double suites with their own bathrooms.

Aquatic adventure is one of Fiji's great highlights and the crystal clear waters and coral reefs are a haven for extraordinary marine life. Snorkelling equipment, kayaks and a Hobie catamaran are all available for guest use within the tariff. You can walk around the entire edge of the island at low tide, looking at the reef life and remains of ancient Fijian fishing pools.

FACILITIES

Accommodation
2 LUXURY SUITES

Recreational facilities
PRIVATE BEACHES
DEEP SEA FISHING
SNORKELLING
WINDSURFING
BOATING
SAILING
DIVING

Meeting facilities
NONE

International Airports
NADI INTERNATIONAL AIRPORT (NAN)
120 MINUTES DRIVE AWAY

RESERVATIONS

Prices
SUITES FROM 1,500 EURO PER COUPLE PER NIGHT

Credit cards
AE, MC, V

GDS Reservation Codes
NONE

Yearly Closing Dates
NONE

CONTACT DETAILS

DOLPHIN ISLAND
P.O. BOX 369
RAKI RAKI
FIJI
TEL +679 6694 699
FAX +679 6694 699
RESERVATIONS@HUKALODGE.CO.NZ
WWW.DOLPHINISLANDFIJI.COM

OWNER: MR ALEX VAN HEEREN
GENERAL MANAGER: MR CO ENGELS

AFFILIATIONS
NONE

HUKA LODGE

Taupo

In the 1920s, a young Irishman, Alan Pye, heard word of an angler's paradise in Taupo. Built on the banks of the Waikato River, Huka Lodge soon established a reputation for fine food and hospitality amidst great natural beauty and tranquility. In 1984, Alex van Heeren purchased Huka Lodge. His resources and passion have added luxury to location, creating one of the world's most famous retreats.

Huka Lodge is set in seven hectares of park-like grounds and has just twenty guest suites. These are all tucked along the riverbank for privacy and nestled amongst the trees. The suites offer every comfort and are light, spacious and very peaceful.

Within the Lodge grounds you can take a leisurely stroll in the gardens or soak in our own hot pool, enjoy a game of tennis on the all-weather court or try a relaxing game of petanque.

The 'Condé Nast Traveller' Annual Readers' Travel Awards 2002 ranked Huka Lodge No.1 in the Overseas Leisure Hotels, Australasia & The South Pacific. Huka Lodge was also ranked No.4 out of 100 in the 'Best of the Best'.

FACILITIES

Accommodation
20 LUXURY SUITES

Recreational facilities
FLY FISHING
HIKING & BIKING
TENNIS
GOLF
RAFTING
BOATING
HORSE RIDING
HEATED SWIMMING POOL
2 SPA POOLS
HELIPAD

Meeting facilities
MEETING ROOM FOR UP TO 40 PEOPLE

International Airports
AUCKLAND INTERNATIONAL AIRPORT (AKL)
30 MINUTES FLIGHT AWAY
180 MINUTES DRIVE AWAY

RESERVATIONS

Prices
SUITES FROM 300 EURO PER PERSON PER NIGHT

Credit cards
AE, MC, V

GDS Reservation Codes
AMADEUS LX TUOLAK
GALILEO LX 67462
SABRE LX 22743
WORLDSPAN LX TUOLT

Yearly Closing Dates
NONE

CONTACT DETAILS

HUKA LODGE
271 HUKA FALLS ROAD
TAUPO
NEW ZEALAND
TEL +64 7 378 5791
FAX +64 7 378 0427
RESERVATIONS@HUKALODGE.CO.NZ
WWW.HUKALODGE.COM

OWNER: MR ALEX VAN HEEREN
GENERAL MANAGER: MR CO ENGELS

AFFILIATIONS

The Leading Small Hotels
of the World

PREFERRED TRAVEL PARTNERS
Providing Travel Excellence

There are many ways to organise one's travel plans throughout the world these days. Travel information and reservation possibilities are numerous and easily accessible through travel agencies, the Internet and even through travel channels on television. It only takes a phone call or a click on the mouse to book a flight, reserve a room or rent a car.

Luxury travel in the true sense of the word, however, requires much more than that. When one only has limited time to enjoy holidays and/or seeks to escape the every day life hustle and bustle in search for some enjoyable quality in life, travel gets a totally different definition. Travel no longer means getting from A to B or staying at hotel Z. Luxury travel requires a totally different approach and is based on such ingredients as: hasslefree, comfort, reliability, personalisation, service and discretion.

At XO, we've just started our search for specialist operators around the world which stand out for their commitment to providing travel excellence. On the following pages, please find a selection of Preferred Travel Partners which rank among the very best in their respective fields.

ALL OF THE FEATURED PREFERRED TRAVEL PARTNERS OFFER TAILORMADE SERVICES FOR THE MOST DISCERNING OF LEISURE TRAVELLERS.

HOWEVER, THEY ALSO OFFER AN EXTENSIVE RANGE OF POSSIBILITIES FOR CORPORATE MEETINGS AND INCENTIVES.

FOR A MORE EXTENSIVE LIST OF OPERATORS WORLDWIDE, PLEASE VISIT US AT WWW.XOPRIVATE.COM

ELITE LIMOUSINE

When travelling for business or leisure, a successful journey always requires timetables to be met and schedules arranged that suit needs and plans. When a booked vehicle fails to turn up on time or when service standards are below what you expect, travelling can quickly become frustrating, stressful and very expensive!

Elite Limousine provides a chauffeur drive service unparalleled in its quality and attention to detail with drivers that understand and appreciate the need for high quality customer service. The Elite Limousine chauffeurs, all uniformed, are trained to exacting driving and safety standards and deliver a personal but discreet service.

Elite Limousine is an official representative of Carey Worldwide Chauffeured Services. Operating as Carey Switzerland, Elite Limousine provides its customers instant access to a global network covering 480 cities in 75 countries.

Excellence in Motion.

ZURICH • GENEVA • MONTREUX • PARIS • CANNES • NICE • MONACO • MUNICH • MILAN • ROME • MOSCOW

PROFILE
Fleet
ELITE LIMOUSINE IS A BRAND OF ELITE RENT-A-CAR AND OFFERS CHAUFFEUR SERVICE THROUGHT 480 CITIES IN 75 COUNTRIES.

EXECUTIVE SALOONS, STRETCH LIMOUSINES, LUXURY 4 WHEEL-DRIVE OR MINIVANS ARE JUST SOME OF THE PRESTIGIOUS VEHICLES AVAILABLE THROUGH ELITE LIMOUSINE.

Reservations
ELITE LIMOUSINE HAS PREFERRED AGENTS AND AN EXTENSIVE NETWORK OF OFFICES THROUGHOUT THE WORLD. FOR THE AGENT NEAREST TO YOU, PLEASE CONTACT ELITE RENT-A-CAR.

CONTACT DETAILS
ELITE RENT-A-CAR, LIMOUSINE SERVICE 51, RUE DE PÂQUIS CH-1201 GENEVA SWITZERLAND
TEL +41 (0)22 909 89 90
FAX +41 (0)22 901 06 09
ELITELIMOUSINE@ELITERENT.COM
WWW.ELITERENT.COM

PRESIDENT: MRS GRAZIELLA ZANOLETTI
COO: MR MORENO PATTHEY

CAREY Switzerland
Worldwide Chauffeured Services

ELITE RENT-A-CAR

Indulge yourself in driving some of the world's most exceptional cars. Ranging from sports cars over elegant convertibles and luxurious limousines to powerful 4x4's, Elite Rent A Car boasts the largest and most diverse fleet of luxury cars in Europe.

Whether adding that extra touch to your private holiday or making that business trip more enjoyable and comfortable, Elite Rent A Car offers you a personalized service that is second to none. Delivery and collection of your car at the airport, hotel or even at your private residence come standard in Elite Rent A Car's extensive range of services for its valued customers.

Elite Rent A Car has developed an extensive network of offices all over Europe and beyond to ensure that customers can always rely on its professional team whenever and wherever they wish to travel.

Emotions in Motion.

ZURICH • GENEVA • MONTREUX • PARIS • CANNES • NICE • MONACO • MUNICH • MILAN • ROME • MOSCOW

PROFILE

Fleet

ELITE RENT A CAR OFFERS A FLEET OF 500 LUXURY CARS THROUGHOUT EUROPE.

MASERATI, JAGUAR, FERRARI, ASTON MARTIN, LAMBORGHINI, BENTLEY, PORSCHE, LOTUS, BMW, MERCEDES-BENZ, RANGE ROVER, AUDI AND MINI COOPER ARE JUST SOME OF THE LUXURY CARS AVAILABLE THROUGH ELITE RENT A CAR.

Reservations

ELITE RENT A CAR HAS PREFERRED AGENTS AND AN EXTENSIVE NETWORK OF OFFICES THROUGHOUT THE WORLD. FOR THE AGENT NEAREST TO YOU, PLEASE CONTACT ELITE RENT A CAR.

CONTACT DETAILS

ELITE RENT A CAR
51, RUE DE PÂQUIS
CH-1201 GENEVA
SWITZERLAND
TEL +41 (0)22 909 87 87
FAX +41 (0)22 731 90 87
BOOKING@ELITERENT.COM
WWW.ELITERENT.COM

OWNER: MRS GRAZIELLA ZANOLETTI
CEO: MRS GRAZIELLA ZANOLETTI

PROAIR

Book cloud number nine

ProAir lands you closer to your final destination than larger airlines normally can. Imagine your car awaiting you just a few steps away from the terminal, no tedious immigration procedures, no queuing in public areas. No time wasted at all. With ProAir, you arrive and take off swiftly in the greatest possible comfort whilst the private crew takes care of your personal luggage.

One highlight in ProAir's portfolio of aircrafts is the Boeing Business Jet where you can enjoy two main cabins, each boasting seating for up to 12 persons and featuring only the finest of creature comforts: Connolly hide leather seating, large sofas covered in luxurious fabrics, tables finished in walnut, soft lamps and an elegantly appointed bedroom with lavish en-suite facilities. It is clear that this interior is more generous than anything found in the best first class airlines and could easily compete with the finest boutique hotels.

Whether your requirements are simple or complex, whether you prefer to fly a helicopter, a turboprop or a jet such as a Gulfstream, Falcon or Challenger, be assured that ProAir's team of professionals understands your needs and takes great pride in fulfilling them. Enjoy the safe and private surrounding, fine tailor-made catering and first class service that comes standard at ProAir.

PROFILE

Fleet

PROAIR OFFERS A LARGE FLEET OF BUSINESS JETS (FALCON, BOMBARDIER, GULFSTREAM, ETC.) OR EXECUTIVE AIRLINERS (BOEING BUSINESS JET, AIRBUS CORPORATE JETLINER, ETC.) WORLDWIDE.

BUSINESS CHARTER SERVICE
AIRCRAFT MANAGEMENT & SALES
INCENTIVE SERVICE

BRANCH OFFICE AT CANNES MANDELIEU AIRPORT, CÔTE D'AZUR (FRANCE)

Reservations

FOR SPECIFIC REQUESTS, RESERVATIONS AND/OR FURTHER INFORMATION ON THE WIDE RANGE OF SERVICES PROVIDED, PLEASE CONTACT PROAIR.

24H-HOTLINE: +49 (0)711 70839-0

CONTACT DETAILS

PROAIR-CHARTER-TRANSPORT GMBH
ECHTERDINGER STRASSE 111
D-70794 FILDERSTADT
GERMANY
TEL +49 (0)711 70839-0
FAX +49 (0)711 70839-11
CHARTER@PROAIR.DE
WWW.PROAIR.DE

MANAGING DIRECTOR: MR THOMAS GODAU
MANAGING DIRECTOR: MR ELMAR MONREAL

SEA CLOUD CRUISES

On the world's oceans as well as on Europe's waterways, Sea Cloud Cruises makes dreams come true. Historic towns, picturesque scenery, exotic beaches and many other highlights provide an ideal contrast to delightful relaxing hours and days on the water. Exclusive shore excursions guarantee memorable experiences.

Whether on the legendary ship Sea Cloud and her sister Sea Cloud II or the river vessels River Cloud and River Cloud II, you can be assured to enjoy the ultimate in personalized travel.

What began in 1979 with the legendary private yacht Sea Cloud has been consistently refined over the years. Today guests can reach the most exciting destinations in Europe and the Caribbean aboard these elegant and intimate vessels. They provide a relaxed yet tasteful atmosphere in which to sample the culinary delights of innovative chefs. Welcome to Sea Cloud Cruises.

PROFILE
Fleet
SEA CLOUD CRUISES BOASTS A FLEET OF 4 VESSELS: SEA CLOUD (32 CABINS), SEA CLOUD II (47 CABINS), RIVER CLOUD (45 CABINS) AND RIVER CLOUD II (44 CABINS).

THE SEA CLOUD VESSELS ARE SAILING SHIPS WHILST THE RIVER CLOUD VESSELS ARE RIVER CRUISE VESSELS.

Reservations
PROGRAMS AVAILABLE UPON REQUEST

CONTACT DETAILS
SEA CLOUD CRUISES GMBH
BALLINDAMM 17
D-20095 HAMBURG
GERMANY
TEL +49 (0)40 30 95 920
FAX +49 (0)40 30 95 92 22
INFO@SEACLOUD.COM
WWW.SEACLOUD.COM

REPRESENTATIVE OF OWNERS: SEA CLOUD CRUISES GMBH
GENERAL MANAGER: MR CHRISTER MÖRN
VP INT'L MARKETING & SALES: MRS ANJA RINGEL

SUNSEEKER CHARTERS

The chauffeur-driven Bentley is waiting outside your front door, the executive plane is standing by. You're about to be magicked away to some beautiful corner of the Mediterranean to glide elegantly across turquoise seas with not a care in the world.

A holiday with so much of you in mind that the moment you step aboard your powerful Sunseeker yacht you'll find your favourite wines chilling in the fridge, your preferred magazines neatly arranged . . . even your chosen brand of sun cream. And your expert crew waiting for your commands.

Want to chill out and moor in a secluded bay off the shores of Malta? Explore the dramatic coastline of Croatia? Party with the glitterati in the bustling, cosmopolitan glamour of the old harbour at Cannes, moored alongside fellow pleasure-seeking yacht people? The choice is yours – just say the word.

PROFILE

Fleet

YOU MIGHT WANT THE SHEER HEDONISM OF THE SUNSEEKER 105, A FLOATING MINI-PALACE FOR UP TO 10 GUESTS OR THE MORE INTIMATE MANHATTAN 74. IF YOU'RE LOOKING FOR SPEED AND THRILLS, CHOOSE ONE OF THE FLEET'S PREDATORS. THE LATEST ADDITION TO THE FLEET IS THE MIGHTY 82-FOOT LONG PREDATOR 82. WHATEVER YOU'RE LOOKING FOR, THERE'S A YACHT TO SUIT, WHETHER IT'S A FAMILY OR A GROUP OF FRIENDS.

Reservations

A YACHT OF YOUR CHOICE CAN BE RESERVED FOR SAILING IN THE FOLLOWING LOCATIONS: BALEARICS, CARIBBEAN, CROATIA, FLORIDA, GREECE, ITALY, MALTA, SOUTH OF FRANCE AND IN THE UNITED KINGDOM.

THE YACHTS ARE EQUALLY AVAILABLE FOR DAY CHARTERS AND CORPORATE EVENTS.

CONTACT DETAILS

SUNSEEKER CHARTERS
23 WEST QUAY ROAD
POOLE
DORSET BH15 1HX
UNITED KINGDOM
TEL +44 (0)1202 682890
FAX +44 (0)1202 682827
INFO@SUNSEEKERCHARTERS.NET
WWW.SUNSEEKERCHARTERS.NET

DIRECTOR: MR DAVID WARD
DIRECTOR: MR STEFAN WERTANS

THE PRIVATE COLLECTION

QS PUBLISHING

QS Publishing is a division within Quattro Services publishing lifestyle books, agendas, calendars and directories for clients.

We set up our dedicated corporate publishing division with the simple premise of bringing the best of our expertise to the field of contract publishing. In essence this means applying our skills as publishers to the objectives of our clients and providing a service to their customers that delivers meaningful response.

In the end it is only through response that the success of a publication can be measured. We are happy to be judged on this principle.

We recognize that each piece of literature needs to do two things.
It needs to effectively communicate your message, whilst also enhancing the brand.

PRODUCT RANGE
- BOOKS
- AGENDAS
- CALENDARS
- DIRECTORIES

CORPORATE GIFTS
WHY NOT OFFER YOUR PRIVILEGED CLIENTS A PERSONALIZED COPY OF THE PRIVATE COLLECTION? PLEASE CONTACT US TO DISCUSS THE DIFFERENT POSSIBILITIES WE CAN OFFER YOU.

64A, RUE MIDDELBOURG
B-1170 BRUSSELS
BELGIUM

TEL +32 (0)2 674 28 68
FAX +32 (0)2 674 28 69
INFO@QUATTROSERVICES.COM
WWW.QUATTROSERVICES.COM

CORPORATE INFO

X O PRIVATE

IS A DIVISION OF

QS PUBLISHING

64A, RUE MIDDELBOURG
B-1170 BRUSSELS
BELGIUM

TEL. +32 (0)2 674 28 68
FAX +32 (0)2 674 28 69
INFO@QUATTROSERVICES.COM
WWW.QUATTROSERVICES.COM

EDITOR
ISABELLE VAN PASSEL
IVANPASSEL@QUATTROSERVICES.COM

PUBLISHER
YVAN VERMEESCH
YVERMEESCH@QUATTROSERVICES.COM

ASSOCIATE PUBLISHER
MAURICE VERMEESCH
MVERMEESCH@QUATTROSERVICES.COM

BUSINESS DEVELOPMENT
PASCAL GERKEN
PGERKEN@QUATTROSERVICES.COM

PRODUCTION

PREPRESS & PRINTING BY

Roels printing n.v.

TEL. +32 (0)3 270 90 30
WWW.ROELS-PRINTING.BE

A SPECIAL THANKS

A special thanks to
Fabienne Delhez, Bea Verreydt,
Rita Van Goethem, David Bagley,
Ludo Herrewijn and Yves Janssens
for their precious assistance,
much appreciated patience and, again,
fabulous work!

334

ISBN 9080908517

WWW.XOPRIVATE.COM

Visit us online:

- Order your personal copy of The Private Collection.

  The Private Collection is exclusively available at the featured properties & preferred travel partners, at select events throughout Europe (Brussels, Cannes, Monaco, Knokke-Zoute, Amsterdam, St. Moritz, Verona & Barcelona) and online at www.xoprivate.com

- Discover all featured properties online.

- Search for the finest travel products throughout the world.

- Choose your preferred airline: updated airline cabin comfort survey.
  (Business Class - First Class)

- Stay informed about our latest publications.